WAR IS OBSOLETE
THE DIALECTICS OF MILITARY TECHNOLOGY
AND ITS CONSEQUENCES

Paul K. Crosser

PHILOSOPHICAL CURRENTS

Vol 3

David H. DeGrood
Editor

Edward D'Angelo
University of Bridgeport

Marvin Farber
State University of New York at Buffalo

Dale Riepe
State University of New York at Buffalo

Associate Editors

The important views expressed by our writers are represented without necessarily implying concurrence of either Editors or Publisher

B. R. GRÜNER N.V. – Amsterdam – 1972

War Is Obsolete

The Dialectics of Military Technology

and Its Consequences

Paul K. Crosser

B. R. Grüner N.V – Amsterdam – 1972

Library of Congress Catalog

Card Number 74–185999

ISBN 90 6032 005 0

1972 by Paul K. Crosser
Printed: Wolters-Noordhoff Printing, Groningen

TABLE OF CONTENTS

INTRODUCTION

This book undertakes to prove a thesis and to spell out the consequences of such a proof. The thesis, which is presented here, sets out
with the observation that the instruments with which wars have been
conducted were always instruments of production. It is further observed
that, during the period when industrially produced weapons were gradually replacing weapons produced in a pre-industrial manner, the application of the most up-to-date industrially reproduced weapons in the
most skillful manner brought victory. It is granted, that factors of war
technology, the perfection and use of the most up-to-date weapons in
the most skillful manner, were always coupled with social as well as
economic factors.

In the pre-nuclear stage of weaponry technology, it is demonstrated
in the First Chapter, each successive stage in the development of weaponry added to the speed of delivery and intensity of firepower of the
technologically more advanced type of weapon over the technologically less advanced type of weapon. The country which used the
weapon of greater speed in delivery and greater intensity of firepower
in the most skillful manner was always the country which won a particular war, it is brought out.

In the nuclear stage of weaponry, technology with missiles applied as
means of delivery of hydrogen bombs, the speed and firepower of
weapons, it is argued, has reached such proportions that any country
made subject to an attack by thermonuclear bomb-laden missiles is
threatened with annihilation. Speed and firepower have increased to
such a degree with the change to thermonuclear firepower and missile
delivery that the application of such weapons has become prohibitive.
The change to thermonuclear bombs and missiles as means of delivery
thus constitutes a qualitative change in the evolution of weaponry technology, it is concluded. The qualitative change signifies the preclusion
of the winning of a war by way of the application of the most up-to-date
weaponry technology, as represented by thermonuclear bombs and missiles.

That qualitative change can well be called a dialectical change.
Dialectical, in the stated context, means the turning of a set of conditions,
in this case a set of conditions pertaining to military technology, into
its very opposite. From a means of winning a war in a military sense,

1

as was the case with regard to the military technology of the pre-nuclear age, the military technology of the nuclear age has become a means of losing a war in a military sense.

The Second Chapter of the book is devoted to the demonstration of the above stated qualitative dialectical change in the development of weaponry technology. A disproof is undertaken in that chapter of the thesis that the most up-to-date weapons – hydrogen bombs delivered by missiles – could win a war. A demonstration is undertaken in the second chapter that the army, the navy and air force, as organized institutional entities, can be expected to disintegrate in the course of a nuclear exchange.

Chapter III, in turn, provides a demonstration of the effects of the qualitative dialectical change in military technology which can be expected to result in the disintegration of the army, navy and air force as organized, institutionalized entities. That disintegration of the organized, institutionalized military entities can, in turn, be expected to be accompanied by the disintegration of the entire institutional framework of the country subjected to a nuclear attack. Any attempt to maintain production, distribution and consumption of civilian goods, in terms of physical and chemical processes, in the course of a nuclear saturation exchange, it is maintained, is doomed to failure.

Chapter IV undertakes, on the basis of the dialectical turn in military technology, to demonstrate the futility of the attempt to form strategic concepts on the basis of which a nuclear war could be fought. Any strategy conceived for the fighting of a nuclear war can only prove to be self-defeating, it is brought out. The cohesive institutional framework of the national state, the preconditioning factor for the conduct of such a war, will cease to exist in the course of a nuclear exchange it is maintained by this writer. Such strategic concepts as limited war, preventive war, pre-emption, deterrent, first strike and second strike, are subjected to a critical examination in Chapter IV.

From Chapter V on, the book tries to spell out the consequences which have to be faced were massive disarmament to take place. The second part of the book, starting from Chapter V, presents the military, social, economic and political results were a massive disarmament drive to be effected. While the first part of the presentation (Chapters I to IV) is to be regarded as presenting a dysfunctional analysis, the second part (Chapters V to VIII) is, in turn, to be viewed as constituting a functional analysis.

The functional analysis starts with a discussion in Chapter V of the measures which, it is suggested, be taken to attain what this writer calls demilitarization. Demilitarization refers to a wider range of measures than what goes by the name disarmament. Disarmament refers but to the reduction and elimination of arms production and the stockpiling of weapons. Demilitarization is viewed as a policy directed towards a re-shaping of the entire cultural and educational system, in order to make subsequent rearmament unpalatable.

Chapter VI discusses what this writer calls economic mobilization for peace. The stated problem-complex is wider in range than the usually referred to problem-complex of economic demobilization. Economic demobilization pertains only to the discontinuation of war goods production. Economic mobilization for peace, in the form in which this writer discusses it, refers to the replacement of war goods production with the production of goods for peacetime pursuits with all its attendant financial, social and economic factors.

Chapter VII entitled International Economic Cooperation places the aspect of the relationship of the industrially developed countries with the industrially underdeveloped countries in a historical perspective. It further evolves principles on the basis of which the industrially developed countries, and in particular the United States and the Soviet Union, could cooperate in assisting the development of the industrially underdeveloped countries. Such cooperation could, in turn, be accompanied by a growing exchange of goods between the United States and the Soviet Union, it is argued.

The last chapter of the book, Chapter VIII, provides a historical account of the Cold War. The conclusion is drawn that the Cold War has become meaningless since it was stipulated on turning the Cold War into a hot war. Such a hot nuclear war, as the first part of the book undertakes to demonstrate, has become senseless. The Cold War can thus be left to fade away, in the wake of successive accommodations between the United States and other Western countries with the Soviet Union and other Eastern European countries. By concentrating on the promotion of the welfare of their respective peoples, the Western and Eastern governments, and in particular, the governments of the United States and the Soviet Union, could lay the basis for an international policy of live and let live.

A definite role in bringing about a better international understanding will have to be assigned to organizations which have their aim in the promotion of peace in all countries of the world. All those organizations devoted to the promotion of peace will have to broaden their outlook. Instead of being merely negative in their approach, i.e., against war, those organizations will have to include in their activities programs which are to contain broad outlines of a peaceful world to replace the warlike world.

The positive aspect of reshaping the social, economic, cultural and educational aspects of the world, in which war in all its inhuman manifestations will be outlawed, is to become the task of all those genuinely interested in peace. This is a formidable task, but a task which is well worth the ingenuity and resourcefulness of all persons of good will.

When the degrading prospects of mass killings of humans by humans will be made to vanish from the earth, the sea and the air, ever advancing technology could be made to focus on life enhancing ends. In pursuing those life enhancing ends, advancing technology could be directed towards the banishment of the scourges of ignorance, poverty and sickness from the inhabited world.

New York, 1971   Paul K. Crosser

PREFACE

When this author started writing this book in the second year of the John F. Kennedy Administration, the thesis on which this exposition is based was not complete. The incompleteness of the thesis resulted from the insufficient evidence that a limited war conducted by the United States on the territory of a foreign country could not be won in the military sense. To be sure, a cogent argument could be advanced even in the early aftermath of the post-Korean War period that the particular war was not won in a military sense, because of a fear on the part of the responsible political leaders in the United States that an escalation of that war, and in particular, an escalation to the point of an inclusion of the use of atomic weapons on the part of the United States, would have resulted in a global conflagration.

The conclusion which United States writers on military strategy had drawn from the cessation of military actions in Korea on the part of all belligerents was not, however based upon the strategic result of that conflict. The United States writers on military strategy, among them Henry Kissinger, the present advisor on national security policy to President Nixon, and a former Chairman of the United States Chiefs of Staffs, Taylor, based their strategy theories of a limited war on the presumption that a war of that type had been won in Korea in the military sense. In actuality, the war in Korea had ended in a draw in a military sense, which the said writers on military strategy did not care to admit. This lack of candor and the misconception of the winnibility of a limited war in the age of nuclear weapons resulted in a repeat performance, with certain variations of the Korean conflict, in the war in Vietnam.

As in the Korean conflict, the war in Vietnam was not won in a military sense. Again, in a military sense, the Vietnam war is about to come to an end in a draw. The settlement of the Vietnam conflict has to be sought in non-military, political terms. Those non-military, political terms, which are to form a basis for a settlement of the Vietnam conflict, could well have been attained before the Johnson Administration in Washington, D. C. and its advisors, made the tragic decision of escalating the conflict in military terms.

The United States, to be sure, possesses the military means to make the whole of Vietnam a wasteland, with no one left in that little country

5

to serve as a party to a peace settlement. That total devastation of Vietnam by United States military forces did not take place because the responsible United States leaders feared involvement of mainland China and the Soviet Union in that kind of conflict, with the prospect of atomic bombs to be used by all the parties possessing such weapons. It is further to be noted that the people of the United States, the United States electorate, has shown uneasiness about the prospects of a further escalation of the United States involvement in the Vietnam conflict. That uneasiness, which could well be called popular resistance, showed itself clearly in the pre-nomination period of the 1968 Presidential election campaign. The voting strength of Senator Eugene McCarthy in the primaries and the subsequent withdrawal of the former President, Lyndon B. Johnson, from the candidacy for his renomination are but the highlights of the dramatic events of the popular distaste for a prosecution of the war in Vietnam as a limited war, with no military victory in sight.

It is of interest to notice in this connection, that an important section of the United States business world formed a council of business leaders which pleaded with the then President of the United States, Lyndon B. Johnson, to desist from further military action in Vietnam, by placing ads to that effect in leading United States newspapers. It is further relevant to state that leading United States newspapers, "The New York Times," as well as "The Wall Street Journal," took editorially a position which pointed out the senselessness of a further prolongation of military action in Vietnam. All in all, there is hardly any doubt that the vast majority of the United States population has come to realize, that the more than 45 thousand lives of United States soldiers and officers killed in Vietnam and the more than 200 thousand maimed as well as the more than 100 billion dollars spent so far in the prosecution of the Vietnam War have been expended in vain. The kind of peace settlement to which the United States would be willing to be a party at present could well be had at the time before the conflict in Vietnam erupted in a full scale limited war at the very start of the reign of the Johnson Administration in Washington.

It is highly unlikely that a repetition of the kind of "limited war" experience which the United States has gone through in Korea and Vietnam would ever be condoned by the political representatives of the United States electorate in the United States Senate and the rank and file citizens of the United States. That such is the case has been dramatically demonstrated when in the spring of 1970 the Nixon Administration had undertaken a military incursion by United States forces into Cambodia. That incursion was taken to be by a vast majority of the United States population as a reescalation of the war in Indochina. That was rightly interpreted as contradicting the policy of deescalation of the

Vietnam War which had come to be pursued by the Nixon Administration since its inauguration. Coincidentally the incursion of United States forces into Cambodia coincided with the shooting and killing of some students on the campuses of Kent University in Ohio and Jackson State College in Mississippi.

Within days after those occurrences over five hundred college and university campuses closed down, most of them for the remainder of the semester. Those actions were taken to protest the invasion of Cambodia by United States troops as well as the invasion of U.S. campuses by police and national guards. This spontaneous mass protest is unprecedented in the history of the United States as far as an expression of displeasure on the part of the academic community with the actions of the government is concerned. What was almost equally significant was the instantaneous reaction of the Nixon Administration which pledged a United States troop withdrawal from Cambodia within two weeks. As a follow-up, the Cooper-Church resolution was adopted in the United States Senate, which forbids the re-entry of United States troops into Cambodia. The lesson which the mass protests of the United States academic community and the firm resolve of the majority of the United States senators taught the Administration in Washington is likely to have a lasting effect. The impact is likely to effect not only the present administration in Washingtion but any other administration which is to follow. In regard to the subsequent invasion of Laos, it should be noted that United States ground troops have been kept from invading that country. Whether the air support which the United States provided for South Vietnamese troops entering Laos is compatible with the letter and the spirit of the Cooper-Church resolution is doubtful.

In the above stated respect, one can safely state that the theory of a limited war, which had blossomed out in the wake of the Korean conflict, is bound to wither away in the wake of the Vietnam debacle. Under those circumstances, the change in the structure of rearmament which aimed at reequipping the United States military forces with conventional weapons after the cessation of hostilities in Korea has also to come in for revision. Reequipping military forces for the kind of "limited wars" which cannot be won in the military sense hardly makes sense. Therefore, if a war is to break out in which the United States military forces are to be engaged, it is by the logic of history and the dialectic of military technology bound to become a nuclear confrontation.

That a nuclear confrontation cannot lead to military victory for either side of the nuclear powers, this author has undertaken to demonstrate in the first four chapters of this exposition. The consequences, in

7

turn, of the realization of the impossibility of winning a nuclear war in a military sense are spelled out by this writer in the last four chapters of this exposition.

In view of the futility of conducting a nuclear war with nonconventional nuclear weapons, or a "limited war" with conventional weapons, massive disarmament has come to become a most pressing problem. Massive disarmament will have to replace massive rearmament before the Twentieth Century comes to a close.

As far as the United States is concerned, massive disarmament would have to be effected not only because military technology is coming to naught in military and political terms, as far as the national security of any nuclear power is concerned. The discovery that what is known as the most affluent society and economy in the capitalist world is afflicted with a widespread and deep rooted poverty among its people, has put the very survival of the United States as a capitalist country under question. Only a massive reallocation of the United States' resources from use for war purposes to the use for purposes of peaceful existence can insure the restructuring of the United States economy and society, in which all segments of the population could be made to have a stake in the preservation of the given social and economic order.

What is involved is not just an increase in the allocation of funds for housing, schools and hospitals. What in needed is not only additional employment for the less skilled and their training. What is required is no less than a social and economic elevation of more than half of the people of the United States.

The much publicized high standard of living of the United States population appears now as but a standard which only a minority of the people are enjoying. More than half of the population of the United States can be counted as socially and economically deprived, in terms of a satisfactory standard of living, in United States terms. A study published in the United States in 1968 by the Department of Labor has demonstrated that a family of four required close to $ 10,000 to be able to purchase the set of consumers goods which are to be considered a minimum by United States living standards. If that contention is accepted, and there seems to be little doubt that the stated appraisal is realistic, one can conclude that above 70% of the United States families did not have the means to live by United States standards. Only about 30% of the United States population had family incomes of $ 10,000 and more in 1968. The raising of the income and spending level of 70% of the United States population from a substandard range, in United States terms, to a standard range presents an undertaking of gigantic proportions.

That such a vast undertaking is not beyond reach can be gathered by comparing the amounts of money spent on war and warlike activities in the United States and the amount of money which would be needed for the stated restructuring of the United States society and economy geared to peaceful purposes. It is a fair estimate that since the end of World War II, which includes the periods of the Korean War and the Vietnam War as well as the war preparedness expenditures incurred by the conduct of the Cold War amounted to about one trillion dollars. The amount of money which is required for a massive restructuring of the society and economy of the United States lies within that range.

Gunnar Myrdal, the well-known Swedish economist and sociologist, had calculated that the elimination of the Negro ghettos, and it is in those that the high percentage of the people of the United States live, who are forced to exist on a substandard level, in United States terms, would require the expenditure of several trillion dollars. This writer did not see the spelling out by Myrdal of his estimates, but he assumes that Myrdal as a highly perceptive economist, as well as a highly perceptive sociologist, realizes that the building of new houses to replace the ghetto structures, whether in the places where the Negro ghettos now are situated, or in places other than where the Negro ghettos are at present located, is not going to solve the problem of the elimination of ghettos.

Pertinent sociological studies have revealed that the moving of low income people from slums to new housing developments resulted in not too long a time in turning the new housing developments into slums. The reason for that is to be seen in the low income level of the people who were moved from decaying buildings to new buildings. The reason for a decay of buildings is not so much due to physical obsolescence of the buildings, as it is due to neglect and disrepair, which is caused by the dwellers in the structure, who are constantly themselves in a state of neglect and malfunction, because they are unable to make ends meet. The solution of the problem is to be seen in the elevation of the slum dwellers, after they have been moved to new structures, to a level of social and economic existence which could be considered adequate by United States standards.

Would an annual expenditure of an amount equivalent to the present annual war and war preparedness budget in the United States be sufficient to finance the stated restructuring of the United States society and economy? At present, with the inclusion of the Vietnam War the Defense Department budget in the United States is coming close to about one hundred billion dollars a year. Suppose the one hundred billion dollars or so, which is earmarked for war and war preparedness spending, would be turned wholly into the spending program for the restructuring of the United States society and economy, would that be enough? In giving an answer one has to ask, enough for what or enough to what extent? It depends for how long such a program is to be stretched and what priorities are to be allocated for such a program.

Let us assume the program is to be stretched to bring tangible results within a generation, which would be about thirty years. It is about thirty years, let us recall, since the beginning of World War II. During the period following World War II, as it has been pointed out here, about a trillion dollars was spent for hot and Cold War purposes in the United States. Considering that the total national income in the United States at present is about one trillion dollars and that 100 billion dollars were to be added to elevate the living standards and the income level of the people living on a substandard level. It does not seem that the 100 billion dollars which, say, could go into new housing and income subsidies would really be sufficient to lead to a restructuring of the United States society and economy. The expenditure of but 100 billion dollars annually is more likely to perpetuate the present level of the social and economic structure for the vast majority of the people.

Have then the sights to be lowered to comply with the prevailing social and economic reality? Are the sights then to come down to the level of the anti-poverty programs which had been put into effect during the Johnson Administration and which to some extent were continued during the Nixon Administration? Is a roughly $ 3000 annual income to be considered the level at which the United States Government will undertake to subsidize the low income people, as is the case at present? About one fifth of the United States income receivers are considered to be within that range. Or, is the United States Government to up the low $ 3000 income level to a $ 5000 annual income level and thus bring all income receivers below the $ 5000 range up to that level through government income subsidies? Were one to settle for the last stated levels, it could result in reducing the number of poverty stricken people, but could not bring about the abolishment of economic deprivation in the United States.

The sights have to be heightened, in order to assure a restructuring of the United States society and economy. Should a restructuring as a goal not be lost sight of, a sum lower than 100 billion dollars annually would certainly not do. One hundred billion dollars stretched over thirty years would amount to 3 trillion dollars. What one has to consider is that prices are likely to rise due to inflationary trends and what 100 billion dollars could buy now will require at least 150 billion dollars fifteen years or so hence. It would therefore, be a realistic estimate to assess the buying power of three trillion dollars extending to a period thirty years hence, as one third of it in present purchasing terms. That means in purchasing terms the 3 trillion dollars will amount to about 2 trillion dollars in the thirty year restructuring period.

A further question arises in regard to priorities of spending the money for the purpose of social and economic restructuring of the United States. Spending money for new housing and spending money for income subsidies will certainly fall short in attaining the goal of restructuring. Without the spending of a substantial amount of money for production, a restructuring of the United States society and economy could not be effected. It is idle to speculate, that United States business concerns could be made to undertake a vast increase in production and employment in order to restructure the United States economy and society. United States business and, in particular, United States large scale business, would have to be prevailed upon to forego a greater part of its profits, were it to assume the effectuation of a major part of the restructuring program. Such could not be the case, were those businesses to continue to operate for profit. What constitutes a more realistic approach to the production aspect of the restructuring program is the establishment of some mixed production undertakings in which business and government would share financial and administrative responsibilities. In addition, a great number of government financed and government operated productive undertakings will have to be established.

At this point, this writer would like to take issue with the current proposal to introduce a so-called negative income tax as well as a proposal to have an annual income guaranteed to all the people who are unable to find gainful employment. These two proposals are geared to an expectation that the United States society and economy could not be restructured and are, therefore, likely to lead to the perpetuation of low substandard incomes as well as to the perpetuation of a low level of employment. It appears that an economic theory which could be applied in an effort to restructure the United States society and economy is lagging or maybe even lacking. Keynes had undertaken to demonstrate that the level of an equilibrium in terms of a balance of consumption and investment can be of a low level, putting up with unemployment or it can be a high level of equilibrium by not putting up with unemployment. What Keynes did not demonstrate in any convincing manner is that full employment can be attained at the cost of elimination of low earnings and living standards without the government taking part in subsidizing production. A society and economy run by businessmen cannot be expected to be concerned with the upping of wages at the expense of cutting profits. Only a government financed undertaking could place a high priority on employment under the condition of upping wages at the expense of profits. It is in that context that the government financing and operation of productive undertakings assumes a major role in the program of a restructuring of American society and economy.

The just completed outlining of a restructuring of the society and economy in the United States places the question of ethnic antagonism between the white and black people in the United States in a social and economic perspective. Social and economic discrimination, as practiced against the black people in the United States, is but part and parcel of the social and economic discrimination as practiced against other groups of socially and economically disadvantaged people in the United States. Some of those socially and economically disadvantaged people belong to ethnic minority groups in the United States, such as the people of Puerto Rican descent, or people of Mexican descent, or people of Polish descent and so on. Others of the socially and economically deprived can well be identified as being of native American stock, whose ancestors had come here from Europe a hundred and more years ago. Social and economic disadvantage does not know any ethnic boundaries and does not provide for a demarcation line between people of different ancestral groups. It should be granted that the percentage of the socially and economically disadvantaged is greater among certain ethnic groups such as, the black people, the Puerto Rican and Mexican ethnic groups, than among other ancestral groupings. That, however, does not make the underlying factors of social and economic discrimination a qualitatively different problem for the various groups of people; it is to be considered a problem which is only quantitatively different for the various groups.

As far as the Soviet Union is concerned, the elimination or massive reduction in spending for war preparedness and the utilization of comparable funds for the furthering of peacetime pursuits could no doubt have favorable effects on the social and economic development of the U.S.S.R. Increase in capital investment, increase in the range of production and distribution of consumer goods, which would signify an increase in the gross national product as well as the national income, could well be expected to result from the replacement of war expenditures with peacetime expenditures. One could further assume, that massive reduction in war expenditures and their replacement with peacetime expenditures could well hasten the time when shortages of consumer goods will come to an end. This might bring closer the time when the Soviet society and economy will be enabled to turn from a society and economy of relative scarcity to a society and economy of relative abundance of consumer goods.

The replacement of a society and economy of relative scarcity with a society and economy of relative abundance in the Soviet Union would also include the turning of housing from a relatively scarce to a rela-

12

tively abundant factor. Such a turning from relative scarcity to relative abundance would also include greater abundance in the sphere of schools and hospitals as well as health resort facilities. One would not go wrong in rating a changeover from relative scarcity to relative abundance in the Soviet Union as a change in the social and economic structure in that country. Moreover, one could well regard a changeover from paid services, such as city transportation, to free services as a factor of social and economic restructuring. The acceleration of that changeover will no doubt also be the result of the replacement of war production expenditures by expenditures on peacetime pursuits.

It has been estimated that the Soviet Union is spending at the rate of about 30 to 40 billion dollars annually on its defense budget. That is about one half of the 60 to 80 billion dollars which the United States had earmarked yearly for defense before the United States' large scale involvement in the Vietnam War. Were one to add the war destruction suffered by the Soviet Union during World War II and take further into consideration the war production and war prosecution expenditures in World War II, one could well arrive at the 1 trillion dollars or more figure. That would be about the equivalent of the trillion or so dollars spent by the United States on war and war preparations, since the end of World War II. Massive bilateral disarmament would make it sure that neither the Soviet Union nor the United States would have to deprive its respective citizens of the full fruits of their labor, in order to have those fruits destroyed in a nuclear holocaust.

With the United States and the Soviet Union becoming affluent nations, as far as the vast majority of their populations are concerned, they could then turn their vistas towards the development of the underdeveloped third of the world. Up to the present, it had not been generally realized what the magnitude of the problem amounts to, as far as the development of the countries is concerned, in which one third of the 3 billion 300 million people populating the globe live. The reason why the magnitude of the problem of developing the countries, in which $1/3$ of the population of the world is living, has not been fully appreciated is probably due to the awareness that comparable sums for a real try to turn those countries from underdeveloped to developed could not be made available by the technologically advanced countries. So far only token assistance has been provided by the United States as well as the Soviet Union, as far as the development of the $1/3$ of the world population living in underdeveloped countries is concerned. As far as industrialization of the underdeveloped world is concerned, one can regard the assistance given by the United States and the Soviet Union as but a financing of pilot projects. The United States has, in addition, provided funds to help the governments of the countries of the underdeveloped

13

world pay their bills. On balance, the development of the underdeveloped countries in terms of a massive industrialization and a massive mechanization of agriculture did not make much headway.

In many underdeveloped countries, and most South American countries can be taken as an example, the increase in population came to outpace the increase in industrial and agricultural production. The sums needed in order for an increase in industrial and agricultural production to be faster than the "production of babies" are of a hitherto undreamed of magnitude. This writer has made a calculation which shows that about 5 trillion dollars would be needed to put the roughly one billion people in the underdeveloped world on a level of $1/_3$ of the national wealth level of the United States. That would then amount also roughly to putting the approximately one billion people in the underdeveloped world on a per capita level of $1/_3$ of the United States per capita income level. Such a development would then place the presently underdeveloped nations within the social and economic range of the developed nations. The division of the world into developed and underdeveloped nations would thus come to an end. The trillions of dollars needed for that kind of operation could not, however, be made available if the donor nations and, in particular, the main donor nations, would not be able to have their own societies and economies developed to hitherto unattained degrees by a shifting of hundreds of billions of dollars from the financing of production of means of destruction to the financing of constructive undertakings. Only massive disarmament spearheaded by the United States and the Soviet Union could lay the groundwork for such a promising future.

FOREWORD

This exposition gained momentum when the United Nations General Assembly approved the nuclear non-proliferation treaty which had been jointly submitted to that body by the governments of the United States of America and the Union of the Soviet Socialist Republic. There followed the signing of the treaty by the governments of the United States and the Soviet Union. There further followed the signing of the nuclear non-proliferation treaty by more than eighty member nations of the United Nations. Ratification of the treaty by the respective parliamentary bodies of the signatories was to follow. Ratification of the treaty by the United States Senate took place at the beginning of March, 1969. The Supreme Soviet of the Soviet Union has also ratified the treaty.

While the nuclear non-proliferation treaty is by itself not a disarmament measure, it can well be regarded as a milestone on the road to disarmament. Had the nuclear non-proliferation treaty not been agreed upon by the United States and the Soviet Union and not approved by the United Nations, the spreading of nuclear weapons, the nuclear armament race, would have likely gone out of control. As things stand now, there are still a number of nations, among them France and The Peoples Republic of China, two nations in possession of nuclear arms, who are not signatories of the nuclear non-proliferation treaty. It may be hoped, however, that in due time, all those non-signatory nations including France and The Peoples Republic of China will comply with the provisions of the nuclear non-proliferation treaty, even if they were not to affix their signatures to the treaty. Such expectation will even be more justified when positive steps towards disarmament will be taken by the signatory powers and, in particular, by the two major sponsors of the nuclear non-proliferation treaty, the United States and the Soviet Union.

That the expectation of positive disarmament steps is not just an illusion was made clear by the official announcement of the government of the Soviet Union that it is prepared to enter into discussion with the government of the United States pertaining to the mutual limitation and later reduction of both offensive and defensive strategic weapons, including anti-missile missiles. The United States government had towards the end of the year 1966 suggested to the government of the Soviet Union a bilateral discussion of the prospective mutual limitation of

15

the manufacture and deployment of anti-missile missiles. The government of the Soviet Union through its spokesman Premier Alexei Kosygin had indicated at the time when the proposal was made, that the Soviet Union would be interested in having the matter of the limitation of the anti-missile missiles defense system discussed, only if that discussion were to include the matter of offensive strategic weapons as well. Yet the government of the Soviet Union had not elaborated further on the matter for about a year and a half. Up to the time when the agreement and signing of the nuclear non-proliferation treaty was effected, the government of the Soviet Union had not made any official statements in regard to a more concrete suggestion on the matter.

The acceptance and signing of the nuclear non-proliferation treaty provided for the Soviet government the basis for giving the signal for an actual start of negotiations on the limitation and reduction of offensive and defensive strategic weapons, including the anti-missile missiles.

The readiness of the government of the Soviet Union to enter into bilateral talks with the government of the United States on the issue of limitation and reduction of offensive and defensive strategic weapons was first announced by the Minister of Foreign Affairs of the Soviet Union Andrei Gromyko on June 28, 1968 in a statement before the Supreme Soviet. A reaffirmation of the Soviet government's readiness to enter into bilateral negotiations with the government of the United States on the limitation and reduction of offensive and defensive nuclear weapons was subsequently made by Premier Alexei Kosygin on the occasion of the signing of the nuclear non-proliferation treaty in Moscow on July 2, 1968.

The government of the United States, as represented at that time by President Lyndon B. Johnson, expressed satisfaction over the pronouncements of Premier Kosygin and Foreign Minister Gromyko and added an expression of hope that the talks would start as soon as possible. The start of those talks came to be delayed by the outgoing Johnson administration on account of events which had taken place in Czechoslovakia in August, 1968. The talks, abbreviately called SALT, did actually start in 1969 during the Nixon Administration. Those talks are still continuing.

In his address on the occasion of the signing ceremony of the nuclear non-proliferation treaty in Moscow, Premier Kosygin made public on July 1, 1968 a memorandum which specified a number of disarmament proposals which the Soviet Union would like to have put on the agenda for further disarmament talks. The proposals specified in the memorandum were submitted by the Soviet government to the Seventeen Nations Disarmament Conference upon its reconvening on July 17, 1968 in Geneva. The proposals were as follows:

16

1. The prohibition of the use of atomic weapons.
2. Measures aimed at discontinuation of production of atomic weapons, the reduction and liquidation of stockpiles of such weapons.
3. Limitation and subsequent reduction of means of delivery of strategic weapons.
4. Prohibition of flights of bombers carrying nuclear weapons beyond the borders of national boundaries.
5. Prohibition of testing of nuclear weapons under the surface of the earth.
6. Prohibition of use of chemical and bacteriological weapons.
7. Liquidation of foreign military bases.
8. Measures aiming at regional disarmament.
9. Peaceful utilization of beds of seas and oceans.

The United States government had reiterated at the reconvening of the Seventeen Nations Disarmament Conference in Geneva in July, 1968 its interest in a discussion of the matter of limiting ballistic missiles. In a message to the Conference the then President Johnson said on July 17, 1968, "should progress be achieved on limiting rockets and other systems for delivering nuclear warheads, the United States was prepared to consider reduction of existing systems." "In this way", Mr. Johnson continued, "we would cut back effectively – and for the first time – on the vast potentials for destruction which each side possesses". Then President Johnson urged the conference to begin consideration of a "workable verifiable and effective international agreement to bar the use of the sea beds for the emplacement of weapons of mass destruction". In a message read by William C. Foster, then head of the United States Arms Control and Disarmament Agency, Mr. Johnson further said "the United States is ready to respect any regional arms pact. It would support", Mr. Johnson continued, "any reasonable measures affecting the activities of the major weapons producers that would make a regional agreement more effective". The then President Johnson suggested that one such measure could be a requirement that suppliers publicize or register their arms shipments to a particular region.

The Soviet Union through its spokesman Alexei A. Roshchin proposed at the Seventeen Nations Disarmament Conference at Geneva, that the Conference take up the questions of demilitarization of the sea beds and regional arms agreements. The Soviet's spokesman at the disarmament conference referred to the above stated proposal by formally introducing the memorandum of arms reduction measures which the Soviet Premier Alexei N. Kosygin had announced on July 1, 1968.

In comparison with the Johnson disarmament proposal, the Kosygin proposals appear much more comprehensive. One cannot help getting the impression that the Johnson proposals were somehow haphazard;

they had but a casual character. The United States Arms Control and Disarmament Agency might have worked on more comprehensive disarmament schemes, such a scheme has, however, not been officially presented to the Seventeen Nations Disarmament Conference in Geneva.

Let us take, for instance, the Johnson proposal which the Johnson Administration pressed for about a year and one half for putting on the agenda of a bilateral United States and Soviet Union discussion of the matter of limitation of the production and deployment of anti-missile missiles. In strategic terms it is well known that production and deployment of the anti-missile missiles defense system is of secondary importance. The issue of production and deployment of missiles is of prime strategic importance in this connection, since no anti-weapon weapon, as is the case with the anti-missile missiles, has ever been able to reduce greatly the effectiveness of the weapon, in this case the missile.

Mr. Kosygin had pointed it out at the time, when the issue of the desired limitation of the production and deployment of anti-missile missiles was first brought up by the Johnson Administration, that the anti-missile missile, which constitutes a defense weapon, is a less objectionable weapon as well as a less important weapon than the offensive weapon, the missile. Therefore, Kosygin concluded, if the question of the limitation of the defensive weapon, of the anti-missile missile, is to be brought up, it has to be tied up with the limitation of the respective offensive weapons. What actually prompted the Johnson Administration to bring up the matter of the limitation of the production and deployment of anti-missile missiles was the difficulty of budgeting such a program, lying within the 100 to 200 billion dollar range, in the face of a mounting United States budgetary deficit which had been brought about by the skyrocketing expenditures for the Vietnam War.

The stated occasion is symptomatic, it does indicate that even in a highly developed country, such as the United States, the device to have guns as well as butter cannot be fully carried out. The Vietnam War which started on a small scale had come to become a major military engagement for the United States. The Vietnam War expenditures coupled with the increasing expenditures in an accelerated arms race had come to lead to budgetary, fiscal and monetary difficulties. Those difficulties will not disappear, even if the Vietnam War abates, they could only become less intensive and acute, in short terms. As far as long term development is concerned, the budgetary, fiscal and monetary difficulties of an accelerated arms race in the United States will persist, and even be intensified, if no comprehensive arms limitation scheme comes to be effected.

Both Premier Kosygin and President Nixon have expressed themselves on the tasks which have been laid before the 17 Nations Disarmament

Conference which had been reconvened on March 18, 1969 in Geneva as reported in *The New York Times* on March 19, 1969. Premier Kosygin expressed his views and recommendations in a message addressed to the reconvened 17 Nations Disarmament Conference. Mr. Kosygin's message made the following key points: "Solution has to be found", Mr. Kosygin stated, "of such problems . . . as stopping the manufacture of nuclear weapons, the reduction and destruction of their stockpiles, the limitation and subsequent reduction of means of delivery of strategic weapons, securing the prohibition of chemical and bacteriological warfare . . .". "It would be highly important", Mr. Kosygin's message emphasized, "also to bring about agreement to the effect that the seabed and the ocean floor are not used for military purposes . . .". In line with the last stated recommendation of Mr. Kosygin, the Soviet delegation at the 17 Nations Disarmament Conference introduced a draft treaty on the prohibition of the use for military purposes of the seabed, the ocean floor and the subsoil thereof.

President Nixon, in a letter addressed to Mr. Gerard C. Smith, newly appointed chief United States delegate at the reconvened 17 Nations Disarmament Conference, outlined his views on the tasks before the Conference. "The United States", Mr. Nixon stated, "is interested in working out an international agreement that would prohibit the emplacement or fixing of nuclear weapons or other weapons of mass destruction on the seabed". In line with Mr. Nixon's recommendation, the United States delegation at the 17 Nations Disarmament Conference had prepared a draft of its own on the prohibition of the use of the seabed for military purposes. Mr. Nixon further outlined his views by stating in his letter to Mr. Gerard C. Smith, that "the United States delegation supports the conclusion of a comprehensive test ban adequately verified". In addition Mr. Nixon's letter contained the following statement. "The United States delegation will continue to press for an agreement to cut off production of fissionable materials for weapons purposes and to transfer such materials to peaceful purposes". Mr. Nixon's letter had the following to say on chemical and biological warfare: "While awaiting the United Nations Secretary General's study on the effects of chemical and biological warfare, the United States delegation should join with other delegations in exploring any proposals or ideas that could contribute to sound and effective arms control relating to these weapons". Mr. Nixon added the following general observations in his letter: "Regarding more extensive measures of disarmament, both nuclear and conventional, the United States delegation should be guided by the understanding that actual reduction of armaments and not merely limiting their growth and spread, remains our goal".

To the stated official pronouncements of Mr. Nixon and Mr. Kosygin, the proposal made on March 30, 1971 at the opening of the 24th Congress of the Communist Party of the Soviet Union by its General Secretary – Leonid Brezhnev is to be added. Mr. Brezhnev proposed the convening of a conference of the five powers in possession of atomic weapons, namely the United States, the Soviet Union, England, France and the Peoples Republic of China, for a discussion of atomic disarmament. Mr. Nixon reacted to that proposal by saying that the so-called SALT talks, the talks conducted by the United States and the Soviet Union about limitations of offensive and defensive weapons, should be accorded prime attention. Subsequently Mr. Brezhnev's proposal was endorsed by the 17 Nations Disarmament Conference in Geneva.

Another proposal by Mr. Brezhnev to the effect of entering a discussion on mutual troop withdrawals in Europe by the NATO and Warsaw Pact countries, was more favorably received by the Nixon Administration. Preparatory studies on the said matter by the NATO powers are reported to be under way. Such preparatory studies are likely to be under way too by the Warsaw Pact powers.

PART I:

THE DIALECTICAL TURN IN MILITARY TECHNOLOGY

Chapter I

MILITARY TECHNOLOGY AND ITS APPLICABILITY IN THE PRE-NUCLEAR AND PRE-MISSILE AGE

There have been voices heard in the past, coming from either theoreticians or practitioners of warfare, who have maintained that no general rules for the conduct of warfare can be devised. The contrary position, however, that general rules for the conduct of wars can be evolved as well as tested by the lessons of history, appears to be more reasonable. Both the well-known theoretician of the eighteenth century, de Saxe, and that notorious practitioner of war, Napoleon Bonaparte, have attempted to present war as a cluster of incidents and a series of improvisations.

While there should not be any doubt that incidents, that is, unplanned and unpredicted occurrences, do take place in great numbers in any conduct of war and that innumerable improvisations to meet the situation created by incidents have to be effected, there can, likewise, be little doubt that a general approach to the planning of a given war, as well as a general pattern for its conduct, can and should be devised.

Reference to a given war, of course, is, first of all, to place it within a stated historical period. The historical period, in turn, refers to such matters as political, social, and economic forms of organization; it would, furthermore, signify the status of development of technology.

It is to be considered as an outstanding contribution of Clausewitz, the ranking post-Napoleonic theoretician of warfare, that in his writings on the principles of conduct of warfare, he specifically linked political and social factors with the planning and conduct of war. In that connection, Clausewitz's often-mentioned saying, that the conduct of war represents but an extension of the political activities of a given national state, is to be cited. Clausewitz's contemporary, the ranking post-Napoleonic theoretician of warfare, Jomini, was more specific than Clausewitz in regard to the correlation of the status of technology and the planning as well as the conduct of war.

Both Clausewitz and Jomini made the basic distinction between planning the realization of the aims of war, which they called "strategy," and the undertaking of the series of actions which were to lead to the attainment of these aims, which they referred to by the name of "tactics". Clausewitz was more specific than Jomini in linking the aims of the war with political aspirations of the state which becomes engaged in it. Jomini, however, was one with Clausewitz in linking the war aims with the national interest of the state. It is in that sense that both Clausewitz and Jomini made a distinct break with the pre-Napoleonic war theory and practice, which was rooted in attempts to further dynastic ambitions.

Both Clausewitz and Jomini were, in turn, insistent that the form of conduct of warfare in the post-Napoleonic period has to be linked with the proposition of *levee en masse,* i.e., the mobilization of the whole population, as it had first come into practice during the French Revolution and had subsequently been employed in supplying manpower for the Napoleonic armies. It is this emphasis on the mobilization of the whole population for military services which presents a break with the practice of dynastic wars, which were fought by mercenaries.

Both Clausewitz and Jomini were further insistent that the actual conduct of the war, which they discussed under the name of tactics, is not to be limited to a range of discussion on how to conduct a given battle. No battle can be properly fought, Clausewitz instructed, and was echoed in that respect by Jomini, without taking into consideration the presence of all the military forces of a given country at a specific time.

In this connection, Clausewitz formulated the concept of "forces in being," by which he meant the forces which are facing each other in a given battle at a given time, plus the forces which remain mobilized, but are not used in the specific battle at the given time. Jomini provided but another formulation of what Clausewitz had called "forces in being." He referred to "zones of operation" and "lines of operation" to indicate that there is a continuous relationship between the conduct of a series of battles. "Lines of operation" refers to the contact of those troops which are in actual combat with those not in actual combat, but in the immediate vicinity of the fighting. "Zones of operation" refers, in turn, to the contact of troops in actual combat with troops not in actual combat in the whole theater of given war operations. In referring to the aspects of lines and zones of operations, Jomini pointed to the specific need of keeping lines of communication and transportation open.

As far as actual combat is concerned, both Clausewitz and Jomini were well aware that the very employment of armies drawn through mobilization of the whole population allows for much fiercer and bloodier combat than the combat of dynastic armies of mercenaries, which were small fighting units and which could not easily be replaced. In that context, the saying of Clausewitz which referred to war as a series of transactions in blood must be cited.

Some of the dynastic wars of the eighteenth and preceding centuries were conducted more in the form of marching exercises and camping, than in the form of actual combat. With respect to the intensity of bloodletting, the post-Napoleonic wars, as defined by Clausewitz as well as

Jomini, were in a sense a throwback to the times when knighthood and chivalry had not yet entered the social sphere in general and the military sphere in particular.

The employment of mass armies and the resulting intensification of combat called, in turn, for the reappraisal of the role of offensive and defensive actions in war. Although both Clausewitz and Jomini emphasized offensive actions as a factor which alone can bring about a decision in war, they were careful not to discount the need for defensive operations, when the situation did not permit an attempt to bring about a decision through the launching of an offensive. Clausewitz has been criticized by some later writers on military subjects for having unduly emphasized the need for defensive operations.

This kind of criticism can be refuted by citing Clausewitz's explicit statement to the effect that retreats and evacuations can never be expected to win a war. Although siding with Clausewitz in bringing out the need for the preponderance of offensive operations in the conduct of war, Jomini was careful to point out that surprise attacks are the most likely to result in a tactical, i.e., short-term, advantage. They are not likely, according to Jomini, to affect the final outcome of a war.

Both Clausewitz and Jomini considered the destruction of the armed forces of the enemy as the ultimate strategic aim of national warfare. Clausewitz added that the actual physical destruction of all the armed forces of the enemy is not to be considered the sole strategic aim. Cessation of the will to fight on the part of a national leadership is tantamount to the physical destruction of the armed forces, as far as its effect on the termination of hostilities is concerned, according to Clausewitz. His added observation that no war can ever be considered lost, unless the national leadership of an armed force specifically acknowledges it to be lost, restresses that physical and psychological factors are interwoven in the conduct of war, as well as in its termination.

Neither Clausewitz nor Jomini considered the acquisition or loss of national territory a decisive factor in national warfare. Acquisition and loss of national territory could be reversed, they maintained, as long as the armed forces retained the power of action. It should be kept in mind that the de-emphasis on the acquisition and loss of territory was a distinctly post-dynastic development in the theory of warfare. In the dynastic period of warfare, acquisition of territory was considered the ultimate war aim, as far as bringing about victory is concerned. Conversely, loss of territory was considered a decisive factor in bringing about defeat. In this period of warfare, the destruction of the armed forces was not regarded a desirable goal, since the dynastic contestants shied away from situations which would require the replacement of the dearly bought and professionally trained mercenaries.

25

In the summary evaluation of Clausewitz's and Jomini's contribution to the evolvement of the post-dynastic theory of warfare, one can say that the two co-founders of the national theory of warfare demonstrated how the social effects of the replacement of the feudal with the post-feudal order on the continent of Europe have affected the formation of military forces and the character of warfare. What the two co-founders of the theory of national warfare failed to point out is how and in what form stages in technological advancement, which were ushered in by the Industrial Revolution, affected the conduct of wars. Jomini is known for having made the statement that the tools of war can be expected to change, but that such change will not affect the principles of war. If this statement is to mean that the ultimate aim of war, the destruction of the army of the enemy, is to be considered the immutable aim of a national war, then Jomini's reference to unchanging principles can be accepted. If, however, the factor of principles includes the whole range of strategic considerations, then Jomini's proposition of the immutability of principles has to be highly qualified at best.

The experience of the Napoleonic Wars, on which both Clausewitz and Jomini drew, was not an experience, in a technological sense, of a fully industrially geared war. This may explain why industrial technology does not play a decisive role in the war theory offered by either Clausewitz or Jomini. A war fully geared to industrial technology has to be fought with weapons which have all the aspects of a machine: they have to be self-propelling weapons. Blatant examples of such self-propelling weapons are machine guns and tanks, as well as missiles. Fire power had been used in the course of the Napoleonic Wars and can, as such, well be regarded as the preconditioning factor of industrial weaponry. It should be conceded, however, that fire power, if it must be effected manually, as was the case during the Napoleonic Wars, does not constitute the complete counterpart of an industrial process in the use of weaponry.

The stage in the development of weapons which were applied during the Napoleonic Wars can be characterized as the stage which had its counterpart in the period of manufactories; as such, it is to be considered as a transitionary stage from the pre-industrial to the industrial technology. In the same way as the manufactories did away with the medieval artisan method of production, in which all phases of production had been handled manually, so the introduction of fire power, as exemplified by the use of guns and gunpowder, did away with the fully manually-handled armor of the medieval fighting man. Manual operations continued to play a large part in the manufactories, where the new technology presented itself in the form of a division of labor: the production process was broken down into the making of small parts with a view towards saving time and increasing productivity and efficiency. The machine-driven factory, in turn, superseded the manually-operated manufactory at a later date.

Similarly, manual operations continued to be the main factor in the handling of guns and gunpowder. The difference between the operation of medieval arms and post-medieval guns and gunpowder is seen in the intensification of the hitting power of the guns geared to gunpowder. This increased intensity of hitting power can well be regarded as the factor of timesaving productivity, and thus made to fall fully in line with the kind of production process which took place in the manufactories. It should, therefore, be regarded as proper to call the stage of warfare which had been conducted during the Napoleonic period as the stage of manufactories in the history of weaponry. The stage can be extended back to the period at which gun and gunpowder first made their entry. The first systematic application of guns and gunpowder in a European war took place in 1494, which antedates the Napoleonic Wars by about three centuries.

The manufactories, in their turn, represented the technologically most advanced production units during the Napoleonic Wars. It is during those wars that weapons and military supply objects were produced in a technologically advanced manner. In this connection, it is worth mentioning that the Continental Blockade, which constituted an act of economic warfare, was instituted by the Napoleonic administration to prevent British products, particularly textiles, from reaching the European continent.

The blockade necessitated the establishment of production units on the continent of Europe under the sponsorship of the Napoleonic administration. It is in this manner, in particular, that textile manufactories first sprang up on the continent. The need for textile products was greatly augmented during the Napoleonic Wars because the Napoleonic armies, as well as those of the opponents, had been established through the mobilization of masses of people who had to be put into uniforms. The very word *uniform,* as a noun, it is to be recalled, appeared in that period to designate the uniform clothing worn by the military personnel.

Guns and gunpowder were also produced during the Napoleonic Wars in manufactories, i.e., in establishments which lacked machinery, but in which traditional time-wasting artisan methods of production had been replaced by a time-saving division of labor, i.e., by a technologically geared subdivision of the process of production of the whole into production of parts, and with the subsequent assignment of the work on the parts to different workers. Ships also were produced in the same kind of production establishments, as were textile products, guns and gunpowder. The name of the production units where ships were made retained the time-honored name of "shipyard." Technologically, the shipyard in the Napoleonic period was operated on the same level as the production unit called manufactory, in which products other than ships were produced for the Napoleonic and the anti-Napoleonic armed forces.

Some of the production work, as for instance the making of uniforms out of textile products, which were produced in the manufactories, were farmed out by the Napoleonic administration and by the administrations of the anti-Napoleonic coalition to so-called "factors". Those factors, in turn, placed the orders with defunct master-artisans or lifetime journey-men, who performed the work in their homes according to the pro-duction devices of the traditional medieval time-wasting technology. Reference in this case is made to the operation of the so-called "domestic system," or as it is also called, the "put out system." In this case, the post-medieval aspect is present in the introduction of the market and the pricing of goods on the basis of the demand and supply factor. The guild which controlled production standards and fixed the price had disappeared, and production standards and prices were set in line with the requirements of the market for goods and services, but as stated above, medieval technology persisted.

Agricultural production in continental Europe had undergone little technological innovation since the medieval period. There, too, pro-duction methods had remained largely unchanged and time-wasting. The breaking up of the big estates and the parceling of the land during the French Revolution did result, to some extent, in the introduction of some methods of intensification of the cultivation of the soil.

In England, the process of the intensification of agricultural pro-duction had set in about 100 to 150 years before that process had been started on its way on the continent. The social upheaval which brought about the Civil Wars in Britain during Cromwell's time and its immediate aftermath had the effect of starting the process of the intensification of agricultural production on its way a century and a half before that development took place on the continent of Europe. Yet, the intensifica-tion of agricultural production was a far cry from the mechanization of agriculture. One can safely say that the agricultural products which had been used by all belligerents in the Napoleonic Wars were produced under conditions which pre-dated the application of industrial imple-ments in agricultural production.

Special mention must be made of the factor of transportation, which constitutes an important aspect in the conduct of any war. Industriali-zation, i.e., the mechanization of transport through self-propelling transportation equipment, was entirely absent in the kind of transportation which had been used in the Napoleonic Wars. Transportation during that period was either by foot or by horse-driven carriages. In regard to the aspect of transportation, the Napoleonic Wars were strictly wars of the horse-and-buggy age. Mechanization of transport is first presented in the introduction of railroad cars driven by steam engines. The widespread use of railroads powered by steam engines did not take place until two generations after the end of the Napoleonic Wars in 1815. It is only in the wars of the latter half of the nineteenth century that the transportation of troops, provisions, and ammunitions could be effected in mechanized means of transportation.

Mention must be made also of the means of communication, as another important aspect of the conduct of war. Mechanization of means of communication, which started with the introduction of the telephone and the telegraph, constitutes a development which started at the beginning of the twentieth century. During the Napoleonic Wars, and well through the nineteenth century, communication in the conduct of war was, as a rule, entrusted to speeding messengers, so-called "runners;" important messages were entrusted to special envoys riding in horse-driven carriages. With regard to the aspect of communication, the Napoleonic Wars lie definitely within an age of non-mechanized means of communication.

It is interesting to relate, in this connection, that it was the aspect of transportation and communication which played a decisive role in Field-Marshal Kutuzov's strategy which led to the defeat of the Napoleonic armies. Napoleon's famous order of retreat, after his army had occupied the city of Moscow, cited the matter of "over-extended supply lines" as the reason for the withdrawal. The need to shorten the supply lines, which the retreat order by Napoleon cited as the aim of the withdrawal operation, was necessitated by the cumbersome and slow operation of the transportation system in the horse-and-buggy age. That was a circumstance which Kutuzov took into account.

Harassment of the French supply lines by the Russian guerrilla fighters, as foreseen by Kutuzov, was an additional factor which made it impossible for the Napoleonic armies to supply its troops in central Russia. It must be kept in mind, however, that harassment by guerrilla fighters can lead to a major destruction of a military transportation system only if the transportation is carried on either by foot or by horsedriven wagons. It is much more difficult to disrupt the operation of mechanized means of transportation, such as railroads. It is, therefore, again the character of the means of transportation in its non-mechanized form which must be regarded as the underlying factor in the failure of Napoleon to supply his troops stationed in and around Moscow.

The slowness, and, hence, the unreliability of the communication systems during the Napoleonic Wars is highlighted by the following occurrence. When Napoleon, after having been driven all the way from Moscow to Paris, arrived at the French capital, he was unaware that his army in Russia had ceased to exist as a fighting force. This incident was reported by one of the closest aides who accompanied Napoleon, General De Caulaincourt. All through the long journey, General De Caulaincourt reports, Napoleon was under the impression that his armies in Russia continued to function as fighting forces. The rather belated information which was passed on to Napoleon after he had reached Paris made him realize that he had to draft an entirely new army to replace the fighting forces which had ceased to exist in Russia.

As far as communication in actual combat is concerned, it can be conjectured that the indecisive outcome of the major battle which the Napoleonic armies fought a hundred or so miles to the west of Moscow, near the village of Borodino, was to some extent due to faulty and unreliable information on the part of the French General Staff. The Russian armies which faced the French in that battle can be considered as having had much more adequate information about the actual situation of the French "forces in being" (to use the term of Clausewitz), which refers to the forces taking part in combat, plus the readily available reserves. In a war situation, regardless of whether or not the means of communication are mechanized, the side which fights on enemy territory is always at a disadvantage, as far as getting and relaying information through given means of communication is concerned. Conversely, the side which fights on its own territory is at a comparative advantage, as far as the getting and relaying of information is concerned, no matter what the means of communication are.

The situation which prevailed in the battle of Borodino throws, in addition, a sidelight on the combination of transportation and communication factors as they affect actual warfare. Some war historians have contended that the reason why Napoleon and his aides decided to let the battle of Borodino end in a draw lies in the realization of Napoleon's commanding staff that, by forcing the Russian armies to retreat and then having to pursue those armies, the French would have been unable to move sufficient supplies with adequate speed to support that advance of their armies.

It is doubtful, as it has been stated here, that the commanding officers of the Napoleonic armies had adequate information on the number and location of Russian military forces as well as their sources of supply. The conclusion, therefore, which the French commanders had drawn in regard to letting the battle of Borodino end in a draw, can be regarded as having been based on the inadequacy of the factor of information, which, in turn, resulted in an inadequate evaluation of the efficacy of the factor of transportation.

In this connection, it might be of interest to dwell on the matter of how much importance is to be attached to what is generally called the "psychological factor" in military decisionmaking. Clausewitz had stated that, with regard to a specific evaluation of the psychological factor, a battle is never won or lost unless the commanding officer decides to claim victory or accept defeat. While the decision, as such, to be made by the commanding officers, can well be regarded as a psychological factor, the basis for making such a decision must be viewed as non-psychological. The inadequacies in the functioning of the communication and transportation systems are certainly not psychological propositions. The degree of the inadequacy in the functioning of the communication and transportation system can be made subject to an appraisal into which the psychological factor does not enter.

It should be the aim of any proper conduct of war and, in particular, of a proper conduct of combat, to increase, as much as possible, the range of objective factual information and to decrease, to the extent possible, the non-objective, psychological range of information. The objective factual aspect of the conduct of warfare and, in particular, of the conduct of combat, was well understood by Clausewitz. He had made the statement that the conduct of warfare can be termed as having its function in the exchange of blows, and that this exchange of blows can be likened to the function of trading which is characterized by the passing on of goods and money from one party to another party. He thus did not make an attempt to overrate the non-objective psychological factor in the making of military decisions.

Taken together, in terms of non-mechanized weapons, non-mechanized transportation, and non-mechanized communications, the Napoleonic Wars must be regarded as pre-industrial wars in the technological sense. In the social sense, however, the Napoleonic Wars fall within the industrial age, because mass mobilization constitutes but a counterpart of the social mobility which presents a pre-conditioning factor for the introduction of industrial technology. The factor of social mobility is rooted, as has been pointed out in this chapter before, in the *levee en masse,* which had first come into practice during the French Revolution and which was reshaped into mass mobilization during the Napoleonic Wars.

The need of the anti-Napoleonic coalition to resort to mass mobilization must, in turn, be regarded as a factor which accounts for the acceptance of the revocation of feudal bondage as a permanent institution in all the countries conquered by Napoleon. The latter, in his turn, hastened the freeing of the serfs in the wake of the advance of his armies so that he might facilitate the mass mobilization of the native population of the conquered European countries in order to bolster his fighting forces. It is known, for instance, that of the six hundred thousand men in the Napoleonic armies which invaded Russia about two-thirds were not Frenchmen, but natives of European countries which had been conquered by Napoleon.

Why feudalism remained intact in Russia in the wake of the Napoleonic invasion can only be explained by the fact that Napoleon never fully conquered Russia and, therefore, lacked authority to abolish serfdom there. Had the conquest of Russia been completed, and had a Napoleonic administration of Russia decreed the abolishment of serfdom, it can safely be assumed that serfdom would have remained abolished in Russia, as it did in other European countries after the Napoleonic armies were defeated.

The first industrial war which was fought in Europe was the Prusso-Austrian War of 1866. That was masterminded on the Prussian side by Moltke the Elder. The designation "Elder" is necessary in order to differentiate between the Moltke who was the Chief of Staff and chief military advisor to the Prussian Crown in the period immediately preceding the unification of Germany, and his nephew, who played an important role in Germany's part in World War I. Moltke the Elder must be given credit for having revolutionized the concept of the conduct of a war by bringing the role of mechanized transportation, i.e., the railroads, into a strategic range of the conduct of war.

Moltke the Elder was an early railroad enthusiast and anticipated the importance of the railroads in the conduct of wars in the early stage of railroad building in Germany. He was fully aware that time and space – the two fundamental aspects of strategy – had become greatly affected by the speed of the transportation of troops by railroad. Troops and provisions could be moved by rail six times faster than the time it took the armies to march in the Napoleonic period. Moltke realized that the country which had a greatly developed system of rail transportation was definitely at an advantage in the conduct of a war.

Moltke the Elder considered the speed of the mobilization and concentration of the fighting forces as essential elements in strategic considerations. Thus he made the timetable of mobilization, of the assembling of troops, and of the initial marching order of the fighting forces the core of the strategic plans which he drew up. In 1859, he used the then existing Prussian railroads in a test mobilization of the Prussian armies. The occasion for that mobilization was the then pending Italian war. The real test of the use of railroad transportation as a means of carrying troops with the utmost speed came in the Prussian War against Austria, which Moltke the Elder directed in 1866. Railroad transportation of troops became an integral part of the whole campaign of Prussia against Austria.

The strategy of the Austrian command, masterminded by the chief advisor on strategy for the Austrian Crown, General Krismanic, was yet the strategy of the eighteenth century. This concept of strategy stressed what can be called "positional warfare," which emphasized massed military formations coupled with a stress on strong defense of fixed positions. This eighteenth century strategic concept of the Austrian armies, which the main strategic advisor of the Austrian Crown, Krismanic, forced upon the Austrian commander-in-chief, General Benedick, regarded the holding and acquisition of territory as the main strategic aim in the conduct of war.

The Prussian forces were led according to a new strategic principle which had been enunciated by Moltke the Elder. He regarded the loss and acquisition of territory a secondary consideration, since it could be overriden by the speed of the movement of troops. Thus, what Moltke the Elder taught, and what the Prussian armies, which were led according to his principles, executed, was to trade space for time. This trading of space for time had an effect on a major tactical device which had been the stock-in-trade of the eighteenth-century war pattern: the use of the so-called "inner lines of operation." The "inner line of operation" was a device by which the separation of the armies of one belligerent could be used by the other belligerent to bring about tactical, and even strategic advantages, for itself.

Moltke the Elder realized that a speeding up of troop movements, in case contingents of troops were divided and separated from each other, could deprive the other belligerent of the opportunity to use this division and separation of contingents to his own advantage. He further maintained that the division of troop contingents of one belligerent party could be turned into a comparative disadvantage for the other party, if a quick movement of the separate contingents could result in a rapid concentration of the initially separated contingents.

If the opponent were not able or willing to move his troops as fast, the rapid concentration of the initially separated contingents could, in turn, result in the encirclement of the enemy's fighting forces. In this case, Moltke demonstrated, all tactical and strategic operations had a relative application, and their significance, depending upon changed conditions, could be turned into their very opposites. In this case we are confronted with a dialectical transformation of tactical and strategic concepts.

In the battle of Sadowa, which constituted the decisive final battle of the Prusso-Austrian War, the Prussian armies failed to draw a noose around the Austrian armies because of a Prussian marching directive, which made the separate contingents of the advancing Prussian army get into each other's way, thus slowing down the advance of the Prussian forces towards the position where the Austrian forces were concentrated at Sadowa. It was not a faulty strategy which enabled the Austrian army to escape the noose which the Prussian armies were supposed to close upon the Austrian. It was the faulty application of Moltke's principle of speedy movement, which was present in the battle of Sadowa.

Moltke the Elder and those who executed his strategic plan in the Franco-Prussian War rectified the mistake made by the Prussian armies at the approaches to Sadowa. In the final battle of that war, the separated contingents of the Prussian armies completed their concentrated movements towards Sedan with such rapidity that all escape routes of the French army were cut off, so that the French were left no alternative to complete surrender.

The rapidity with which the successful army contingents reunited in the case of Sedan was not brought about by the use of railroads only. Marches on foot were definitely a part of the plan of concentration devised by Moltke and executed by the Prussian generals. However, the marches on foot always were closely coordinated with the troop movements by train. What must not be forgotten in this connection is that continuous day-after-day marches of troops always resulted in great fatigue among the soldiers. Were a battle to be fought right after a prolonged march, the weakened physical condition of the troops employed was most likely to have an adverse effect on the chances of winning such a battle. With transportation by rail used to supplement marches, the fatigue element affecting the troops was greatly reduced.

It is apparent, therefore, that railroad transportation of troops plays a considerable role, even if not all troop movements are made by train. As far as the movement of troops on foot itself is concerned, it should be kept in mind that roads had been greatly improved during the nineteenth century, which meant that even the movement of troops on foot could be speeded up. The improvement of roads is, in turn, also to be considered a factor of technological advance in road building techniques and equipment.

As far as the general conduct of the Franco-Prussian War is concerned, it should be admitted that France also had railroads when the war broke out, and that railroads were used for the transportation of French troops as well. What the French military command in that war did not have, however, was a strategic plan in which the railroads as carriers of troops played as important a part as they did in the strategic plan of Moltke the Elder, which was executed by the Prussian generals.

From the experience of the Franco-Prussian War, Moltke the Elder learned more about the relativity of strategic and tactical concepts. It was a strategic device which had come down from the experience of the Napoleonic Wars and was codified by Clausewitz and Jomini, that an early concentration of troops, or, as the Napoleonic expression had it, "the massing of troops," was an extremely dangerous proposition, which could not be reversed in the whole campaign. According to the Napoleonic rule, once the armies had been massed, battle had to be given, no matter what the other circumstances were at the given time.

Moltke the Elder realized from the experience of the rapid movement of troops by means of railroad transportation, and in particular, from the rapid advancement of the Prussian armies to the battle scene of Sadowa, that a reversal of the concentration of troops (or, as the Napoleonic expression went, "the massing of troops") could be undertaken with a fair chance of success, if speedy railroad transportation were to be provided. In that case, early concentration or marshalling of troops does not have to be accepted as an unalterable situation. Therefore, according to latter-day reflections of Moltke the Elder, the mere marshalling of troops cannot be regarded as a decisive factor in forcing a military decision under otherwise unfavorable circumstances.

The impact of the speed of movements of the Prussian troops brought about through the use of railroads and the integration of railroad transportation of troops in the Prussian strategic plans of Moltke the Elder is but re-emphasized when one takes into consideration the other comparative factor of those campaigns. In the Prusso-Austrian War, the Austrian cavalry was generally considered superior to the Prussian cavalry. But horses were no match to the railroads, as far as speed of transportation is concerned. In this sense, one can say that the Prusso-Austrian War for the first time specifically demonstrated the superiority of mechanized equipment to animal driving power.

It was also generally agreed that the Austrian artillery formations were more efficiently organized than those of the Prussians. But here again, the speed of the movement of the Prussian troops and the coordination of railroad transportation with marches first determined the timing of the decisive battle, and then determined its short duration, as a result of which there was not even sufficient time for artillery action to come into full effect.

It is generally conceded that the so-called "needle gun", which the Prussian armies used, was to some degree superior to the rifle with which the Austrian infantry was equipped. It is also generally conceded, however, that the mere superiority of the Prussian rifles could not have brought about victory for Prussia, were it not for the speedy and concentrated movement of troops, for which the railroads have to be given major credit.

In regard to the Franco-Prussian War, it should be kept in mind, that the French artillery units had been overhauled just before the war, in the course of the reforms by which Marshall Neil sought to increase the efficiency of the French Army. The French artillery equipment was, on the whole, superior to that of the Prussians. However, the speed of the Prussian troop movements, which brought the whole war to an end in five weeks, deprived the French armies of a chance to use the potential of their artillery.

The French armies had also received new rifles, the so-called *chassepot,* a new breech-loading rifle which was greatly superior to the Prussian needle gun. In addition, a new type of machine gun, called *mitrailleuse,* had been provided for some French infantry units. But again, the swiftness of the advance of the Prussian troops, in the main through the mechanized transportation equipment of the railroads, nullified all the relative advantages of the more intensive fire power of the French infantry units, which, had the war lasted longer, could have had some effect on its outcome.

The victories which Prussia had scored over Austria and France signified to the leading military circles in Germany that Moltke the Elder had found a sure device for winning modern wars. Count Alfred Schlieffen, who succeeded Moltke the Elder as head of the German General Staff, devoted himself to a further spelling out of his predecessor's plan of military operations. Schlieffen, as did Moltke, geared his plan for military operations to the utilization of railroads for purposes of mobilization and combat. Schlieffen realized that the rail network of Germany had spread out since the days of Moltke the Elder, and that the greater density of the German railroad system was to be utilized to bolster the German military mobilization and combat plan.

Schlieffen also became aware that, in addition to the perfection of the railroad system, great changes had taken place in Germany, as well as in its neighboring countries, in the sphere of communication. Mechanization of transport had been followed by mechanization of the means of communication, with telephone, telegraph and wireless becoming standard communication factors. Schlieffen, therefore, in working out his plan of operations, included full reliance on mechanized means of communication along with full reliance on mechanized means of transportation.

Schlieffen went further than Moltke the Elder so far as the range of his plan of military operation is concerned: Schlieffen included not only the factor of mobilization up to the point of readying the military forces for battle, but also the actual combat itself. The widening of the range of the military plan, and in particular the inclusion of the actual conduct of battle in the plan, required a great deal of precision in planning. Schlieffen thought that the perfection in the operation of mechanized means of transportation, as well as communication, provided a secure basis for minute precision in planning.

The political aspect of the Schlieffen plan of operation was based on the assumption that Germany would have to fight a war against two adversaries, France and Russia, at the same time. With the dismissal of Bismarck, the German foreign policy which was on the whole friendly towards Russia came to an end. Under William II, Germany instituted a foreign policy which was as unfriendly towards Russia as it was to France. In any future European war, Germany had to expect to be forced to fight simultaneously against both Russia and France. Schlieffen, therefore, had to draw a plan of operations on two fronts, an Eastern as well as a Western front.

The first phase of the drafting of the Schlieffen plan was underlined by the assumption that the major part of German forces was to be concentrated against Russia and the minor part of the German forces was to face France. In the later phase of the drawing up of the Schlieffen plan, the order was reversed; the major part of the German forces was to face France, and the minor part of the German forces was to face Russia. In neither case could Schlieffen assume that Germany would have a superiority of forces against either potential foe. To make up for the comparative disadvantage of numbers with which Germany expected to be confronted in any future European war, Schlieffen emphasized the high mobility of the German troop movements based on the use of mechanized means of transportation and communication.

Schlieffen did not live to see his plan put into operation. When the plan was put to test under the direction of Moltke, Jr., a nephew of Moltke the Elder, it was found sorely wanting. Schlieffen had overemphasized the factor of mobility geared to a technologically advanced transportation and communication system; what he forgot in drawing up his plan was the impact of technologically advanced weapons.

Thus, the First World War, which erupted in August, 1914, and which was supposed to be the most mobile war fought in modern times, turned out to be the most immobile. What happened was that the offensive operations planned by Schlieffen were made impossible by the employment on a wide scale of a mechanized weapon, a machine gun, which forced defensive operation upon the Germans as well as upon their French, English and Russian adversaries. Neither the French nor the Russians had offered any strategic plans which took the defensive character of the widespread use of the machine gun into consideration. The French and the Russians, as well as their allies, the British and the Italians, were as perplexed as the Germans and the Austrians and their allies, when, at the very outset of World War I, they found themselves forced to settle down to four years of immobile warfare.

The French, on their part, under the direction of Colonel Grandmaison, also had planned for offensive operations, as they were provided in the Schlieffen plan. The only difference between the Schlieffen and Grandmaison plans is seen in the comparatively narrow range of the Grandmaison plan, which, unlike the Schlieffen plan, did not include the planning of actual combat. In their respective major strategic aims, which were directed toward a quick military decision in the field, with an ensuing breakthrough of enemy lines and subsequent envelopment and possible encirclement of enemy troops, the Schlieffen and Grandmaison plans were identical.

A specific conditioning factor must be kept in mind as far as the Schlieffen plan is concerned; not only did Schlieffen overemphasize the mobility of troops at the expense of a de-emphasis of fire power, but he overemphasized the mobility of troops at the expense of their number. Confronted, as he was, with the necessity of planning a war on two fronts, and thus faced with the prospect of an inferiority of numbers, as far as the German troops *vis-à-vis* the Russian and French troops were concerned, he counted on the mobility of German troops as a squaring factor. He traded too much in terms of numbers of German troops for what he considered to be their superior mobility. Had Germany at all times during World War I had a superior number of forces on both the French and the Russian fronts, Germany conceivably could have won that war.

That the inferiority in numbers of German troops played a decisive role in first stalemating, and in the end defeating, Germany can be seen from the following. Germany did not win the important battles of the Marne because the German generals, who were responsible for the fighting of these battles, overestimated the number and the fighting strength of the allied troops which faced the Germans in the battle area. The estimate which the commanding German generals made of their foes in the Marne battle area compared unfavorably with the depleted number of their own German troops at the scene.

Had the German troops at the battle area of the Marne consisted of say, fifty per cent more of what they actually were at that time, the battle might have been won by Germany. Whether this alone would have decided the war in the West appears to be doubtful, however. Only if the overall strength of the German troops on the Western front had been fifty percent greater than it actually was could Germany conceivably have won the war in the West after winning the battles of the Marne. That kind of German troop concentration was, however, an impossibility for Germany, as long as she had to fight a war on two fronts.

The same relative inferiority in numbers of troops which kept Germany from conceivably winning the war in the West kept Germany, too, from conceivably winning the war in the East. In the battles of Tannenberg and the Masurian Lakes in East Prussia, General Hindenburg scored the kind of victory which had been envisaged by Schlieffen.

Russian troops which had entered East Prussia at the beginning of World War I had been encircled at Tannenberg and the Masurian Lakes and were forced to surrender. That victory à la Schlieffen and Moltke the Elder did not, however, bring about an overall victory for the Germans over the Russians. Faced with the overall inferiority in numbers on the Russian front, the Germans had to settle down there, too, for a trench war.

Instead of a war of annihilation, as planned by Schlieffen and his French counterpart, Grandmaison, World War I became a blatant example of a war of attrition. The maxim which had been laid down by Clausewitz and reaffirmed by Schlieffen, to the effect that the struggle for maintaining and acquiring positions in warfare was outdated, had been turned into its very opposite in the course of World War I. The bloodiest battles ever fought in modern times for one inch of territory were those which were fought in the immediate vicinity of the trenches. World War I might yet have continued for quite a number of years after the four years which it lasted, and could possibly have ended in a draw, were it not for two developments.

Both developments were in their major aspects political. The first pertains to the revolution in Russia, the second to the entry of the United States into the war against Germany. The overthrow of the Czarist regime had, in no small measure, been brought about by the lack of munitions and provisions for the front-line Russian troops. The Provisional Russian government which took over, first under Prince Lvov and subsequently under Kerenski, decided to continue the war against Germany.

An offensive was launched in June of 1917 on the Austrian front, with the aim of effecting a breakthrough. This strategic aim was not attained, however, and the political repercussions from the inability of the Provisional Russian government to bring the war with Germany to a speedy conclusion, set the stage for the overthrow of that government by Lenin and his followers. Lenin was set on getting Russia out of the war. Soviet Russia concluded a separate peace treaty with Germany in Brest-Litovsk.

With Russia out of the war, Germany could add a number of divisions, which were no longer needed on the Eastern front, to its forces on the Western front. However, those added divisions could not bring about a superiority or even a matching in numbers with the troops of the Western powers at that time. When the dictated peace settlement of Brest-Litovsk, which the Lenin government had signed with Imperial Germany, took effect, the United States expeditionary corps had been added already to the armies of France and England which manned the Western front.

On the Western front, the cards had been stacked against Germany. Not only could Germany not match the vast numbers of allied troops to which the United States expeditionary corps had been added; the United States forces had, in addition, just entered the war and were not as battle-weary as the German troops, or, for that matter, the French and British troops.

But the military decision on the Western front turned against Germany not solely because the Western troops were numerically superior, and not even on account of the physical battlestrength of the Americans. What decided the military issue against Germany was the addition in great quantities of a new mechanized weapon – the tank. The American tanks manned by fresh American troops overran the German positions and sealed Germany's doom.

The pendant to the significant role which the self-propelled machine gun and tank played in land warfare in World War I can be seen in the significant role which the self-propelled torpedo played in sea warfare in this war. All authoritative evaluators of the conduct of the war at sea during World War I agree that fear of the self-propelled torpedoes of the submarines and destroyers checkmated the action of the surface ships.

For all practical purposes, the surface fleet of battleships and cruisers was immobilized as a mass fighting force during most of World War I. The only major attempt to use battleships in formation to fight a decisive sea battle was made by the British fleet at Jutland at the beginning of the war, but the fear of torpedoes made the British commander, Jellicoe, call off the battle before any decisive action could be undertaken by either the British or the German fleet. Forays by a few British or French surface ships, or of the German fleet for that matter, were undertaken from time to time, but these forays were not meant to have any strategic significance.

The self-propelled torpedo of the submarine also played a nearly decisive role in the war against commercial vessels. In the main, the effort of the German submarine fleet to cut off British supply lines from the overseas sources of food and raw materials has to be mentioned. Authoritative evaluation of the effectiveness of German submarine warfare against British commerce is united on the point that the rate of sinking of British and allied commercial vessels which tried to supply Britain with food and raw materials reached such proportions that a further prolongation of the war would have starved Britain to the point of capitulation.

It is of interest to notice that neither the officially adopted German naval strategy nor the officially adopted British naval strategy made any allowance for the decisive role of the self-propelled torpedoes fired from submarines. German naval strategy in World War I was based on the Tirpitz doctrine of offensive warfare by super battleships. This theory, to which Tirpitz and his American counterpart, Mahan, subscribed, aimed at obtaining a decision through sea battles in which the major battleships of one nation were to be arraigned against the major battleships of another nation. It was based on an outdated concept of naval warfare, in which surface vessel-formations were to try to attain a major military decision, it constituted a different projection of a pattern of naval warfare, which had a valid basis in the days of the sailing boats.

The decisive battles between the Dutch, the Spanish, and the British fleets which resulted in decisive victories for either side, were fought at the time when no threat to surface vessels existed except by other surface vessels. With the presence of self-propelled torpedoes geared to submarines, the potential of the fighting power of surface vessels had to be judged not only against that of the fighting power of enemy surface vessels, but against the fighting power of submerged enemy vessels armed with self-propelled torpedoes as well.

The fighting power of the submerged enemy vessels armed with self-propelled weapons had reached such a degree of intensity at the time of World War I that it placed surface ships practically out of commission, as far as any attempt to bring about a major military decision by their actions is concerned. British Admiral Jellico's move to withdraw the Grand Fleet from Jutland before any decisive naval battle with the German High Seas Fleet could be fought is not only symbolic of the preponderance which a submarine armed with the self-propelled torpedo assumed over the battleship; Jellico's action actually signified a decisive step towards the abandonment of the doctrine of surface naval warfare, which had come down to the age of steamships from the age of the sailing vessels.

The role of the steamship in naval warfare can be compared to the role of the railroads in the conduct of land warfare. Transportation of military manpower, munitions and provisions was accelerated by the use of steamships instead of sailing vessels. Military personnel on the high seas, and their ammunition and provisions, could speedily be brought into close contact with military personnel and their munitions and provisions on the land. But the comparative speed of transportation cannot by itself be considered a factor on which a military decision as such could be expected to rest; neither was this the case in regard to the role which railroads came to play in modern war, nor was this the case in regard to steamships and the role they came to play in modern warfare.

The role of railroads as well as steamships could be assayed as having but an auxiliary function in the war geared to modern technology. The roles of railroads and steamships in modern warfare can well be regarded as contributing factors in the effectuation of strategic plans. But it cannot be regarded as the factor which, by itself, can be responsible for either victory or defeat, whether in a land war or in naval warfare.

World War II, even more than World War I, demonstrated the role of the Navy as a transportation medium. The operation of the American fleet, which was the largest and most powerful of all the belligerents by the end of World War II, was in the main concentrated on establishing land bases. The so-called "island-hopping campaign" in the Pacific theater of operations was not in any way aimed to deliver a decisive blow at the Japanese fleet.

Nor, for that matter, did the Japanese fleet seek a military decision on the high seas. The kind of military action which took place in the Pacific during World War II was reminiscent of the forays of the surface vessels, in which all the belligerents engaged in World War I, after the abortive sea battle at Jutland. The forays which led to the United States conquest of Japanese-held islands in the Pacific were on a somehow larger scale than those in which surface vessels engaged during World War I. They were forays, nonetheless.

The defensive naval actions which the Japanese undertook against United States naval assaults on the Pacific islands were in the line of raiding activities. At no time and in no place during the United States-Japanese naval warfare in World War II did sizeable fleet formations of the Americans and the Japanese face one another in battle. The Japanese naval strategists, it appears, never subscribed to the precepts of naval strategy of the West, as they had been expounded by the British and German naval strategists prior to World War I. The action of the Japanese fleet during the Russo-Japanese War of 1905 was based on the aim of outmaneuvering, and then cornering, the Russian fleet, thus avoiding open battle. In their strategy of avoiding large-scale naval battles, the Japanese strategists were chronologically ahead of their British and German counterparts.

While the Russians as well as the Japanese had a number of submarines armed with self-propelled torpedoes during the Russo-Japanese War, it is doubtful whether the lurking submarine menace played a major role in making Japanese naval strategists reluctant to take a chance and face the enemy fleet in open battle. It appears likely that, in the evolution of the Japanese naval strategy, it was rather the application of the rational strategic principle of Clausewitz, pertaining to the economy of forces, which played a major role in the Japanese naval strategy. The aspect of the economy of forces was no doubt a factor in the Japanese naval strategists' decision to counsel their naval commanders to caution, and in their insistence upon gaining superiority in maneuverability over the enemy.

In World War II, however, the substantial increase in the number of submarines armed with self-propelled torpedoes in the fleets of all belligerents made it imperative for the Japanese naval strategists to prevail upon their naval commanders to avoid large-scale sea battles, because of the technological military superiority of the submarine-based self-propelled torpedoes over the surface battleships armed with guns.

As far as the Atlantic waters are concerned, the submarine warfare against surface ships played a less decisive role in World War II than in World War I. British anti-submarine warfare, which was spearheaded by destroyers and mine sweepers, was successful in reducing the losses to the British surface fleet to bearable proportions towards the latter part of the war. It is interesting to note that, in contrast to World War I, when submarine and anti-submarine warfare were not included in the strategic plans of either the German or the British navy, submarine warfare as practiced by the German Navy against the allied vessels, and, in particular, against those which serviced British supply routes, proved a more decisive factor in the conduct of sea warfare.

To some extent, the more telling effect of submarine warfare on the British supply routes during World War I is to be ascribed to British unpreparedness for anti-submarine warfare. This unpreparedness had been overcome by the British and their allies in World War II. The less telling effect of German submarine assaults on British and allied shipping is to be ascribed to that comparative allied preparedness. Attacks on British surface shipping from the air also were unable to attain decisive results. British as well as Russian supply routes were kept open in the face of indecisive German submarine and aircraft attacks during World War II.

The use of allied aircraft based on aircraft carriers definitely added to the number of enemy vessels sunk. The paucity in the number of aircraft carriers limited their contribution to the successful prosecution of the allied war effort. The carrier-based aircraft cannot be considered as a potent means of destroying battleships, but it can be considered an effective weapon for the destruction of armed commercial vessels or their convoys. De Seversky's total negation of the role of the aircraft carrier appears to be an unjustified, extreme position. However, it would be an extreme position, in turn, to rely upon the aircraft carrier as a decisive factor in sea warfare.

As far as actions of battleships are concerned, they were limited, on both the allied and the German side, to hit-and-run activities. Open battle of battleships in formation was not even attempted during World War II. The major positive role of surface vessels in the Atlantic during World War II was to provide transportation for troops, munitions, and provisions. This is the same role which surface vessels, in the main, played in the conduct of the war in the Pacific.

The major aim of aircraft activity as a whole was to facilitate the movement of troops in the respective theaters of operations. The initial superiority in numbers of German fighter aircraft is greatly responsible for the swift advances of German troops in Poland at the beginning of World War II. The gain in numbers and fighting strength of British and American bombing and fighting planes in the latter part of the war is, in turn, responsible for the slowing down as well as the retreat of the German ground forces. The destruction of German production centers and communication lines, on which allied bombing missions concentrated, was in line with Douhet's concept of air warfare.

What Douhet had overestimated was the time required to obtain decisive results. Instead of days, as contemplated by Douhet, months and even years were required to get telling results in the destruction of German production and communication centers. German aircraft, in turn, as far as their major use against Britain is concerned, were used as a weapon of terror. Since the air raids failed to break British civilian morale, German aircraft did not attain the strategic aim which the German command had set for itself, in the stated campaign. In the Russian campaign, German aircraft were used as a tactical weapon, in coordination and cooperation with ground forces.

The militarily decisive battles of World War II were fought on land. The strategy and tactics of the French Army had been geared to the twin concepts of defense and fire power. Mechanization of the army had been neglected, and offensive operations were ruled out. The Maginot Line and the fire power sheltered in it were to guarantee France's military invulnerability. Pétain's defensive position behind the concrete wall surrounding Verdun in World War I was intended to serve as the prototype of the French defensive posture in World War II. A war of movement geared to offensive operations was decried by Pétain and those who followed him as too costly in terms of arms and men. The fire power of heavy artillery was to make any offensive operations unnecessary.

British strategists, led by Fuller and Hart, concurred with Pétain and his followers in emphasizing the reliance on defensive operations. Fuller and Hart did not, however, advocate reliance on fire power to the exclusion of the mechanization of the army. Mechanization of the army, as conceived by Fuller and Hart, however, was but the means of further strenghtening the defensive position of the British. Hart went as far as to suggest a ban on the removal of British mechanized forces from British territory.

The German General Staff, operating with direct personal interference by Hitler, placed, in turn, its sole reliance upon offensive operations. In addition, the German General Staff pressed for the mechanization of troops, placing the major emphasis on the speed of movement. Fire power was not stressed as much as easy maneuverability and speed in the execution of military operations. The Soviet Russian General Staff operating in coordination with the Supreme Defense Council headed by Stalin accepted an approach which was to try to balance defensive and offensive operations. At the same time, the Russian General Staff provided for equal stress on mechanization and fire power.

When the battle was joined, the mechanized forces of Hitler's armies had no difficulty in outmaneuvering the French and the British. The forced evacuation of the British army from Dunkirk as well as the military collapse of France were due to the technological inferiority in weapons on the part of Britain and France, as compared with the arms of the Hitlerian troops. In the Russian campaign, the motorization rather than the mechanization played a decisive role in the quick advance of the Hitlerian army in Russia. Mechanization and fire power, with chief reliance upon the tank and heavy artillery, is responsible, in turn, for the Russian counterdrive, which, in the end, brought about the defeat of Hitler's armies.

The technological complexion of the United States armies at the time of the invasion of Europe, and, in particular, at the time the second front in Normandy opened, was akin to the technological complexion of the Russian armies. Tanks and heavy artillery constituted the major striking force of the United States expeditionary corps, as was the case in the Russian army. The incredible speed with which the United States expeditionary force advanced after the invasion of Normandy is, in the main, due to the fact that the major part of the Hitlerian armies were engaged on the Eastern front.

The sapping of the strength of Hitler's armies by the losses in manpower and equipment on the Eastern front must be considered an added factor which accelerated the tempo of the advance of United States troops. World War II, in its decisive final stage, was a war of movement. The decision was rendered by the speed of the movement of the mechanized forces, in the main the tank forces, and by the intersity of firepower, mainly from heavy artillery in anticipation of the movement of the mechanized forces as well as a result of such movement.

Mention must be made of the correlation and synchronization of the movement and the operation of the mechanized and non-mechanized forces. If resistance to the advancing mechanized forces is weak and indecisive, there is little need for non-mechanized forces to come to the support of the mechanized forces. This was the case on the Western front at the beginning of World War II. The French and British armies were left helpless after the Hitlerian mechanized forces had overrun their outer defenses. Hitler's victory on the Western front in the initial phase of World War II was obtained exclusively by the mechanized forces, without any significant supporting action on the part of the non-mechanized forces.

On the Russian front, however, the need for the supporting action of the non-mechanized forces of the Hitlerian armies grew steadily with every advance made by the mechanized forces in Russia. The space which had to be covered in Russia, in addition to the stubborn rearguard action of the retreating Russian troops, made it imperative that the Hitlerian mechanized forces cooperate, and, if possible, synchronize their operations with those of the non-mechanized forces.

This cooperation and synchronization did not, however, take effect to any significant extent in the course of the rapid advance of the German mechanized forces in Russia in the initial phase of the Russian campaign. This lag, as well as lack of cooperation and synchronization in the operations of mechanized and non-mechanized Hitlerian troops, must be considered as the basic drawback in the effectuation of the strategy and tactics in the Hitlerian campaign in Russia. The deeper the mechanized sections of the German armies advanced into Russia, and the longer the initial phase of the Hitlerian campaign in Russia lasted, the more the non-cooperation and non-synchronization of the operations of the mechanized and non-mechanized forces came to weaken the entire position of the invading army.

The initial success of the Russian counter-attack can, to a great extent, be ascribed to the fact that the mechanized Hitlerian forces had been kept detached from the non-mechanized ones, and thus could not withstand sustained Russian pressure. When the Russian counter-attacks gained momentum, the contrast between the forward movement of the Hitlerian troops at the initial phase of the Russian campaign and the forward movement of the Russian troops in the successive phases of the Russian campaign appears striking. The so-called *Blitz* of the Hitlerian armies, which forced the Russian armies back in the initial phases of the Russian campaign, was, for the most part, a succession of vast encircling movements, with very little sustained fighting and comparatively unintensive fire power. When the Russians, on their part, were pressing on the Hitlerian troops and forcing them back, fierce fighting took place, and the intensity of fire power per inch of the contested area became hitherto unmatched. This can be called *"a Grinding Blitz,"* to paraphrase Marshal Sokolovsky; the word *grinding* meaning fierce combat and immense fire power, and the word *Blitz* referring to the speed of the movement of the combat troops. The initial German *Blitz* appears in the succeeding Russian *Grinding Blitz* – a *Blitz* with a vengeance.

In the operation of the American troops after the Normandy invasion, the coordination and synchronization of the mechanized and non-mechanized American forces did not play as much of a role as in the period of sustained Russian counter-attacks. In their active defense during the retreat in the initial phase of the Russian campaign, and then in the series of counter-attacks in the successive stages of the Russian campaign, the Russian troops sapped much of the strength of the Hitlerian armies, which explains why the armies led by General of the Army Dwight D. Eisenhower could make use of the mechanized American forces without any interruption. There was no need to wait for the nonmechanized American forces to come to the support of the mechanized forces.

General Patton's tanks moved through the German lines with the facility of a knife cutting into butter. Only in a side engagement, such as the Battle of the Bulge, which could not be regarded as more than a diversionary maneuver on the part of the Germans, did the Americans have to use fire power to the extent of the capability of their guns. On the whole, it was not necessary for the American expeditionary corps which landed in Normandy and then invaded France and Germany to use the firing capacity of the heavy guns to a full extent for any extended period of time. In a sense, the American expeditionary corps duplicated the Hitlerian armies' *Blitz* tactics, which had been employed at the beginning of World War II, first against the French and British troops in the West, and then against the Russian troops in the initial phase of the Russian campaign. Hitler's chickens had thus come home to roost.

The delay of the Second Front on the part of the Western allies had thus made it possible to dispense with the full application of the American military might in the American campaign in France and Germany. The Americans had been accorded a comparatively advantageous military position vis-à-vis the Hitlerian armies. The German forces, which faced the American troops were inferior in numbers, had sparse fighting equipment, and showed a sagging morale due to the fact that the Russians had applied their fire power as well as their manpower to an almost unimaginable extent before the Americans had reached the soil of France and Germany.

Chapter 2

MILITARY TECHNOLOGY AND ITS NON-APPLICABILITY IN THE NUCLEAR AND MISSILE AGE

In the previous chapter, it was demonstrated that wars have been won by successively more advanced weapons. In the industrial age, each succeeding weapon added to delivery speed and fire power. In this succession of weapons, the addition of speed and fire power provided the margin for victory for that party which made the most efficient use of the most up-to-date weapons. At the present stage of technological development, however, the addition to the delivery speed as well as the addition to the intensity of the fire power of weapons has reached a degree which threatens the very survival of each potential belligerent, if full use is made of those most up-to-date weapons. Under such circumstances, one can no longer speak of victory or defeat in any large scale future war.

The development of an almost instantaneous delivery device in the form of continental and inter-continental ballistic missiles, which have the capacity to carry thermonuclear bombs with a destructive power of one hundred megatons and more, offers the prospect of almost complete annihilation for any belligerent in a war in which such weaponry were to be used.

Weapons, one could argue, always have been devised and applied to inflict as much damage as possible, by one opponent on the other. The invention of continental and inter-continental missiles, coupled with the invention of thermonuclear bombs, it can be argued, was fully in line with the trend which had taken place in all the preceding stages of weapon development in the industrial age. There is a difference, however, in the added degree of destructiveness of the thermonuclear bomb. The added degree of speed and destructiveness in the case of the ballistic missiles and thermonuclear bombs turns the stated weaponry into one of qualitative distinctiveness. The qualitative distinctiveness of the ballistic missiles carrying thermonuclear bombs is to be seen in the threat of absolute destruction which this weapon combination presents. This threat of absolute destruction, which is inherent in the stated weapon combination, would justify our naming that combination the ultimate weapon.

As the arms race, now in progress, advances, it can be safely assumed that each of the potential belligerents among the two world powers, the United States of America and the Union of the Soviet Socialist Republics, have accumulated a sufficient number of missiles and thermo-nuclear bombs of various ranges to be able to stage a saturation attack on the other's territory and population. The saturation point can be expected to be reached within hours after the beginning of the nuclear bombardment. The reaching of the saturation point in a nuclear war would mean the total destruction of the systems of communication, transportation and production, of the factories and dwellings, and of the stockpiles of manufactured goods, raw materials, and consumer products.

Moreover, the reaching of this point of thermonuclear bombing in a series of bomb-laden missile attacks would further mean the destruction of the instrumentalities of war (the ammunition and the provisions of the armed forces), and the destruction of military installations on the ground, as well as those within the territorial waters and within the reaches of the domestic air space. Furthermore, it would mean the all-but-complete annihilation of military personnel, whether stationed on the ground, in territorial waters, or in the domestic air space. And, last but not least, it would mean the almost complete annihilation of the civilian population, whether it be on the ground, within territorial sea limits, or within the domestic air space.

The reaching of a saturation stage in thermonuclear bombing in a series of missile attacks will thus culminate in making an end of both belligerents as social, economic, and political units. Nobody will be left in authority to sue for peace, nor will there be any organized social and economic unit to which a bid for peace could be addressed. For all practical purposes, the nations engaged in nuclear combat will cease to exist when the saturation point of thermonuclear bombing in a series of nuclear attacks has been reached. At that stage, one could safely maintain that, for the belligerents concerned, the war to end all wars will have reached its goal. That this test of proving the irrationality of war as a means of national policy should be considered a possibility, if not a probability, if the arms race continues, is by itself a *reductio ad absurdum* of war as a violent manifestation of human conflict.

Various calculations have been offered as to how many thermonuclear bombs and missiles of various ranges the two potential belligerents, the United States of America and the Union of the Soviet Socialist Republics, possesses or possessed at a given time. These estimates are, at present, beyond the point. They have lost any particular meaning, since it can be ascertained with certainty that thermonuclear bombs, as well as missiles, are now being produced on a mass production basis. And, as one knows from experience, there is hardly any limit to the manufacture of any item, if mass production methods are applied. The only limitation to the amount of mass production is the amount of raw material, the amount of available production equipment, and the size of the available labor force. There does not seem to be any threat of a shortage in the raw materials, the minerals and metals which are used for the production of thermonuclear bombs or missiles; nor may one expect any particular limitation on the amount of production equipment or on the size of the labor force which is required for the continued mass production of either the thermonuclear bombs or the missiles.

Of course, no country has unlimited resources of any kind, and there is a relative scarcity of any given raw material, as well as of equipment and of the labor force for any production purpose in relation to the raw materials and material equipment for all other production purposes. But the allocation of raw materials, equipment, and labor to various production purposes hardly puts any appreciable limit on the production of nuclear bombs and missiles, because with the arms race in progress, the mass production of those instruments of mass destruction will, for the time being, be accorded top priority. The agreement between the United States and the Soviet Union on the limitation of the production of fissionable material does not basically change the situation, in addition it is but a temporary agreement.

It should be inserted here that the production of thermonuclear bombs takes place on a serial basis. One series of tests is followed by another and still another, and so on and so forth. Each test series inaugurates the production of a new type and new range of bombs. In a way, the serial production method of thermonuclear bombs is not basically different from the method applied in the production of missiles. In the production of thermonuclear bombs, the testing of the bombs constitutes but a phase of production, which is known as modeling, and modeling also takes place in missile production.

The modeling phase in the production of thermonuclear bombs is more spectacular and more subject to publicity than the modeling phase in the production of missiles. The production process in the case of the bombs is more of a chemical nature, whereas in the case of the missiles it is more of a physical and mechanical nature. These are but differences in the properties of the material and product. Since it is generally recognized that mass production takes place in both chemical and metal industries, there is no reason why the manufacture of thermonuclear bombs as well as missiles cannot be placed on a mass production basis.

Various estimates have also been made as to how many missiles of various ranges and thermonuclear bombs of various ranges are required for a saturation attack on either of the two potential belligerents, the United States of America and the Union of Soviet Socialist Republics. These estimates can all be considered out of date, since they were not made on the basis of mass production figures of either thermonuclear bombs or missiles, but on the basis of the estimated availability of thermonuclear bombs and missiles of various ranges at a given time. At present, with the mass production of thermonuclear bombs and missiles in progress, it can be maintained with certainty that each of the potential belligerents has accumulated a sufficient number of those instruments of mass destruction to assure itself a safe margin of what has been referred to by the slang term "overkill."

One has to keep in mind that there is a difference between trying to reach a target and actually reaching it. Various estimates can be given as to how many times one side has to try to reach a given target in order, in all probability, to reach it. Naturally, the more times a party tries to reach a target, the greater is the probability of reaching it. The continuous adding to the stockpile of thermonuclear bombs of various ranges and missiles of various ranges increases the number of those instruments of mass destruction and, therefore, increases the capability of escalating the series of potential raids. This, in turn, increases the probability of hitting a target.

With the present arms race in progress, there is hardly any doubt that, in a war in which missile-borne thermonuclear weapons are employed, a saturation point can be reached within no more than a number of hours. Such a certainty can, in turn, be used as a taking-off point for a demonstration that any other weapons or instrumentalities of war could hardly play any decisive role in any such conflict. It could well be ascertained that the development of military means of communication and transportation, and the buildup of the armies, navies and air forces continues to take place not on account of any military necessity in this age of missile-geared thermonuclear warfare, but out of sheer inertia.

To start with the military communication system, much emphasis has been placed since World War II on the development and installation of the radar system, the function of which is based on the application of electronic devices. The spreading of the extremely costly radar network has been geared to an expectation of an attack by manned bombers. It has been estimated that if the approach of manned bombers were recorded on a radar screen, a warning time of about fifteen minutes could be given to the population on whose territory the attack is made. Such warning can be expected to take effect only if the radar screens function properly and the personnel servicing the radar installations properly interprets the recording.

The nebulousness of any radar recording as well as the subjectivity of the interpretation of the recording by the personnel impairs the reliability of the operation of the radar system. As far as the approach of thermonuclear bombs in unmanned missiles is concerned, the radar screen can be rendered insensitive by that kind of object. Except for some people who might be able to spot an approaching bomb-laden missile with the naked eye immediately before it strikes, the potential victims of the attack will not be able to detect the missile and its bombs before they actually hit the ground. This is a crude system of detection, indeed, in which all the costly and intricate radar installations are becoming superfluous.

The radar screens which will be rendered insensitive to the approach of bomb-laden missiles can well be expected to become wholly inoperative as the bomb-laden missiles attack progresses. One or two direct hits by bomb-laden missiles on radar installations centers could well knock out the operation of the radar system in wide regions, if not on a national scale. In that case, the approach of any other military object, to whose approach the functioning radar screen could be expected to be sensitive, will go undetected, too.

The inoperativeness of the radar system will, in turn, form a major link in the wave of inoperativeness which will affect other means of communication in the wake of bomb-laden missile attacks. The inoperativeness of the radar warning system will deprive such means of communication as radio, television, the telegraph and telephone, of the recordable data which might effect, first, the transmission of a warning, and subsequently of any other information. Thus, the radio, the television, the telegraph, and the telephone will be rendered useless for the dissemination of directives for the armed forces and the civilian population in the time immediately preceding, as well as in the time succeeding, a bomb-laden missile attack. The physical destruction of the respective equipment within minutes, if not seconds, in the course of the bomb-laden missile attack can be expected to lead to a complete inoperativeness of the radio, television, telegraph and telephone.

The only way of communication left open would be communication by word of mouth and the dispatching of messengers. The havoc wrought on the ground and in the air, the flying debris and the raging fires, coupled with the high radioactivity of the air, can hardly be considered conducive to an organized attempt to establish a communcation system by using humans as communication media. The conclusion is rather that no communication system whatsoever would be in existence immediately following the landing of a few scattered bomb-laden missiles in different parts of a given country.

The paralysis of the communication system, coupled with the physical destruction of the means of communication, will be matched by a paralysis of the transportation system, which will be coupled, in turn, with the physical destruction of means of transportation. Intercity means of transportation, such as streetcars, buses, trucks and aircraft, will be deprived of an effective basis of operation the minute a few scattered bomb-laden missiles land. The first principle on which the operation of any transportation system is based is the certainty that it provides a continuous link between specified geographical points. In other words, the effective operation of any transportation system is based on the reasonable expectation that the medium of transportation will reach its destination.

This reasonable expectation will not be present any more after a few scattered bomb-laden missiles attacks. In view of the absence of the operation of communication media, to which reference has been made above, the identification of the areas in which bomb-laden missiles have landed, as well as identification of the ranges of devastation, as a basis for the redirection of the means of transportation will become an insurmountable task. Therefore, streetcars, buses and subways in intracity traffic, and trains, buses, trucks and aircraft in intercity traffic, will be racing into nowhere, so to speak, immediately following an attack by a few scattered bomb-laden missiles. None of these transportation media, even if they are not physically destroyed while they are moving, will be sure of reaching their destination.

The actual, as well as the threatened destruction of the means of transportation, regardless whether or not they were moving, will increase with each succeeding landing of additional bomb-laden missiles. The way to escape the continuous wave of physical destruction will be open only to aircraft off the ground. Yet, a landing of such aircraft could be assured only with a certain degree of probability, if it were to leave the airspace of the nation which has come under attack by bomb-laden missiles. Within the range of the airspace of a nation under attack by bomb-laden missiles, the safe landing of aircraft could not be assured after a few scattered bomb-laden missiles have landed on the territory of that nation. The entire transportation system will, as the attack progresses, be as much put out of commission, as will the communication system.

What chance is there, one is bound to ask, for the maintenance and the functioning of the armed forces in a country under attack by bomb-laden missiles? The answer will be given step by step. The armed forces, one must point out, depend to some extent on their own communication and transportation systems. The air force and the navy, in particular, are composed of movable vehicles which are provided with means to communicate with each other. The army has a number of units, such as artillery and tanks, which consist of self-propelling vehicles. Those components of the armed forces, as well as the rest of the armed forces, will no doubt be affected by a progressing bomb-laden missile attack.

It should also be kept in mind that the paralysis and the subsequent destruction of the communication and transportation systems which, aside from the radar warning system, are not part and parcel of the maintenance and operation of the armed forces cannot have but an adverse effect on the military effectiveness of the armed forces. The military effectiveness of the armed forces will, in turn, be affected by the relative effectiveness of the ultimate weapon, the bomb-laden missile. The degree of destructiveness of the ultimate weapon must be considered as the basic factor in a reappraisal of the role of the armed forces in relation to the military missile units. The paralysis and subsequent destruction of the means of communication and the means of transportation in itself constitutes but a practical manifestation of the military impact of bomb-laden missiles and of their power of destruction.

At first sight it might appear as if the impact of bomb-laden missile attacks could be compared with the aim of attaining air control, as laid down by Douhet and later implemented by Mitchell and De Seversky. In that case one could say that at least the concept of air supremacy is bound to attain practical application. This conclusion, however, is not warranted when a more careful scrutiny of the matter is undertaken. The concept of air supremacy and air control as expounded by Douhet, Mitchell, and De Seversky, was based on the postulation that bombing by aircraft would leave the bombed country defenseless. The navy and the army, Douhet, Mitchell, and De Seversky argued, would cease to be decisive military factors, either in defense or offense, after the aircraft had gained control of the air over the opponent's territory. The military decision then, the air strategists argued, would be attained through strategic bombing.

The attendant impossibility of the country, over whose air space superiority was attained by the opponent's bombing aircraft, to defend itself effectively through the use of navy and army forces will result in a quick capitulation. The bulk of the country's production system, as well as the bulk of the country's population, the capitulation of which was to be brought about by the attainment of air superiority over that country, would then be expected to remain intact. This cannot be expected to be the case, however, in an attack by bomb-laden missiles, and in particular in the case of a saturation attack.

Arguments have been advanced in support of an assumption that an attack by bomb-laden missiles might be undertaken solely with the purpose of terrorization, so as to bring about disorganization, disorientation, and subsequently, panic. Arguments have also been advanced in support of an assumption that only selected military installations and selected production centers are likely to be hit in such an attack. If either of these assumptions turned out to be correct, total devastation would not result. The bulk of production centers, as well as the bulk of the population would, in such a case, remain unscathed. Any damage after such limited attacks could then be compared to the damage wrought in the course of attacks by manned aircraft. A situation could then arise in which one belligerent could obtain air control over another country, as foreseen by the writings of Douhet, Mitchell, and De Seversky.

It is, however, highly unlikely that attacks by bomb-laden missiles will remain limited. It is much more likely that a war in which bomb-laden missiles are employed will be pursued to the point of a saturation bombing. The reason for this expectation is the utter impossibility for either the attacked or the attacking party to assess properly the extent of the damage which any particular bomb-laden missile attack or a series of bomb-laden missile attacks has caused. The inoperativeness and subsequent destruction of the communication and transportation systems in a country under such an attack will make the assessment of the damage inflicted by bomb-laden missile attacks next to impossible.

There are other reasons why an all-out saturation attack may be expected. The information which one country could be expected to have about another's missile launching sites must be considered to be incomplete as well as misleading. It stands to reason, therefore, that the attacking opponent, in the effort not to leave any conceivably hidden missile launching sites intact, could not and would not take any chances in leaving any part of the opponent's territory unscathed.

The possibility that production centers will remain unscathed, or that limited attacks will be concentrated only on production centers, seems slight in view of the inability of directing bomb-laden missile attacks to hit specific production centers and to exclude others. The destructiveness of the bomb-laden missiles is so large that the production targets which, from a strategic point of view, are important or unimportant will have to be hit indiscriminately. The same can be said with regard to a possible differentiation between military and non-military targets.

Again, the range of destructiveness of the bomb-laden missiles at present has reached such proportions as to make it impossible to aim at military installations to the exclusion of non-military installations, or vice-versa. A like argument can be advanced to show that it will be next to impossible, in view of the extensive range of the destructiveness of the bomb-laden missiles, to make a distinction, as far as targets are concerned, between structures and people.

There has been some talk of the possibility of the invention of a so-called "neutron bomb," which will kill only people but leave structures unaffected. So far, the neutron bomb is only in the talking stage. Were it to become a reality, the question could be asked, for whom are the structures to be preserved? Structures, as we know, cannot take care of themselves, and the people who might care for the structures cannot be expected to exist. Presumably the neutron bomb would be more effective in killing people than the thermonuclear bomb, since it could expend all its power of destruction exclusively on putting humans to death.

As things now stand, thermonuclear bombs will have to do, and these bombs can be expected to do quite a thorough job of mass destruction. There will be hardly any structures left, and there will hardly be anybody left to attempt to take care of the remaining structures after a saturation attack with nuclear bombs has taken place. In that regard, the situation is entirely different, and it is not incorrect to say that a qualitatively different situation has arisen, as compared with the situation which the air strategists, Douhet, Mitchell, and De Seversky expected to find, after an aerial bombardment by non-nuclear boms dropped from manned aircraft.

The total devastation that can be expected to be wrought on the territory of all major belligerents in a nuclear war makes it wholly impossible to conclude such a war, in the way the air strategists propounded it. There would not be anybody with sufficient authority left to extend either a bid for yielding or to do the yielding, not to speak of the absence of a means of communication and transportation by which such imaginary bids could be conveyed.

In this connection, one must take up the question as to whether the manned aircraft, laden with either non-nuclear or nuclear bombs, has in itself become obsolete with the arrival of bomb-laden missiles. Neither the manned bomber nor the fighter, to cite but the representative manned military aircraft, can undertake an attack on a moving missile. The difference in the speed limits of the non-manned missile and the manned aircraft alone makes such an attack impossible.

The manned bomber can continue to engage in bombing mission over the opponent's territory. The opponent's fighter planes can, in that case, try to chase the attacking bomber away or to direct it to lesser targets. The fighter planes can also continue to attempt to shoot down the attacking bombers. The comparatively low speed of the bomb-laden manned aircraft precludes, however, a coordination of the possible missions of the bomb-laden manned aircraft with the bombing activities of bomb-laden missiles. The bombing of the opponent's territory with bomb-laden manned aircraft can assume but an incidental character in a war in which bomb-laden missiles play a preponderant role. The question whether, from a strategic point of view, the continuation of the construction and operation of manned bombing aircraft is warranted, has to be answered in the negative. The bomb-laden missiles appear to be sounding the death knell for a strategic air force composed of manned bombers.

Fighter planes used for purposes of reconnaissance and regular planes built for the transportation of troops, military equipment, and military provisions could continue to play a limited role in the face of the preponderance of bomb-laden missiles. Such a role can, however, at best be called auxiliary and tactical. Yet, even that tactical role might come to an end within a very short time, when a given bomb-laden missile attack gains momentum. Instantaneously, the air, in the course of a bomb-laden missile attack, is likely to become radioactive to a degree which will make the manning of aircraft impossible. Almost instantaneously, too, the launching and landing sites are likely to become unobtainable in the wake of wholesale destruction wrought by bomb-laden missiles.

It seems strange that, at a time when the wildest dreams of the air control strategists, Douhet, Mitchell, and De Seversky, appear to come true, via the strategic supremacy of bomb-laden missiles, the manned aircraft, whose cause had been expounded in the literary labors of these air control strategists, is slated for oblivion. The reason for this paradox is the fact which constitutes the very essence of the ultimate weapon, the bomb-laden missile, namely, its almost incredible acceleration of speed and precision of delivery, coupled with the almost incredible multiplication of the power and range of destructiveness wielded by a thermo-nuclear bomb delivered by a missile. The result can be expected to be close to an instantaneous total range of devastation.

Air control appeared as a desirable strategic role to the air strategists when there was a prospect of gaining control over something, such as territory, with its mineral resources, structures, and equipment, as well as over the population of the opponent. Now that the prospect of gaining control over something has been replaced by the prospect of gaining control over nothing, in terms of material resources and manpower, the concept of air control is becoming an empty shell. There would hardly be any advantage were one of the opponents to gain or regain air superiority over the other's flaming debris and radioactive space. Nothing is to be gained by assuming control over nothing.

Much as the ultimate weapon is bound to dispose of the concept of air power superiority as it had been advanced in the period predating the epoch of bomb-laden missiles, so it is bound to dispose of the concept of sea power superiority as it had been advanced in the pre-missile age. The impact of the bomb-laden missiles on military technology is bound to dispose not only of the doctrine of superiority in sea power *in extremis,* as it had been advanced by Mahan, the United States writer on naval strategy. It is bound also to dispose of much of the more limited thesis concerning the role of sea power, which had been sustained by the continental European naval strategists, as represented by the followers of the Jeune Ecole in France.

Mahan's proposition, as has been pointed out in the previous chapter, already was out of date when it was advanced. Mahan had projected a strategic condition which prevailed in the time of wooden ships and sailing vessels into a period which was characterized by iron ships and steam power. Only in the times of wooden craft and sailing vessels had sea battles decided the outcome of a war, as in the case of the Dutch victory over Spain at Gibraltar, or of the British victory over Spain at Trafalgar.

With the advent of the iron warship driven by steam power, naval battles alone could no longer decide the outcome of a war, particularly when one or both of the parties to the conflict were powers with extensive national territory. The main reason why the era of wooden ships or sailing vessels was the era in which the outcome of a war could be decided by sea battles was the absence of mass land armies in that period. The army contingents which fought on the land at that time, consisted of a loose conglomeration of relatively small bands of people who owed their respective allegiance to a varied number of sovereigns. It is only during the French Revolution and its aftermath that unified mass armies were put into the field under a centralized command. Those mass armies then became the decisive factor in winning a war, and the role of the navy was reduced to an auxiliary function.

Mahan had failed to realize the change in the relative strategic position of the two parts of the fighting forces. The European naval strategists, and in particular the strategists of the Jeune Ecole in France, which advanced the thesis of the *guerre de course,* had taken account of the change in the relative strategic weight of the navy and the army. In the strategic view of the representatives of the Jeune Ecole, the navy was assigned the role of an auxiliary force in the conduct of a war. Preying on enemy shipping, protection of the coast, and the transportation of war goods and military personnel were the functions of the *guerre de course;* these functions were assigned to the navy by the representatives of the Jeune Ecole. The British naval strategists did not basically disagree with the strategic naval concept of the French proponents of the *guerre de course,* although the British naval strategists accentuated the degree of prosecution of the *guerre de course.*

The addition of the submarine, and later of the aircraft, to the naval arsenal did not basically change the role which the French strategists assigned to the navy. More weight, to be sure, came to be placed on the submarine as an instrumentality of attack on enemy shipping, a role, which before the advent of the submarine, had been assigned mainly to the battleship. The cruiser, which before the advent of the submarine had been designated mainly for the role of an auxiliary craft to the battleship, was, in turn, designated to play the role of an auxiliary craft to the submarine.

When the aircraft entered the scene, it was assigned a reconnaissance role, as well as the role of a bombing plane for the facilitation of the landing of naval craft. The aircraft carrier came, in turn, to serve as a floating launching site for naval aircraft operations. The impact of the submarine and of aircraft on naval technology reduced further the strategic importance of naval battles in the over-all strategy of the conduct of a war. The over-all auxiliary role of the navy as an arm supporting land operations became even more pronounced when the submarine and aircraft were added to the naval arsenal.

This was, by and large, the strategic position of the navy before the advent of the bomb-laden missile. With the arrival of the bomb-laden missile, the strategic position of the navy underwent further change. A war in which bomb-laden missiles were to be employed would have to be a war fought mainly with what in general strategy is called "forces in being." This means that the transportation of war goods and troops on land, and the more so at sea, will become less important and could even be said to be a minor factor.

This will be so because the provisions and war material stored up on land, as well as the land-based production centers and the land-based military personnel, as well as the civilian population, will be subject to almost complete physical destruction. There will be nothing to move from the land to the sea. Nor will it be possible to land any provisions, war material, or military and civilian personnel from the sea to the territory of a belligerent. Furthermore, it must be taken into account, that the almost complete destruction on the territories of the respective belligerents will occur almost instantaneously.

Only naval ships which at the start of the missile-geared nuclear war are to be found on the high seas can expect to remain afloat, assuming they were to keep dispersed in order to reduce the danger of their being spotted by enemy planes and being made subject to bombing attacks. The same situation can be expected to prevail for battleships and cruisers, as well as for commercial vessels converted into military transports. The landing of those vessels on either home or enemy territory cannot be expected to take place because of the radiation danger. The only places where those vessels can possibly land will be the territory of a country which will stay out of the conflict and will be sufficiently removed from the territory of the belligerents.

What could be expected to happen in such a case is that the vessels will land on the coast line of a neutral or non-belligerent country, which would result in the internment of their crews and of the confiscation of their loads. The alternative might be for those vessels to roam the high seas until the war ends, and for some time after the nuclear exchange has been completed, in the expectation that the termination of the war and the reduction of the degree of radiation might, in due time, allow for a landing on home territory.

Such a course, however, must be considered as hazardous, since the extent of the devastation in the coastal region of the vessels' home territory will be difficult, if not impossible, to determine ahead of landing, and, secondly, it will be next to impossible to determine the degree of radiation in advance of landing. There simply is not likely to be a sufficient number of normally functioning humans around in the coastal regions in a territory which had been under a saturation attack by bomb-laden missiles. Nor is it likely that any means of communication which possibly could be used to provide information for approaching vessels will be in existence after such a saturation attack.

The above analysis is intended to demonstrate that the role which surface vessels have played up to World War II, either as vessels covering landings or as transportation media, will not be granted them under the conditions of bomb-laden missile warfare. The very concept of assigning auxiliary tasks to surface naval forces, in making them cooperate with operations conducted by land forces, will have to be disposed of. With land forces instantaneously immobilized and subsequently destroyed in the course of bomb-laden missile attacks, there is not going to be any military force on land with which to cooperate. Nor will there be a means of communication between the land and sea forces.

As far as the role which the aircraft carrier and naval aircraft can be expected to play in the course of bomb-laden nuclear warfare, the following may be said. Only in the initial phase of bomb-laden missile attacks on the territory of the belligerents would naval aircraft be able to add their own bomb loads to those of missiles. Such an addition of bombs to be landed on enemy territory could in no way be considered, however, as having a chance to affect significantly the total effect of the destructive power of nuclear bombs.

Such bombings from carrier-based aircraft could only be considered as desperation attacks under conditions of bomb-laden missile warfare. Such attacks, were they to be pursued, could be explained only as a means of unloading bombs somewhere on enemy territory, because there would be nothing else for those bombers to do. Furthermore, it must be considered that only medium-sized bombers could be placed on aircraft carriers, which further reduces the impact of that kind of bombing on enemy territory, even if nuclear bombs were to be used in such attacks.

In regard to the role of aircraft-carrier-based fighter planes, they could of course, be used to accompany the bombers on their missions and thus protect them from the attack of enemy fighter planes. The fighter planes based on aircraft carriers could also serve as escorts for the bombers returning to their carrier base. If the fighter planes are successful on such missions, the likelihood that the bombers will unload their bombs on enemy territory and return to their base will be increased.

The cooperation of the carrier-based fighter planes and bombers could not increase, however, the peripheral impact of the bombing by aircraft-based bombers in relation to the impact of the bomb-laden missiles. In addition, such a peripheral role of bombing by aircraft-based medium bombers could have any effect at all only at the time of the initial attack by bomb-laden missiles on enemy territory. The joining of aircraft-based medium bombers in subsequent attacks by bomb-laden missiles would make little, if any, sense at all. Repetitive bomb-laden missile attacks can be expected to result in such a high degree of devastation of the enemy territory that any additional small-scale bombing is not likely to make any difference to the total bombing effect.

The carrier-based figther planes could also be used for reconnaissance purposes. Such reconnaissance is likely to lose any strategic import after repeated bomb-laden missile attacks on the territory of the belligerents, because the purpose of the conduct of the nuclear war, which is the mutual annihilation of both belligerents, would have been attained within hours. The only purpose of a reconnaissance, after the strategic goal of such a war has been reached, for which carrier-based fighter planes could be used, would be the attempt to detect landing territory which could be considered free of radiation. Detection of such territory, if effected, could then be used in leading the personnel of the aircraft carrier and the crew of the fighter planes to a place where they could possibly disembark and reach comparative personal safety. Such an undertaking, as one can see, has nothing to do with any strategic aim and has no relation to the actual conduct of the war. Such reconnaissance would then be a post-war activity, an activity leading to the gathering of survivors of the nuclear holocaust from amongst those who found themselves on the high seas at the start of the nuclear war.

As far as the operation of submarines in a nuclear war is concerned, it should be realized that the submarines will lose the particular role which was assigned to them previous to the advent of the bomb-laden missile. There will be little point for submarines to attack either battleships or transport vessels, since the decision in the war conducted with bomb-laden missiles will be effected before any sustained activity of the submarines could take place. Depth charges by submarines could be expected to take effect for the most part after the mass devastation of the territory of the belligerents in a nuclear war has taken effect. Under those circumstances, any effectuation of the depth charges of the submarines could not be expected to have any relation either to the conduct of the war or to its termination.

Submarines have of late, however, been supplied with nuclear power.

This device enables them to remain submerged for a long period of time. The lengthening of the period of submergence assumes importance in connection with the supplying of the nuclear powered submarine with bomb-laden missiles. In this context, the submarine constitutes an addition to the land-based missile arsenal and its nuclear bomb load. The submarine thus becomes a moving launching site, which, at that, can become submerged. This combination makes the submarine an extremely effective weapon and provides it with strategic import, as far as the conduct of the war with bomb-laden missiles is concerned.

The speed, the accuracy, and the number of submarine-based bomb-laden missiles might well be considered among the decisive factors which could bring about early results in the nuclear interchange of the major belligerents. The relationship between land-based bomb-laden missiles and submarine-based bomb-laden missiles has to be considered in this context. Much will depend on what the comparative numerical strength of the land-based and submarine-based bomb-laden missiles will be. Of vital importance may also be the extent to which the firing time and the setting of the targets of the land-based bomb-laden missiles are coordinated with those of the submarine-based bomb-laden missiles. The question of the reloading of the submarines with bomb-laden missiles would also have to be taken into consideration.

The chances that the atomic-powered submarine will escape punishment are much better than the chances of land-based missile launching sites, whether they are above or under ground. An atomic-powered submarine will have a good chance to re-load and to return to fire further bomb-laden missiles. Any such firing, however, would make sense only if the saturation point of nuclear bombing on enemy territory had not been reached. In view of the overstocking in land-based bomb-laden missiles, it is most likely that the saturation point in nuclear bombing of enemy territory will have been reached before many reloadings of the nuclear-powered submarines with bomb-laden missiles were completed.

The functioning of the submarine as a movable launching site of bomb-laden missiles constitutes a basic functional change in its operation. The nuclear-powered submarine, functioning as a launching site for bomb-laden missiles, has lost its role as a constituent part of naval operations. The submarine which had been functional as a movable base for depth charges constituted part and parcel of naval operations in the sense that it was designed to attack other naval craft. In its capacity as an attacker, by way of depth charges, of battleships and transportation vessels, the submarine was operated for the purpose of reducing the naval power of the opponent. In its capacity as a naval launching site for bomb-laden missiles, the submarine has been turned into an attacker of enemy territory as well as of enemy land forces. In that capacity the submarine has come to function as an auxiliary of the land-based bomb-laden missiles. It can well be argued that the difference between the land-based bomb-laden missiles and the submarine-based bomb-laden missiles constitutes but a difference in the location of the base of the bomb-laden missiles.

It should be granted that, as far as aiming at land targets is concerned, naval craft (other than submarines with bomb-laden missiles) are known to have engaged in that kind of operation. Battleships as well as cruisers are known to have bombarded land targets, either preliminary to landings on enemy shores or for purposes of disrupting the enemy transportation to and from harbors. The aiming at land targets by battleships and cruisers did not, however, constitute the whole sphere of their operations.

It can well be maintained that the aiming at land targets by battleships and cruisers constituted but an incidental factor in their sphere of operations. Battleships and cruisers were designed in the main to serve as a counter-force to enemy battleships and cruisers. In the contest between two belligerents, each fleet of battleships and cruisers aimed at reducing the opponent's battleships and cruisers.

In the prosecution of this aim, the battleships and cruisers were assisted by the submarines. The submarine, however, which has become a movable site of bomb-laden missiles, is no longer an auxiliary force in the operation of battleships and cruisers. The submarine serving as a launching site for bomb-laden missiles has become an auxiliary part of the land-based bomb-laden missiles. In that sense, it can be said that the submarine which serves as a launching site of bomb-laden missiles ceased to be a naval vessel, since it is used but as an extension of the land-based bomb-laden missile force.

The transformation of the submarine-based bomb-laden missile force into a constituent part of the land-based bomb-laden missiles but underlies the fact that the navy as such has ceased to play any significant role in the conduct of a war keyed to the bomb-laden missiles. The navy as such, whether formed of surface vessels or of underwater craft with emplaced guns and depth charges, is bound to become obsolete in the case of a war geared to a saturation attack by bomb-laden missiles. Under these conditions, the situation of the navy is similar to that of aircraft. With decisive blows expected to be delivered by bomb-laden missiles, the operation of the air force, as has been demonstrated in the preceding part of this chapter, becomes dispensable.

An exception must be granted to those aircraft which could be made to operate as airborne launching spaces for bomb-laden missiles. Aircraft thus operated could not, however, be properly considered as part of an air force setup. The military air force, whether of the bomber or fighter variety, had as its major aim the destruction of as much of the surface aircraft of the opponent as possible, so as to attain control of the air. Control of the air, as has been demonstrated earlier in this chapter, becomes meaningless in case of a full-scale bomb-laden missile exchange. The operation overkill as represented by a saturation attack by bomb-laden missiles deprives the strategic air force of the strategic basis for its existence.

As far as the tactical aspect of air force operations which is linked to the strafing of land targets, whether military or civilian, is concerned, it ceases to have any import in view of the almost instantaneous impact of the overriding hitting power of the bomb-laden missiles. The conclusion, therefore, can be drawn that, in any war geared to a saturation attack by bomb-laden missiles, the military air force is bound to become as obsolete as the navy.

Nor is there much chance for the army to play a strategic or tactical role in a war geared to a saturation attack by bomb-laden missiles. As far as the infantry is concerned, it could be metaphorically stated that the foot soldier, no matter on what part of the territory of a belligerent he may find himself at the start of a conflict geared to bomb-laden missiles, he will hardly have the time to put his feet on the ground. Any large-scale movement of foot soldiers will become impractical after the first exchange of bomb-laden missiles because of the uncertainty as to where the bomb-laden missiles will land in the subsequent exchanges.

With each succeeding exchange of bomb-laden missiles, a movement of foot soldiers will become not only impractical but impossible. The raging fires, the flying debris, and the radioactive air will preclude any movement by persons, whether in or out of uniform, except for those who would be seeking an escape from the inferno. It can well be stated with a degree of certainty that any infantry units which were to find themselves within the range of the falling bomb-laden missiles would turn into hordes of panic-ridden people trying to find some imaginary protection from the horrors surrounding them.

Under such circumstances, any thought of mobilizing additional infantry units must be considered as preposterous. Preposterous, too, is any thought that the infantry forces "in being" could be used as fighting units at any time after the initiation of a war geared to an exchange of bomb-laden missiles. Preposterous, furthermore, is any concern with providing the infantry units "in being" with any additional munition and supplies. The most likely use which infantry units could be expected to make of their munitions in the course of bomb-laden missile attacks and their aftermath is to try to kill fellow soldiers or civilians who might obstruct their road of presumed escape. The most likely use which infantry units could be expected to make of their supplies in the course of bomb-laden missile attacks and their aftermath is to try to salvage some of those provisions for consumption in the presumed place of safety.

Nor is it to be forgotten that quite a number of infantry units will find themselves within the target area of the falling bomb-laden missiles. The innumerable casualties which such direct hits upon the range of the location of infantry units will cause will, no doubt, be a factor in either generating panic or in aggravating an already existing panic. It should, furthermore, be taken into consideration that in any area hit by bomb-laden missiles, it will be impossible to separate military and civilian casualties. As the saturation attacks of bomb-laden missiles progress, the intermingling of military and civilian casualties will, in turn, play an added role in an ever-accelerated transformation of the infantry units into hordes of horror-stricken people.

It must be granted that some cases of exemplary heroism and of the will to maintain military posture up to the very physical end might occur among some members of the infantry units. Such behavior can be expected only from a small number of individuals, however, and then those would-be heroes may be expected to be crushed by the weight of the mass of deserters, to whom the rules of military conduct would have lost any meaning in the wake of the progress of the atomic holocaust.

Any war up to the present, one has to recall, was founded on the assumption that the society from which the fighting forces were drawn would remain intact. In case of survival, an infantry man could expect to rejoin the society out of which he had been called to military service, after the termination of the war. No such expectation could be held by members of infantry units in an atomic holocaust. Under their very eyes, the soldiers are bound to witness the physical destruction of the civilian society from which they were drawn for military service. The mingling of civilian and military casualties will provide for the infantry a patent demonstration of the total dissolution of organized social life, whether in its civilian or its military form.

With civilian life in any organized form expected to be destroyed in the course of hostilities geared to a saturation attack by bomb-laden missiles, the maintenance of a military organization could well be regarded by the military personnel of infantry units as an incongruous proposition. It is most likely that this conclusion will be drawn by the infantry men, and that they will act upon it accordingly. The self-dissolution of infantry units will, in those circumstances, appear as the most logical development.

Nor can much chance be granted to any strategic or tactical role of artillery units in a war geared to a saturation attack by bomb-laden missiles. The thought that fire power of the range of which land emplaced guns are capable could play any role in a nuclear war must be dismissed as lacking any foundation in reality. First, a great many land emplaced guns will become subject to physical destruction in the course of a nuclear holocaust. Second, those few land emplaced guns which might possibly escape physical destruction will of necessity find themselves in the radioactive range. This situation applies to the land emplaced guns in the interior of the country as well as to those in the front lines.

As far as the front line is concerned, the belt of radioactivity is likely to lead to its complete dissolution. As the nuclear exchange progresses, no military units of either belligerent stationed at the front line can be expected to find themselves outside the range of high radioactivity. Artillery units stationed at the front could be expected to be engulfed by radioactivity as much as infantry units.

Radioactivity can well be considered a factor which is likely to lead to an early disorganization and a subsequent dissolution of all front line military units, no matter what their specific identity. The entire front of both belligerents will become one wide radioactive belt. Military discipline and organizational cohesion can be expected to be extinguished at an early period of the nuclear missile exchange. Under such circumstances, any thought of moving guns from the interior to the front line, or from less exposed to more exposed front line positions, will become utterly unrealistic. Nor for that matter could, under the said circumstances, any thought be given to moving any other military forces to front line positions, or from exposed front line positions to less exposed front line positions or to the interior.

Nor is there a prospect for the effective operation of the mobile artillery units, the so-called tanks. Aside from the danger of being hit by a nuclear charge, the area of high radioactivity will preclude any change in the position of the tanks from either the front line or the interior. The whole concept of offensive or defensive operations will have to be considered inapplicable under conditions of nuclear warfare geared to missiles. Nor will it be possible to maintain the concept of the division between front line military units and interior military units. Nor for that matter will it be feasible to sustain the concept of division of military units and non-military entities. Chaos will engulf all front line and interior millitary units as well as all military and civilian entities. The disorganization and early dissolution of military units will be matched by the disorganization of civilian entities.

As a postscript to the above stated blueprint for disorganization and dissolution of institutionalized military entities, a description of the probable effects of the use of biological and chemical weapons has to be added. Pertinent information has been made available in an article by

Elinor Langer entitled *Chemical and Biological Warfare: The Weapons and Policies,* published in the journal *Science,* the publication of the American Association for the Advancement of Science, in the issues of January 13th and January 20th, 1967. Chemical weapons, in terms of lethal and non-lethal gasses, had been used in some instances by the French and German armies in World War I. Hardly any use was made of chemical and biological weapons by any of the belligerents in World War II. As far as the United States is concerned, little attention was paid by the U.S. military planners to the development of chemical and biological weapons up to the middle 1950's. Since then the development of chemical and biological weapons has received increasing attention by the United States Defense Department.

A noticeable spurt in the development of chemical and biological weapons came about with the election of John F. Kennedy to the Presidency of the United States. In line with his aim to diversify the war potential of the United States, the development of chemical and biological weapons was given a distinct place in the United States development of weaponry. Notice was taken of the relatively low costs of developing highly potent chemical and biological weapons on a massive scale, as compared with the extremely high cost of developing nuclear weapons and means of their delivery. Instead of the cost of tens of billions required for the development and manufacture of thermo-nuclear weapons, highly destructive chemical and biological weapons could be had on a massive scale for tens of millions of dollars. Chemical and biological weapons development was assigned a definite auxiliary place in the United States arsenal of thermonuclear weapons by the Kennedy Administration. A whole range of chemical and bacteriological weapons came to be developed, since the Kennedy Administration gave that kind of weapon development a definite go-ahead signal.

The chemical and biological weapons which had come to be developed in the United States since the Kennedy Administration are directed at incapacitation short of death as well as incapacitation with the inclusion of death of a mass of combatants as well as non-combatants of any given adversary of the United States. In addition, the United States developed chemical and biological weapons are aimed at making human existence on the territory of a given adversary impossible. The physical human environment, the soil, air, and the water are slated to becoming contaminated to an extent by the United States developed chemical and biological weapons which would make the country upon which such weapons are visited unliveable for any living creature.

An additional factor in the spurt of the development of chemical and biological weapons since the Kennedy Administration is to be seen in the close attention which that Administration gave to the then developed concept of limited war. The limited war which had been fought in Korea was about to become duplicated, with certain variations, in South Vietnam. Chemical and biological weapons were conceived by Kennedy's military advisors and technologists as a potent means for counter-insurgency military actions against irregular combatants, called in United States military parlance guerrilla fighters. Some of the standard chemical and biological weapons to be used in counter-insurgency military actions became the chemical, napalm, which can burn people alive and the defoliation spread which can destroy crops and forests and render the soil uncultivable for an extended period of time.

The uninhibited use of those chemicals in a country as small as South Vietnam did not, however, bring about victory for the United States. As far as its impact on those who did not themselves become victims of the application of chemical and biological weapons in South Vietnam, such use on an extensive scale by the United States military came to be regarded by the rest of the South Vietnamese, whether they were armed insurgents or just people living under the control of the insurgents, as no more than terror weapons. At any rate, the extensive use of chemical and biological weapons by the United States armed forces in South Vietnam did amply demonstrate that chemical and biological weapons cannot be regarded as having a strategic impact. This brings us back to the onset of this discussion of chemical and biological weapons.

Chemical and biological weapons can have but an added effect in an armed conflict in which strategic military weapons, such as thermonuclear bombs carried by rockets, are applied on a mass scale. That added effect, it should be realized, however, will not be needed, were nuclear weapons carried by rockets to be rained upon any given country. Total mass destruction of the population, as well as its environmental habitat will be effected within hours or possibly within minutes, under those circumstances. Of what use could chemical and biological weapons then be after death and desolation on a mass scale had taken place in the wake of a nuclear attack?

The United States military planners had been continuing, however, their financing and research for greater perfection of chemical and biological weapons and the invention of new weapons of that kind. What those United States military planners probably had in mind is that other limited wars, after the Vietnam venture is discontinued, will provide ample opportunity for applying chemical and biological weapons. What those United States military planners did not take into consideration, however, is that high policy makers in the United States might come to the realization that the time has passed not only for the conduct of an all-out war with the introduction of nuclear weapons, but for the conduct of limited wars as well, in which no nuclear weapons come to be used.

It has been reported by United States Government sources that the Soviet Union has perfected a toxic gas to be used in warfare. There should not be any doubt that the Soviet chemists and biologists are ingenious enough to develop chemical and biological weapons. No information is available to the effect, that the Soviet defense establishment has embarked on a systematic plan to develop a large variety of chemical and biological weapons which could possibly match the arsenal of those weapons which have been developed in the United States since the advent of the Kennedy Administration. It is more likely to assume, that those responsible for weapon development in the Soviet Union accord chemical and biological warfare as but an incidental factor in the conduct of any war whether total or limited.

A contrary view on the place of the development of chemical and biological weapons in the Soviet arsenal had been expressed at a briefing of United States senators and representatives, as reported in *The New York Times* of March 5, 1969. According to the report published in *The New York Times,* Brigadier General James Hebbeler, director of chemical-biological radiological and nuclear operations of the army, briefed the group of United States senators and representatives on the need to expand the United States research and development program of chemical and biological warfare. After the briefing, one of those present, Representative Robert L. S. Sikes, Democrat of Florida, is reported to have advised the press that the Soviet Union has supposedly "seven to eight times (the chemical and biological warfare) capability than the free world". No mention was made of the source of that information. It is quite possible that the figure is not more than a guess and an unintelligent guess at that. Doubts in regard to the accuracy of the above stated figure as related to the scope of Soviet activity in regard to chemical and biological warfare can be well founded.

In the above stated connection some information provided recently at the First National Convocation on The Challenge of Building Peace in New York on March 5, 1969 by Professor Jerome Wiesner, sometime science advisor of the late President John F. Kennedy and at present president of the Massachusetts Institute of Technology, is of interest. Professor Wiesner informed the forum that at the time when he was a science advisor to President Kennedy and it was his task to discuss national security matters with the President as well as the Congress, the take-off for many of his assignments was an imaginary strategic position attributed to the Soviet Union, which subsequently had been established to have had no foundation in fact. But, any time an imaginary strategic position attributed to the Soviet Union exploded in the face of subsequent factual information, a different imaginary strategic position came to be attributed to the Soviet Union, which, in its turn, came to be disproven on a factual basis. The ingenuity of conjuring up imaginary strategic positions to be attributed to the Soviet Union never came to an end, Professor Wiesner stated, as long as he was science advisor to President Kennedy. Whether the information which alleges that the Soviet Union is embarked on seven to eight times of the scope of the United States range of chemical and biological warfare is not of the same order as the conjuries which have been put in circulation in Professor Weisner's time as a science advisor to the White House is not definitely known. That such might be the case, at least as far as characterizing the scope of Soviet chemical and biological weapons program is concerned, cannot be entirely ruled out of order.

In the meantime voices came to be heard in Congressional circles which supported an expanded United States program of chemical and biological weaponry on the basis of the allegation that the Soviet Union is engaged in a vastly accelerated chemical and biological warfare program. It should be noticed, however, that there were voices in Congress which opposed any acceleration of the United States program of chemical and biological warfare and who advocated restraint in the possible use of such weapons. As to the Nixon Administration, it went on record as being opposed to any continuation of a large scale program of testing and developing chemical and biological weapons. The Nixon Administration has, moreover, through its authorized spokesmen declared that it is in principle agreeable to become a party to the international agreement on the banning of chemical and biological weapons. In a follow-up move, some centers of testing and developing of chemical and biological weapons in the United States have been ordered closed and some stores of chemical and biological weapons have been slated for disposal.

In consequence of the changed stand of the United States administration, the matter of a ban on biological and chemical warfare came up for discussion at the 17th Nations Disarmament Conference in Geneva in the first half of 1971. In the course of those discussions, the United States representative wanted some chemical weapons, in particular those which have been used by United States military forces in Vietnam, excluded from a general ban on chemical weapons. Faced with the refusal of the United States to have all chemical weapons prohibited, the Soviet Union took the position that the matter of a ban on all chemical weapons is to be deferred. In the stated connection, the British representative at the 17 Nations Disarmament Conference in Geneva suggested that the matter of a general ban on chemical weapons is to be taken up within the time range of five years after a general ban on biological weapons comes to be agreed upon. That is where the matter rested when this book went to press.

Chapter 3

THE MYTH OF PREPAREDNESS

The dissolution of the armed forces in the wake of successive attacks by bomb-laden missiles, which has been described in Chapter II, can be expected to have its counterpart in the dissolution of the social fabric of the civilian population, the demonstration of which will be undertaken in this chapter. In the post-dissolution stage, it should be kept in mind, a distinction between members of the armed forces and members of civilian entities will hardly be maintained. The process of dissolution itself will differ somehow, however, in the way in which it will take place among the members of the armed forces and among the civilian populace and its organizations. Though civilian, non-military organizational forms are less pronounced and rigid than those of the armed forces, they are more intricate in their relation with each other as well in their relation with the armed forces.

In a sense, the very existence of the military as an organized force is predicated upon the existence of civilian organizations. The dissolution of the civilian organizations will thus make the reorganization of the military structure impossible after its dissolution has set in. The dissolution of the civilian organizations can, on its part, be subdivided into the dissolutions of the economic, social, and political structures. The dissolution of the economic, social and political organizations can, in turn, be expected to be preconditioned by the initial malfunctioning and eventual destruction of the communication and transportation system.

The malfunctioning of the communication system will begin, as has been pointed out in the previous chapter, by the malfunctioning of the radar warning system. The radar system, as we have seen, can be made insensitive to the approach of bomb-laden missiles and thus cannot be expected to be of any use in case of such an attack. The civilian population will first become aware that a missile-driven hydrogen bomb attack is under way when the first bomb is detonated. Some people could possibly spot the approaching bomb-laden missile seconds before the actual detonation takes place, but detection at that time will hardly put the person who detected it to any advantage over the person who becomes aware of the attack only after the actual detonation of the bomb has taken place. The difference in time between the time of detection by eyesight and the time of detection by sound is not likely to be more than a difference of a split second.

After the detonation of the first series of bombs, means of communication other than the radar system cannot be expected to function in any reliable manner. This phase, too, will be characterized first by malfunctioning and next by ultimate destruction. Radio and television which are designated to disseminate warning signals will be deprived of their function from the very onset of the attack, since the basis for dissemination, the recording on the radar screen, cannot be expected to take place, as has been indicated above. With the progress of the bomb-laden missile attack, the radio and television stations will experience ever-growing destruction. The accelerated destruction of the radio and television sets in the homes will take place at the same time.

The central telephone switchboard, as well as telephones in the homes, will be subject first to malfunctioning and, closely thereafter, to physical destruction. The same sequence, first malfunctioning and subsequently physical destruction, can be expected to take place in regard to the telegraph. The sending and receiving of messages will be first impeded and, in the wake of successive bomb hits, be discontinued. Nor for that matter can it be expected that one might fall back on a messenger service. Falling debris and radioactive air will prevent anybody from taking even a few steps from the place where he finds himself during the progress of the attack to any other place. Uncertainty as to where the next bomb might fall will, in turn, frighten away those not within the immediate radius of an attack in progress and thus preclude them from serving as messengers.

The proper functioning of any communication system, as is well known, is predicated upon one basic factor, the reasonable expectation that the message sent by one party will reach the party to which that message has been sent. That reasonable expectation will cease to exist with the initiation of bomb-laden missile attacks. With the progress of the attack, the physical facilities for either sending or delivering a message will, in turn, cease to exist.

Similarly, it can be said of the transportation system, that proper functioning is predicated upon the reasonable expectation that a person boarding a vehicle will reach his destination. This reasonable expectation will no longer be present from the very initiation of a missile-driven bombing attack. With the progress of the attack, the physical destruction of means of transportation will follow.

The malfunctioning of the transportation system, which will take place in the initial period of a bomb-laden missile attack, will affect long-distance as well as short-distance transportation. Even an immobilization of an intermediary link in a given transportation network during the initial phase of a sustained attack will affect the operation of the whole of that transportation network. Even if only short stretches of the tracks were to be destroyed in the initial phase of a sustained bombing attack, the whole rail line is likely to become inoperative.

The destruction of a few short stretches of tracks on a subway can be expected to render the whole subway system inoperative. With the destruction, during the initial phase of a sustained bombing attack, of but a few stretches of a road on which buses operate, the operation of the entire bus line might well become impossible.

Considering the time factor alone, one has to keep in mind that any rerouting and rescheduling of either long-distance trains or subway and buses will hardly be feasible. The time span stretching from the initial phase of a sustained attack to its saturation stage is likely to be so short as to make rerouting or rescheduling wholly useless from any practical point of view.

In some cases it might be possible to operate parts of long distance trains on parts of their routes after a part of the track has been severed from the rest of the rail line through bomb destruction. It is doubtful, however, whether this partial operation of a railroad could continue for an extended period of time. With the progress of the saturation attack, within a few hours at best, the major part of all the tracks on all rail-roads will become subject to wholesale destruction, and the wholesale destruction of transportation equipment will take place within the same short period of time.

The use of the means of transportation, whether for passengers or freight, can be expected to be discontinued even before the wholesale destruction of the roads and the equipment has taken place. The fear of the impending destruction of roads and vehicles will keep any person, who has not lost the ability to think and conduct himself rationally, from boarding or entrusting freight to a public vehicle right after the initial phase of the sustained bombing attack has taken place.

In desperation, a number of people might well jump into their cars during, or immediately after, the initial phase of a sustained attack. Those persons might be motivated by a spontaneous urge "to get away from it all." Any such attempt is likely to lead to nothing more than to the destruction of the car, either by falling debris or by burning, not to speak of the danger to the passengers in the car that is subjected to the effects of radioactivity.

In some out-of-town places, which did not at once fall within the range of the detonation of missile-driven hydrogen bombs, some travelling in private cars might be possible for a while, yet only for a short while. The danger of arriving in an area which is becoming subject to direct hits in the wake of successive bombing attacks will be ever present for such travellers. There will hardly be any escape from the car once it has become a death trap.

The roads within the radius of the hydrogen bomb explosions will become impassable. Falling debris and raging fires, as well as radioactivity, will make the roads impassable not only for vehicles, but for persons as well. Nor would there be, for that matter, any point why a person who finds himself in an inhabited area within the range of a hydrogen bomb explosion should try to get to an area where such an explosion in the initial phase of a sustained missile-driven hydrogen bomb attack has not yet taken place. Within an hour or so, at the most, the entire territory of any nation under sustained hydrogen bomb attacks will become enveloped in flames and radioactivity. In the saturation stage, falling and fallen debris will be added to the raging fires and radioactivity. In the non-inhabited places, we can expect debris to be absent, but fires might well extend to those areas and engulf trees and other plants. Radioactivity will be carried from one part of the country to another by air currents and winds.

Under those conditions, one can well assert that any person and any object not directly subject to the impact of fallen debris, fire, or radioactivity, or any combination of these, will be frozen in the space in which he were to find himself at the initial phase of a sustained missile-driven hydrogen bomb attack. In addition to the physical obstruction to the movement of persons or objects from the place in which they were to find themselves following the initial phase of the sustained attack, the fear that any movement of persons or objects might be blocked by fallen debris, raging fires and radioactivity, in an ever extending area, is to be cited. That fear will tend to freeze any person and any object close to that person in the place in which they were to find themselves at the time of the initial phase of the sustained attack.

Any attempt on the part of any person to move and any attempt by a person to move an object after the initial phase of a sustained hydrogen bomb attack has taken place can well be considered irrational from the point of view of the effect. Such an attempt, it can be foreseen, will not offer any reasonable chance to escape the impact of the falling debris, the raging fires, and the radioactivity in the place in which the person or the object were to be found in the initial phase of the sustained attack. This does not mean that many persons will instinctively, on the spur of the moment, not attempt either to move themselves or to move objects after the initial phase of the sustained attack. Such moves, however, can be expected, under the given circumstances, to have a good chance to but hasten the destruction of the persons and the object.

Special attention must be given here, in this context, to the discussion of the bomb-shelter program. As far as the United States is concerned, the building of bomb-shelters, which could protect the population at large from blasts and fires, has for a time not been under consideration. The reason for eliminating bomb-shelters, which could protect the population at large from blasts and fires from the range of possibilities for some time, is related to the prohibitive cost of such shelters. It had been calculated to build shelters which could protect the entire population of the United States from blasts and fires in case of sustained missile-driven hydrogen bomb attacks would require an investment equal to that which has been made in building all privately and publicly owned productive establishments in the nation.

In other words, the money needed for blastproof and fireproof shelters would equal all the money spent on turning the United States from a primitive agricultural country, which it was before the Civil War, into the leading industrialized nation of the world which it became after the Civil War. Such an amount of money cannot be made available without great difficulty and without disrupting the entire national economy of the United States.

One way in which such an amount of money theoretically could be made available would be by instituting a compulsory mortgaging program which would make it compulsory for all real property holders in the United States to get a mortgage on the total value of their property. The real property holders would then turn the proceeds from the mortgages of the total value of their property over to the United States Government, which would build blastproof and fireproof shelters. Another way of financing the blastproof and fireproof shelter program would be to issue bonds to the amount of all real property owned in the United States and to institute a bond buying program either for the entire population or for the real property holders.

Such financing schemes would add about two-thirds to the present total government and private indebtedness in the United States, which is at present somewhat over one trillion dollars. It must be remembered that about three trillion dollars constitutes the value of all property, real and personal, in the United States. This means that one could buy all that has property value in the United States for about three trillion dollars. This, in turn, would mean that, in case the mortgaging for the bond buying program to finance the fire and blast protection shelter program were to be instituted in the United States, the indebtedness of the country would rise to about the total of all the amount of the value of all real property in the United States.

This kind of financing scheme would appear to be unsound even under peacetime conditions. No mortgage in peacetime would consider granting a mortgage amounting to more than 60% of the properly appraised value of the property. Repayment of the vast sums obtained from either the compulsory mortgaging program or the compulsory bond buying program definitely would be in doubt, even if peacetime conditions were to be prevail. But, with the war – and a missile-driven hydrogen bomb war at that – looming, the repayment of such a vast amount of money could not even be attempted. The reason for this is the reasonable expectation that almost all, if not literally all, real estate in the United States will be destroyed in the course of a saturation attack by hydrogen bomb-laden missiles.

The land will still be there after a saturation attack, but it will be covered with debris, and the air above it will continue to be radioactive. Hardly any concrete value could be placed on such land; it will have to be considered wasteland to which no economic value could be attached. All the mortgages and bonds contracted for the purpose of building shelters for the protection of the population at large from blast damage and fire would therefore have to be considered worthless. By rendering the mortgages or the bonds worthless in the case in question, the population of the United States would be deprived of the equivalent of all real property value of the nation. The worthlessness of the mortgages or bonds in the case in question would thus represent quite a radical scheme of impoverishment of the entire United States population.

Aside from the aspect of financing the building of shelters for protection against blast and fire, the question of the effectiveness of those shelters remains to be answered. Though these shelters might withstand the impact of blast and fire, the persons who would remain sheltered in them could not be assured that they will ever be able to get out of their shelters, were they to be erected in populated places. Debris piled in front of these shelters in the course of the sustained hydrogen bomb-laden missile attacks will make it quite difficult, if not impossible, for those who had remained in the shelters to dig themselves out. The falling of additional debris, the spreading of the raging fire, and the spreading of radioactivity, must be added to the hazards with which those persons, who had found protection from blasts and fire in the shelters, will be confronted when they decide to leave the shelters.

Consideration, too, should be given to the factors on which the people who will have survived by taking refuge in blast and fireproof shelters will base the decision to leave the shelters. Were food and water to run out in the shelter, that would be a clearly specifiable reason for attempting to leave the shelter. In that case, one would have to consider, however, the possibility of getting food and water outside the shelter. This possibility is not likely to exist in inhabited places, even if the survivors were to emerge from the shelter after the short-term effects of the saturation attack, such as falling debris, fires, and radioactive air had worn off. With a target area and its environs turned into a wasteland, the possibility of replenishing food and water by the survivors of the blast and fireproof shelters, who emerge from the shelters, will be as good as non-existent.

Were the survivors to emerge from the blast and fireproof shelters before the first effects of a sustained attack had worn off, falling debris, raging fires, and a high degree of radioactivity would necessarily make such an emergence fatal to all those who had survived blasts and fires in the shelter. Exactly when the first immediate effects of a sustained attack, in terms of falling debris, raging fires, and a high degree of radioactivity, were to wear off, would be difficult if not impossible for the survivors in the blast and fireproof shelters to determine.

The building of shelters which could protect people within them from blasts and fires had at any rate for some time been given up in the United States, as far as the protection of the population at large is concerned. Blast and fireproof shelters have probably been erected for persons high in the government and possibly for persons high in the managerial hierarchy of large United States corporations. One can assume that the highranking persons inside and outside the government will survive unharmed from bomb blasts and fires as long as they are in the blast and fireproof shelters.

The danger to the safety of those persons will arise wnen they decide to leave the shelters. First of all, they might not be able to take a step outside the shelter because debris could be expected to block the exit from the shelter in case the shelters were built in a populated place. In addition, the danger from continuously falling debris, spreading fires, and spreading radioactivity might well seal the doom of those privileged few who could be enabled to spend some time after the initial attack by hydrogen bomb-laden missiles in blast and fireproof shelters.

In addition to the few blast and fire proof shelters for persons, a number of blast and fireproof repositories have been built all over the United States to protect documents and money from damage by blast and fire. It is likely that the documents and money placed in those repositories, some of which have been built in caves, will remain undamaged from blasts and fires as long as those documents and money remain in the repositories. Whether authorized persons will ever get to those repositories to take out the documents and money, however, remains in doubt.

Even if some authorized persons ever got to the repositories and collected the documents and the money, they might have quite some trouble in having to carry the documents and money to safety, in view of the danger to the persons, documents and money from continuously falling debris, spreading fires, and high degree of radioactivity, not to speak of roads blocked by debris as well as by fires. Furthermore, where are those few authorized persons, who were to be so fortunate as to emerge from blast and fireproof shelters and then to reach the repositories, to carry the documents and the money? With a wasteland all around, the documents and the money could well be expected to have become nonfunctional.

Very little public debate has taken place in the United States for some time on the issue of blast and fireproof shelters. The prohibitive costs of building such shelters for the population at large had for a time eliminated this issue from public discussion. The matter of fallout shelters, i.e., shelters which are not expected to protect the population at large from the impact of blast of fire has had an almost unchallenged monopoly in the more recent public discussion of the shelter issue. As to what extent exactly the so-called "fallout shelters" could protect the public at large from the ill effects of radioactivity engendered by detonated thermonuclear bombs is still subject to debate. The two variables, the answers to the questions as to how much radioactivity there is going to be in the air in the aftermath of a thermonuclear bombing attack and as to how much radioactivity a person can take without ill effects on this health, remain largely undetermined.

Even if the degree of radioactivity after various time intervals after a single nuclear thermonuclear bomb attack had taken effect could be determined with any degree of certainty, it will hardly be possible to predict the exact degree of radioactivity in a sustained attack, with one thermonuclear bomb followed by another thermonuclear bomb and still another and so on and so forth. As far as the degree of radioactivity which a person can be expected to take is concerned, that will continue to be a matter of conjecture for a long time to come. Predictions have been made in regard to the expected ill effects of a high degree of radioactivity on generations yet unborn. Whether and to what extent such ill effects will take place, one cannot really know until the generations yet unborn are born and grow up.

A warning in regard to the last stated matter has been sounded recently by Professor of Radiation Physics at the University of Pittsburgh, Ernest J. Sternglass. In a letter published in *The New York Times* on February 19, 1969, Professor Sternglass states "a vast body of observations both in animals and man accumulated over the last ten years show that the human ova, sperm and developing embryo are 10 to 100 times as sensitive to radiation from x-rays and fallout as the mature adult. This factor is not considered at all in past military estimates of casualties from nuclear war". Those are indeed somber observations, which so far have not received either public or official attention.

Experts differ as to the immediate effects of a high degree of radioactivity on the part of the population which might survive a sustained nuclear attack. Coupled with it is the unpredictability as to what the degree of radioactivity will be in different parts of a country which is subjected to a sustained nuclear attack. The whole issue of the predictability of the ill effects on the health of persons from radioactivity either in the short run or the long run, after a sustained attack, continues to remain a highly conjectural matter.

There remains, in addition, the problem of the correlation of the degree to which the building containing the fallout shelter can be made impenetrable in regard to the degree of the radioactivity in the atmosphere. As to whether the building containing so-called "fallout shelters" could be made foolproof against any degree of radiation in the air is not known in any exact form.

Even if the impenetrability of so-called "fallout shelters" to radioactivity in the air outside the fallout shelter could be assured, there still will remain the problem as to when a person who has the benefit of the protection from the ill effects of radioactivity, while in the shelter, can safely emerge from the shelter. The blocking of the exit from the shelter by debris and the uncertainty about additional falling debris, the spreading of fire, and the spread of radioactivity, will confront the person emerging from a so-called "fallout shelter" with innumerable hazards.

Nonetheless, the United States Government, as well as a small section of the United States population, have come out in favor of a program to build so-called fallout shelters. The United States administration has embarked on a program which is aimed at building community fallout shelters. Authoritative sources have estimated a number of years ago that to build so-called fallout shelters for the entire United States population would cost about twenty billion dollars. The United States administration was a few years ago contemplating the spending of two billion dollars for fallout shelter construction in a year. Thus, the community fallout shelter construction program as sponsored by the United States Government does not seem to be intended to cover the whole population until many years hence, were such program to be realized.

But even if the whole population were to be provided with community fallout shelters, those shelters would not protect the population from the dangers of falling debris, fire, and physical destruction. Under such circumstances, the whole so-called fallout community shelter program, as it has been devised by the United States administration, can be considered as aiming foremost at a psychological effect. The fallout shelter program in the form which has received the official sanction in the United States is designed to imbue the population with a sense of security. To what extent the subjective sense of security with which the United States population is to be imbued in regard to the so-called "fallout community shelters" has any objective basis remains an open question.

In the absence of blast and fire protection for the bulk of the population, one could expect that the vast majority of the so-called "fallout community shelters" will be either consumed by fire or damaged by blast effects in any sustained thermonuclear attack on the United States. Thus, in the vast majority of cases, the protection against radioactivity, which the fallout shelters are supposed to offer to humans, would become unnecessary for lack of any surviving humans.

What has been said here in regard to the so-called "community fallout shelters" can also be said of the privately owned so-called "fallout shelters" as regards the protection they could possibly offer. The privately owned, privately constructed, and privately financed so-called "fallout shelters" could be expected to be consumed by fire or to be damaged by blast effects as much as the fallout shelters constructed by a public authority and financed through the use of public funds.

In isolated places, far away from population centers, some of the privately owned, privately constructed and privately financed fallout shelters could be expected to remain standing, should those isolated targets happen to be at great distances from the nuclear attack. The survivors in those shelters would still have to face the problem of getting food and other necessities from populated places. Establishing contact with the formerly populated places, which are likely to become depopulated in the case of sustained nuclear attacks, will most likely present insurmountable difficulties for the survivors in shelters in isolated places.

Reports have been circulated in the United States by Government and private sources that the Soviet Union is also engaged in a shelter-building program. These reports are not confirmed by official sources in the Soviet Union. In any inquiry as to what actually does take place or has taken place in the Soviet Union with regard to shelter building, a distinction must be drawn between shelters which are supposed to provide protection for the population at large in the period which predates the period of nuclear bombs and those intended for use in the period in which nuclear bombs are possibly to be used. In the period which predates the use of nuclear bombs, any taking of cover in the lower floors or basements of buildings, or inside subway tunnels, could have been considered as providing reasonably adequate protection. That kind of shelter program, it can be reasonably assumed, had been put into effect in the Soviet Union.

As far as the possibility is concerned that the Soviet Union has embarked on a large-scale program of building blast and fireproof shelters, it can be stated very definitely that the Soviet Union does not have the means to finance such a program. The cost of effectuating a large-scale program of building blast and fireproof shelters is as financially forbidding for the Soviet Union as it is for the United States. One can reasonably assume that some blast and fireproof shelters have been and are being built in the Soviet Union to protect key personnel in the government, the military establishments, and the important productive enterprises of the country. The building of blast and fireproof shelters for key personnel in the Soviet Union probably matches the building of blast and fireproof shelters for key personnel in the government, the military establishments, and the important economic enterprises in the United States.

In the United States, the building of blast and fireproof shelters for key personnel in the government and military establishments is financed by public funds. The construction of blast and fireproof shelters for key personnel in important enterprises in the United States is financed by corporate funds of those privately owned enterprises. In the Soviet Union, all important undertakings are publicly owned and no building of shelters, therefore, can be expected to be privately financed. What could take place, however, as far as the financing of blast and fireproof shelters for the key personnel in the important economic undertakings in the Soviet Union is concerned, is that special funds might be set aside by those publicly owned economic undertakings, for the specific purpose of building blast and fireproof shelters for the key personnel of these undertakings.

It can also be assumed that some form of blast and fireproof repositories have been built in the Soviet Union for the safekeeping and protection of documents and money, as they have been built in the United States. It would be desirable to build, in the Soviet Union as well as in the United States, blast and fireproof repositories for important books and art treasures. While hardly anybody might be left alive of the particular generation in a country which is subjected to a sustained thermonuclear attack, future generations coming from other parts of the world could greatly benefit, were they to unearth those deposited and preserved cultural objects.

It is safe to assume that the Soviet Union is not engaged in a large-scale fallout shelter-building program. The leaders of the Soviet Government do not appear to be in need of embarking on a shelter-building program in order to lull the population into a false sense of security against the impact of sustained atomic bomb attacks. The Soviet leaders have quite frankly told their population that fallout shelters cannot provide any protection in a nuclear war. Thus the allegation that the Soviet Union is embarked on a large-scale fallout shelter program cannot be given much credence. That allegation, it can be assumed, is being circulated in the United States in order to overcome lagging popular support for the fallout shelter program on which the United States administration is considering to embark.

In summing up the analysis of the possibilities and impossibilities of the realization of a shelter program, one can safely conclude that no shelter program which would appreciably reduce the degree of wholesale destruction, which a series of bomb-laden missile attacks will cause, can be effected. The effect which even the most extensive realization of a fallout shelter program might have can be considered as but extending the time limit of the agony of those who will have had a chance to reach the shelter before the falling debris and the raging fires were to prevent them from taking shelter.

The agony of those who were to reach the shelter can be seen in their being placed in a fixed position from which there will be no escape in case the shelter area itself becomes engulfed in the range of the falling debris and of raging fires.

In addition, those few who could conceivably be expected to survive by taking refuge in a fallout shelter will hardly be able to leave the shelter after the cessation of the sustained bomb-laden missile attack, in view of the debris piled up in front of the shelter entrance and of the fires either raging or smoldering all around the shelter area. Nor will there be any reliable way to determine when the air outside the shelter has reached the low degree of radioactivity which would permit human survival, even if the danger of an entrance blocked by debris and fire could be conjured away. Furthermore, it must be taken into account, that even a safe exit from the fallout shelters by those who have found refuge there will confront those emerging with the prospect of a sight of wholesale incineration. Neither normally functioning humans nor objects generally usable for the satisfaction of human needs will be found by those who could conceivably emerge physically unscathed from some fallout shelters.

In some areas, far removed from the sustained attacks by bomb-laden missiles, some people emerging from fallout shelters might be able to detect some psychologically and physically uninjured humans and some objects not wholly unusable for the satisfaction of human needs. Such a situation, however, is likely to prevail only in a few scattered areas. Moreover, those scattered areas cannot be expected to have much chance of establishing contact with each other for a long time to come, because of the absence of a functioning mechanized communication and trans-portation system.

The key personnel, which might well survive a sustained bomb-laden missile attack in blast and fireproof shelters, upon emerging from their shelters, will face a problem similar to that which will confront those emerging from the fallout shelters. Falling debris and raging and smol-dering fires will present, for the most part, insurmountable obstacles for those emerging from blast and fireproof shelters. Piled up debris, raging and smoldering fires might well force those emerging from the blast and fireproof shelters back into the shelters.

In some isolated places, where debris and fires will not present insurmountable obstacles to the safe emergence of key personnel from blast and fireproof shelters, it is unlikely that objects could be found for the satisfaction of human needs, because of the very isolation in which the shelters for the key personnel may be expected to be placed. Aside from the factor of the physical ability to function on the part of those of the key personnel who could possibly emerge from the blast and fireproof shelters is the realization that they could hardly be expected to be able to resume their function as key personnel. The economic, social, and political fabric in which they functioned before taking refuge in the blast and fireproof shelters can well be expected to have ceased to exist, after the sustained thermonuclear bomb-laden missile attack had been terminated.

A similar observation may be made concerning the usefulness of the documents and money, which could possibly remain intact in blast and fireproof repositories. There hardly will be any persons around who could make use of those objects, not to speak of the improbability of the survival of specific persons or those designated to represent deceased individuals and defunct organizations, who could undertake to advance specific claims for a repossession of those objects.

A study sponsored by the United States Government a few years ago suggested "a sharing" of the financial means which could possibly be conserved in blast and fireproof repositories by the survivors of a sustained bomb-laden missile attack in different regions of the country. The study in question even suggested that the more heavily damaged areas be given financial assistance at the expense of the less damaged areas. A rather naive conception underlies this study; it is a conception which somehow reprojects a situation which prevails in a large country in which some strictly limited parts are hit by natural disasters such as flood or tornadoes. But in such cases, the communication and transportation system remain intact so that one cannot expect any difficulty in establishing contact between the undamaged and the damaged part of the country. Nor, in such a case, can one expect any difficulty in ascertaining the extent of the devastation wrought upon a specific part of a country.

Neither of the two stated factors can be expected to exist in the wake of a sustained thermonuclear bomb-laden missile attack. Nor will there be a functioning system of communication and transportation in existence through which easy contact could be established between the damaged and undamaged areas. Nor will it be possible to undertake an estimate of the extent of the devastation effected. What will take place in the wake of a sustained thermonuclear bomb-laden missile attack is the engulfing of the entire country in a nuclear inferno which will leave only a few isolated spots relatively untouched.

The special, geographical problem, as far as the damage wrought in the wake of thermonuclear bomb-laden missile attacks is concerned, will amount to the very opposite of that which takes place in the case of disasters of nature, such as floods and tornadoes. In case of sustained thermonuclear attacks, the undevastated areas will be the exception and not the rule, as in the case of natural disasters. Therefore, any suggestion that the undevastated areas, which at best will consist of a few isolated spots in the country, provide financial or other economic assistance to the devastated areas constitutes a highly unrealistic proposition. With all but a few isolated spots destroyed, the devastation will have to be considered complete, as far as the territory of the nation, which had become subject to a sustained nuclear attack, is concerned. At best, isolated cases of financial or other economic self-help could be expected after a large-scale devastation of the respective national territory has been effected.

Another study made a few years ago by a United States Government agency advances the argument that there will be no food shortage after nuclear attacks because proportionately more people can be expected to be killed than the food supplies which can be expected to be destroyed. The study falls short of suggesting a decrease in food prices on account of the relative superabundance of food in such a situation. Yet, even without the direct suggestion that the survivors of nuclear attacks might possibly benefit from lowered food prices, the whole argument of that study is based on the wholly unrealistic conception of the expected range of devastation in the wake of sustained thermonuclear bomb-laden missile attacks.

With the whole of the national territory devastated, and with only few isolated, undevastated spots remaining relatively untouched, one cannot expect that the price system will continue to operate. Products in the few isolated spots which could possibly remain relatively untouched in the wake of a sustained thermonuclear attack can at best be expected to be distributed on the basis of emergency allotments. Under the stated conditions, such a system of allotments could at best be set up on a local emergency basis. Those allotments could be expected to be regarded as emergency relief allotments, which would not require monetary compensation on the part of those who are to receive them.

In the absence of a normally functioning communication and transportation system in the wake of a sustained thermonuclear bomb-laden missile attack, it will be next to impossible to ascertain whether any food supplies are present outside the immediate locality in which some survivors may find themselves. Nor will it be possible to ascertain reliably, for a considerable time after the termination of a series of attacks, whether the food supplies, either in the immediate vicinity of the locality in which some scattered survivors of a sustained thermonuclear attack were to find themselves, or in areas not within sight of a particular isolated locality with a few scattered survivors, are fit for human consumption.

All the studies pertaining to the effects of thermonuclear attacks, whether those conducted by governmental, semi-governmental, or non-governmental organizations in the United States, lack one particular aspect: they are not directed towards an investigation of what effect a sustained series of thermonuclear attacks is likely to have on the economic, social, and political framework of a country which comes to be subjected to such attacks. The usual approach of these studies, as they have been conducted in the United States, is geared to the question as to what will happen to individuals in case of a thermonuclear attack. The most frequently asked question is how many individuals are likely to be affected, and in what way, by a thermonuclear attack on the United States.

The most publicized study of that kind, the book by Hermann Kahn, *On Thermonuclear War,* presents an attempt to calculate the prospective number of killed and surviving persons in case of thermonuclear attacks of various degrees on the territory of the United States. Kahn does not make any allowance for an all-out sustained attack on the United States by thermonuclear bomb-laden missiles, which is the most likely extent of an attack, should a thermonuclear war break out. Aside from sidetracking the most likely effect of a thermonuclear attack on the United States, Kahn's study has another major defect. It does not deal with the institutional framework within which individuals are known to operate before the beginning of a sustained nuclear attack as constrasted with the institutional framework within which the individuals, who could possibly survive such an attack, could conceivably be expected to operate after such attack had taken place. This second defect of Kahn's study is shared by almost all United States studies dealing with the problem of survival after the nuclear holocaust. This particular defect deprives all those studies of any realistic basis and thus deprives the respective conclusion drawn from them of any real significance.

What significance, one is bound to ask, can there be attached to Kahn's study, which attempts to demonstrate that a varied percentage of individuals in the population could be excepted to survive under varying degrees of thermonuclear attacks? Aside from the fact that Kahn does not deal with the ultimate attack by the ultimate weapon, i.e., the sustained thermonuclear bomb-laden missile attack, he does not attempt to provide a basis for judging the behavior of the potential survivors in reference to an institutional framework. The assumption which underlies Kahn's study is based on the notion that the institutional framework is going to remain intact, no matter what percentage of casualties in the total population can be expected to be. He presumes, without convincing proof, that if, say, less than 30% of the population is killed by a nuclear attack, the institutional framework can be expected to remain intact. Kahn buttresses this presumption with a description of individual attitudes one could expect to find among the prospective survivors of such an attack. What Kahn forgets is the possibility that the institutional framework might not hold, even if the percentage of those killed does not reach beyond a 30% of the total population, no matter what the conceivable attitudes of some individual survivors could be. Moreover, Kahn neglects to mention that the institutional framework certainly will not hold in case the number of fatal casualties reaches 50% or more of the total population. A 50% of fatal casualties, in terms of the total population, is, by the way, close to a figure of projected fatal casualties suggested by the former Secretary of Defense McNamara, in his statement upon leaving office in 1968. This, however, is but an approximate projection of the first strike casualties. No matter what the number of projected casualties, however, Kahn's approach which relies on the description of the attitudes of potential survivors, constitutes an analysis conducted in an institutional void, and therefore, it does not constitute any realistic appraisal of the expected situation.

Kahn's study constitutes no more than a numbers game and is well in line with other studies of the possible effects of nuclear warfare, which also are geared to the application of the so-called "game theory." This kind of theory, one will recall, was inaugurated by von Neumann and Oscar Morgenstern. The game theory, it should be realized, disposes of the major axiomatic propositions of traditional mathematics and reduces mathematical calculations to the level of dice game propositions. This approach presents a deliberate evasion of key mathematical propositions to which empirical data can be linked. It is an approach which deliberately narrows the range of mathematical formulations to a scope from which significant factors of the totality of reality are forced to be absent. Psychologically, the so-called "game theory" and its application operate within the range of the attitude which could be expected to generate and operate within the mind of a dice thrower who is not concerned with anything but the winning of a given dice game. Psychologically, the approach of the game theory and its application likewise can be linked to the mind of the person who is engaged in playing roulette.

One has to remind oneself, in this connection, of the sight with which one is confronted when one enters casinos in which roulette games are in progress. There are always several people present at the roulette tables in the casinos with long sheets of paper, on which they record the outcome of the specific games which have taken place on the particular roulette table during a certain period of time. It has yet to be demonstrated that the recording of the results of specific roulette games of the past has any direct bearing on the results of specific roulette games in the future. Although the variety of combinations which might ensue in any number of roulette games is limited, the recording of the combinations effected in the past, and the results of the application of those combinations by the respective players in the past, will continue to be without predictive value with regard to future games. The element of chance will continue to be overwhelming, since it will remain impossible to predict what specific combinations with what specific results out of an almost infinite variety of combinations and results will ensue in any specific future game.

Conversely, if one could conceivably record possible results of any number of nuclear attacks, that still would not have any predictive value with regard to the actual casualties which could be expected were any such attack to materialize in the future. Any figures in terms of expected casualties from any number of nuclear attacks which Kahn undertakes to record in his book, *On Thermonuclear War,* or which he might undertake to record in any other book in which he were to use the same method of computation, can be considered but as a presentation of random figures within the range of an almost infinite variety of the degrees of devastation which could be expected to result from any number of nuclear attacks. Assuming the very unlikely situation that Kahn were able to record all possible correlations of the degree of the severity of any number of nuclear attacks with the number of human casualties which could be expected to result from any number of attacks in a neatly arranged series of mathematical presentations, such exhaustive recording would still not have any predictive value. The degree of severity of any future thermonuclear attack or attacks and their expected results will be but one, or, at best, just a few, of the almost infinite variety of the degrees of attacks and the respective casualty figures resulting from them.

The application of the game theory to the calculation of expected casualties presents, in reverse, a calculation of the expected non-casualties, i.e., of survivors. Were one to accept the figures of expected casualties offered by Kahn, one would have, by the same token, to accept his reverse contention about the expected number of survivors. This writer here reaffirms that the number of casualties, as well as the number of survivors, presented by Kahn, constitute at best random selections of an almost infinite variety of possibilities and, therefore, can in no way be regarded as representative of a real situation which could arise in the wake of thermonuclear bombing attacks.

In like manner, the present writer argues here that the unrepresentative number of casualties as well as the unrepresentative number of survivors selected, so to speak, at random by Kahn can be taken as his way of unrepresentative presentation of the range of expected devastation and "non-devastation" on the territory of the United States in the wake of thermonuclear attacks. This unrepresentative presentation of the expected range of devastation and "non-devastation" by Kahn can, in turn, be regarded as his unrepresentative projection of what can be expected to happen to the economic, social, and political framework of the United States as a nation, as a result of sustained thermonuclear attacks on its territory.

Kahn's entire range of inquiry does not go beyond the scope of individual reactions, which, in turn, are related to individual reactions, which, in turn, are related to individual reactions, and so on, and so forth, *ad infinitum*. An objective presentation of the economic, social, and political factors of a respective institutional framework is missing from Kahn's inquiry. He thus deprives himself of an analytical tool which could have enabled him to get out of the vicious circle in his recording of expected individual reactions by having individual reactions related to objective factors, i.e., to the given economic, social, and political matrix. The congeries of individual reactions, as presented by Kahn, are meaningless, since they are not linked to an assessment of the question as to whether or not individual United States citizens could be expected to be willing to support the prevailing economic, social, and political institutional fabric of their country in the wake of thermonucnlear attacks on United States territory.

The instant study avoids the methodological deficiencies of Kahn's book *On Thermonuclear War*. This study avoids first the method of random selection among an infinite variety of possibilities of the expected effects of any number of nuclear attacks of various degrees on United States territory by postulating the high probability, if not certainty, of a saturation attack. This study further avoids the methodological pitfall of Kahn's exclusive reference to individual reactions by bringing in objective factors towards which the individual is expected to react. While in Kahn's book, economic, social, and political aspects appear as but vague implications, in this tract the economic, social, and political factors are made explicit in no uncertain terms.

The most fitting approach to the analysis of the range of destruction to which the economic system of a country under a sustained bomb-laden missile attack may be subjected is to assume that not a single human will be motivated to take any part in the working of the economic system, the second after the first series of thermonuclear bomb-laden missiles has landed. It is irrelevant, in regard to this stated assumption, to consider how

90

many humans can be expected to be killed, maimed, or otherwise physically incapacitated by the first series of thermonuclear bomb-laden missile attacks. No rational human being, no matter what his physical status were to be after the first series of thermonuclear bomb-laden missile attacks, can be expected to be motivated to do anything towards the functioning of the economic system as a whole in the nation under attack.

As far as consumer goods are concerned, only those consumer goods which were to be found within the immediate vicinity and within easy reach of the individuals within, and just outside the range of, the attacks could be expected to be considered to have economic value. The economic value attributed to those consumer goods can be expected to have no relation to either the restocking or the reproduction of those particular goods. Those consumer goods can be expected to be accorded economic value only in relation to the satisfaction of the particular consumption need of particular individuals under conditions of dire emergency.

One could expect each individual to be willing to give his last to acquire consumers goods to add to those which he has been able to store in his place of residence. This last, which any individual could be expected to be willing to give – to secure some additional consumers goods, if he continued to act rationally, would be within the utter limits of his personal income and wealth. Though the source of income and the embodiment of wealth can be expected to vanish as a result of physical destruction in either the first or succeeding bomb-laden missile attacks, the particular individual cannot be expected to have knowledge of this factor at the time when he will have to decide about the acquisition of some additional consumer goods. This decision, therefore, can be expected to be made on fictitious grounds, and, therefore, will have no more than symbolic value. In these circumstances, therefore, the price offered by an individual in a bid to acquire some additional consumer goods cannot be regarded as an expression of what, in the technical language of the economists, is called "effective purchasing power," since no calculable economic basis for the effectuation of such a purchasing power can be expected to exist at the time when such price is to be stated. The price aspect itself will, therefore, have to be termed an imaginary or fictitious proposition.

The only real price affecting factor which can be expected to exist at the time when a bid were to be made by an individual, who found himself within the range of a series of bomb-laden missile attacks, could be related to the cash an individual were to have on hand at the particular moment when he makes his bid for the acquisition of additional consumer goods. It is doubtful, however, whether under the stated circumstances, many individuals in possession of a surplus of consumer goods could see any particular value in turning some of these goods over to any other person for cash. In an area within or close to the range of bomb-laden missile attacks, the seller of such goods could hardly expect to replenish his stock. The only use he could make of additional cash, were he to continue to think and act rationally, would be to turn that cash over to somebody who might possibly be in possession of some other kind of consumer products which would be otherwise unavailable. In this case, it will again be a factor within the range of emergency consumption needs which will determine the price asked and paid for by particular individuals, without regard either to the cost of replenishment of the stock or to the continuation of the production of goods.

The individually determined prices, whether fictitious or non-fictitious, would, in turn, have no relation to each other under the given circumstances. They would be prices which could be explained in terms of an individual who no longer expects to act as a functioning economic entity, but who would be willing to dispose of his material and financial resources in an effort to save his very life at the given instant. Life is of course of the highest value to any normally functioning individual, but how much any person could rationally afford to offer for the preservation of his life differs from person to person.

The malfunctioning of pricing can be expected to be matched by the malfunctioning of the basis on which price formation depends. The malformation of prices is of necessity connected with malformations in the sphere of income. To state it in plain language, prices paid or not paid depend upon how much people earn or do not earn. There are only four ways in which one can make a living in a capitalist economy. One can establish a claim to profits, or a claim to interest, or a claim to rent, or a claim to wages. It can easily be demonstrated that none of these claims will be made by any rationally thinking and acting person, once the initial phase of a bomb-laden missile attack has begun. Under the circumstances of a sustained bomb-laden missile attack, the motivation to engage in profit making, interest taking, rent collecting, or wage earning, cannot possibly prevail over the motivation to escape death.

Immediately following an attack, some people might be motivated to dispose of their businesses as the source of profits, or of their capital funds as the source of interest, or of the land as the source of rent, in the anticipation that each succeeding bomb-laden missile attack will greatly enhance the physical destruction of the objects upon the existence of which those property rights are based. Whether such owners of businesses, capital funds, or land will be able to find buyers for their prospective sales under the given circumstances is doubtful, unless there are some adventurous speculators present among other prospective victims of successive sustained bomb-laden missile attacks. Yet, even granted that adventurous speculators on the misery of their fellowmen could be found under the given circumstances, and that some such speculative deals could be effected, it is highly doubtful whether any such deals could be consummated.

It cannot be expected that such prospective deals will be cash transactions, since the objects involved are to be considered capital goods of comparatively high economic value. The deals would require the drawing up of documents, and this one could not possibly expect in the given circumstances. Agreement could, of course, be reached by word of mouth, but whether such an agreement could ever be expected to be held is extremely doubtful. Even if legal documents could be drawn up under these circumstances, it is doubtful whether any court sitting in the wake of the termination of a sustained bomb-laden missile attack would validate such a claim, since any such deals could be expected to be adjudged as deals made under duress. It is assumed that, in the stated instance, survivors would be in a position to press claims and that judges would be present to adjudge those claims after the termination of the sustained attack, of which assumptions, of course, one cannot be certain.

As regards the claims to wages, no rationally thinking and acting person can be expected to be motivated into continuing or resuming work from the initial phase on of a sustained bomb-laden missile attack on. No formal notices of termination of the work contract can be expected, however, under the stated circumstances. The work contract of any employment can be expected to come into a state of suspense with the initiation of the attack. The state of suspense will soon be followed by the actual termination of the work contract through death, maining, or other forms of incapacitation in the course of succeeding bomb-laden missile attacks.

Claims to wages earned before the initiation of the attacks, and claims to wages earned prior to the termination of the work contract through death, maiming, and other forms of incapacitation can be expected to be maintained. Whether such claims will ever come to be pressed after the termination of a sustained attack will depend on the number of survivors and the relationship of those survivors to those who established those claims to wages, or to their respective heirs.

As far as the economy of a country in which the means of production are not privately but publicly owned, as in the case of the Soviet Union, is concerned, the economic impact of the initial phase of a sustained bomb-laden missile attack can be expected to be somewhat different from the economic impact on a business economy. In the Soviet Union, prices, by and large, are fixed; however, any fixed price, no matter what particular agency of the government has the authority to fix it, has to have some relationship to the amount of the goods available and to the prospects of having identical goods or their substitutes produced in the future.

With the initial phase of the landing of bomb-laden missiles on the territory of the Soviet Union, and with each successive series of landings of bomb-laden missiles on Soviet territory, the stock of available goods as well as of the production facilities can be expected to be destroyed in ever increasing numbers. The material basis on which prices are fixed in the Soviet Union can be expected to be successively reduced. Fixed prices for products, were they to continue to be maintained, would then lose any real material content and would amount to nothing more than empty economic shells.

Some pricing could be expected to take place in the Soviet Union in regard to the consumer goods available in close proximity to potential consumers, either within the range of the sustained bomb-laden missile attacks or on territory adjoining that range. With all the stores in which consumer goods are offered for sale owned and operated by the government, a change in the price tags of the goods offered for sale in the wake of successive bomb-laden missile attacks – provided no physical destruction of the particular store is effected – could not be expected.

In peace time, any change in the price tags of state owned and operated stores must be initiated by the central authority which supervises the operation of these stores. Since no communication between the administrators of the individual stores and the central administration of all the stores in the particular line of trade can be expected to exist in the wake of sustained bomb-laden missile attacks, no approval of any price change by a higher authority can be expected under the stated circumstances. Whether some administrators of individual stores would take it upon themselves to change the price tags under the given circumstances is doubtful.

It is conceivable, however, that some emergency legislation, authorizing administrators of individual stores to change the price tags in an emergency, such as one caused by sustained bomb-laden missile attacks, might be enacted in advance of such at attack. Were such legislation to be passed, and were individual administrators of stores in which consumer products are sold authorized to change price tags, such changes, in the wake of sustained bomb-laden missile attacks, could be expected to be made with a view toward providing income for the personnel, so as to enable them to weather the sustained attack in an economic sense, provided they were not killed. The pricing thus would be detached from the assessment of supplies available in any place other than that particular store, as well as from any consideration of the prospect of future production of identical goods or their substitutes. Again, the price formed in the stated instance would not constitute the regular form of price formation; it would amount to no more than a pricing which could but be expected to reflect emergency conditions.

It is conceivable that some deals for the acquisition of consumer products could take effect among individuals in the wake of successive bomb-laden missile attacks on the territory of the Soviet Union. Cash could conceivably be offered by some individuals to others, for the acquisition of individually owned consumer goods. Such deals, if effected, would reflect the emergency needs of the respective parties, and thus again would have no relation to either restocking or reproduction.

As far as the relationship of price formation to the formation of income in the Soviet Union is concerned, the following observations are in order. Claims to profit, interest, and rent can as a rule be advanced only by state authorities, by virtue of the state's titles of ownership to either productive or distributive economic undertakings, as well as the state's titles of ownership to capital funds and land. Individuals, as a rule, have only the right to advance claims to wages on the basis of the work they perform.

Deals between different state authorities for the exchange of titles to the particular state property they hold could be expected only if one state authority could be expected to have a better chance to protect its particular state property from destruction than any other state authority. Yet, even in that case, which can be considered a rather remote proposition, a deal for passing state property from one state agency to another could not be expected to be effectuated, since, in the absence of means of communication in the wake of a succession of bomb-laden missile attacks on the territory of the Soviet Union, it will be impossible for a local state authority to get the approval of any higher state authority.

Conceivably, legislation to the stated effect could be passed in the Soviet Union for just such a contingency. Such legislation would enable local administrators of specific state economic units to take emergency measures aimed at the best possible protection of state properties in case of bomb-laden missile attacks. Any such emergency action, however, even if it were authorized, would be geared to the salvaging of government owned property and not to the actual operation thereof.

As far as the work contract, on the basis of which individuals establish a claim to wages, is concerned, we must note that such a contract, as a rule, is in effect in the Soviet Union between the individual and the respective state authority which operates a given productive, distributive, or other undertaking. This contract cannot be expected to expire in the wake of a succession of bomb-laden missile attacks. The basis for the effectuation of the work contract can, however, be expected to cease in the wake of a succession of bomb-laden missile attacks on the territory of the Soviet Union, for such attacks are likely to destroy productive and other government operated properties as well as the individuals who are supposed to man them. Claims by possible survivors or their heirs to wages earned in the past as well as claims to severance pay in case the productive or otherwise used government property is physically destroyed could be expected to be pressed after the termination of sustained bomb-laden missile attacks.

Continuation of work, even in essential undertakings, after the initial phase of a sustained bomb-laden missile attack, can hardly be expected for any length of time in the area within the range of that attack. To what extent work in essential undertakings in the Soviet Union could be expected to continue in the wake of successive attacks in scattered areas not under direct attack, in view of the expected absence of means of communication and transportation with wide areas coming under direct attack, is very difficult to say.

It is, of course, conceivable that in the Soviet Union, as well as in the United States, the distribution of consumer products free of charge will be authorized in preparation for the expected emergency, the bomb-laden missile attacks. Special legislation to this effect could be passed in the Soviet Union as well as in the United States. Such legislation and its possible application would, however, have no direct bearing on either the functioning or the malfunctioning of the respective economic systems of the two countries. The effectuation of such an emergency legislation will present a mere humanitarian measure and thus be non-economic in character.

Yet, whether passage of such legislation and the stocking up of food and clothing in certain localities for distribution free of charge would actually result in the distribution of these supplies in case the contingency arises remains highly doubtful. The degree of physical destruction of buildings, equipment, and humans, in the wake of successive bomb-laden missile attacks, can be expected to be of such vast magnitude that in the end there will be neither any supplies which have not been physically destroyed or been made radioactive, nor will hardly any people be left to request such supplies. In the area under direct attack by bomb-laden missiles, survivors will, for the most part, be trapped in partially destroyed buildings, while falling debris and radioactivity will threaten those who would undertake to leave the sheltered places which enabled them to survive.

In the wake of the progress of the sustained bomb-laden missile attack, the whole range of activities pertaining to the production, distribution, and consumption of products will increasingly become a non-economic activity. With buildings, production implements, raw materials, semi-finished products, and finished products becoming increasingly destroyed

96

or radioactive, the very basis for a correlated effectuation of goods and services will cease to exist. At that advanced stage of destruction, it will become impossible even to think of a formation of prices or of income. Conversely, it will become pointless to inquire, at that advanced stage of destruction, about the malfunctioning of price formation or of formation of income. Furthermore, it will become pointless, at that advanced state of destruction, to refer to the breakdown or absence of a functioning communication and transportation system as a factor impeding the operation of the economic system. Not much will be left to be operated at that stage.

The low level economic stage which will be reached in the wake of the progress of the sustained bomb-laden missile attack can well be called a "grab bag" stage. It can be expected to be a stage in which those individuals who remain alive will try to put their hands on such products as might conceivably continue to be available in the immediate vicinity of such individuals. Under such circumstances, it really will not matter very much whether initially, before the beginning of a sustained bomb-laden missile attack, the economic system in operation was geared to the functioning of individually or corporatively owned economic undertakings, as is the case in the United States, or whether the operation of the economic system was initially geared to the functioning of publicly owned undertakings, as is the case in the Soviet Union.

This so-called "grab bag" stage may be regarded as one in which no organized economic activity can be expected to take place. As such, it can be regarded as a stage which lies below the level of the primitive tribal economy. In a stage in which a primitive tribal economy functions, there definitely is a set of organizations which extends over an interconnected territory. No organizations of any kind can be expected to exist in the so-called "grab bag" stage. In this "grab bag" stage of the economy the satisfaction of the most elementary human wants will have to be effected under conditions of all but total physical destruction of production and distribution facilities and their respective organizational framework.

Along with the dissolution of the economic organizational framework the social fabric will become subject to disintegration in the course of bomb-laden missile attacks. The distinction between rich and poor as the basis for social stratification will cease to exist. As rich will come to be regarded a person who, in the so-called "grab bag" stage of the economy, finds within his reach a product fit for human consumption. As poor will be regarded a person who does not find the products fit for human consumption within his reach. The distinction between propertied and non-propertied, as a basis for social stratification, likewise will vanish in the wake of bomb-laden missile attacks. With documented titles to property increasingly divorced from their holders, because either the documents and/or the property holders are destroyed, the legal aspect of property holding will become an increasingly remote proposition.

Material property, such as houses, factories, and machines will become increasingly subject to destruction and thus make the basis for property titles rather illusory. Property as a means of making a living will lose all its significance. Hardly any person will be concerned with the continuous conduct of a business or will report to his job after a few bomb-laden missiles have reached their target. The only activity a person can be expected to pursue in the course of the bomb-laden missile attacks is that of maintaining one's physical integrity. Such integrity one, if uninjured, can be expected to maintain for the most part at the expense of social cohesion.

The rule "dog-eats-dog" will become the overriding factor in individual's conduct. With wholesale destruction taking place all around him, the probability of an individual's survival will be reduced to an infinitesimal chance. Such chance could be enhanced were the individual to free himself of any social obligation tying him to any other individual.

This crass individualism will extend not only to the wider ranges of the social fabric, such as the division between the propertied and the non-propertied or between employers and employees, but the "dog-eats-dog" attitude will extend to the relationship within families as well. It is most likely that in the dire emergency which will arise in the course of progressing bomb-laden missile attacks, a situation will prevail in which one member of a family will be given a chance, no matter how slight, to save himself at the expense of other members of his family. It is most likely that such chances will taken.

That such crass individualism will prevail even among members of a family can be explained by the expectation of any surviving member of a family that all the other members of his family will have been killed in the course of the progressing bomb-laden missile attacks. If such were to be the expectation, considerations such as a guilty conscience born out of regret that family ties have to be broken, in an effort to save one's physical existence, will hardly play any role.

The split second decision which the individual would have to make to save himself could not be expected to leave room for the consideration of the survival of any other individuals. The infinitesimally small chance of any individual's surviving could well be reduced to zero, were he to try to save himself with due consideration for any social ties, including the family ties which had existed prior to the start of the sustained bomb-laden missile attack.

One can expect, to be sure, that some spontaneous individual cases of unselfish heroism will take place. However, since the prospective hero and those for whom he was to risk his life can all be expected to meet with certain death, any such heroic attempts will have to be regarded as merely pathetic. It can also be expected that some heroic individual efforts will be made to preserve cohesion among members of a family. Those efforts can, however, be expected to be foredoomed. The probability of entire families meeting death will be so great that any attempt to preserve family unity could, in the end result, amount to no more than an empty gesture. It can also be expected that some sporadic individual efforts will be made on the part of heroic individuals to preserve social ties going beyond the family unit. Such individual heroic efforts are likely, however, to come to naught. Not enough people will survive to make any sustained social cohesiveness a reality.

With the economic framework and the social fabric dissolved, the political superstructure can also be expected to collapse. Deprived of its economic and social content, the national state, the existence of which is at the base of political institutions, will completely disintegrate.

Chapter 4

FUTILITARIAN STRATEGIES

In the face of the prospect of nearly total annihilation, the aspects of which have been spelled out in the foregoing two chapters, military strategists, in and out of uniform, continue to draw up plans and to discuss moves for the fighting of a nuclear war. In the United States, in particular, the updating of military strategy, geared to nuclear weapons, has blossomed into a new kind of science. This new kind of science appears, however, to have been placed in a vacuum. This vacuum can be said to be of two dimensions.

First, it is entirely ahistorical. It leaves the experience with past military strategy out of consideration; it starts its argument from scratch, in the assumption that the experience of past military strategy is nonexistent and does not count. Second, this new United States military strategy confines itself to a strictly operational range, within whose scope it constructs models, which are not required to stand an empirical test.

What one gets, therefore, is an assortment of cobwebs which basically reflect the working of the mind of the particular military strategists, whether in and out of uniform. These military stratagems are no more than subjective speculations, as far as their relation to the prospects of the actual fighting of a thermonuclear war is concerned. The only relation these subjectively conceived military stratagems have to objective factors is to the continuation and acceleration of the arms race.

By disregarding the experience gained from the application of past military strategy, the contemporary American military strategists, in and out of uniform, may be subconsciously assuming that nuclear weapons geared to missiles ushered in an entirely new era in military strategy and warfare. This assumption of the United States military strategists could then lead to the belief that the military strategy applied in past wars had no relevance in the present. To a certain degree, the United States military strategists, who deliberately disregard experience with military strategy in past wars, are right. Nuclear weapons geared to missiles constitute a break with the use of weaponry, as it has been practiced in the past. There is a qualitative distinction between pre-nuclear and nuclear weaponry and between the respective applicability of these two types of weapons in actual warfare.

What the qualitative distinction amounts to has been spelled out, in its basic aspects, in the preceding two chapters of this tract. The conclusion at which this writer arrived makes it clear that the qualitative distinction between the weaponry of the pre-nuclear age and of the nuclear age, and between their respective applicability, must of necessity rule out nuclear war as an instrument of a rational national policy of any nation.

Were the military strategists in the United States, in and out of uniform, to accept the stated conclusion, they would have to give up their positions as military strategists and would have to engage in other pursuits. By ignoring the effects which an all-out nuclear war is most likely to have on the very physical existence of any national state which becomes involved in nuclear warfare, those military strategists manage to perpetuate themselves in their positions, and thus play an important role in the continuation and acceleration of the arms race.

In all fairness, one has to grant that there are some military strategists, in and out of uniform, in the United States who are critical of specific military stratagems which have been devised by other military strategists in the United States, in and out of uniform. But the critical stand of the particular military strategists in the United States, in and out of uniform, does not go beyond the range of a criticism of a given military stratagem. After the specific criticism of the particular military stratagem is completed, the given critic then goes on to provide a stratagem of his own. Thus, the critics are in reality using their critical stand in regard to a particular military stratagem as but a springboard for joining the ever growing number of those who devise military stratagems in the United States.

A patent example of how a criticism of prevailing military stratagems resulted in but adding another stratagem is Henry A. Kissinger's book, *Nuclear Weapons and Foreign Policy*. Kissinger has become in 1969 the chief military strategy advisor to President Nixon. Kissinger's book expounds the thesis that an all-out nuclear war is not the only possibility in the age of nuclear weapons. Limited nuclear warfare, as well as warfare with conventional weapons, Kissinger argues, are to be included in the range of possibilities in the nuclear age. The effect of Kissinger's book was the inclusion of these other ranges of warfare in the military planning of the United States administration. The impact of the book thus resulted in a widening militarization of the United States, not in the narrowing of it.

The prospect of all-out nuclear war is not excluded from actual military planning in the United States, but other forms of warfare have been added to the military planning of the United States government. That limited warfare, and, in particular, limited warfare with conventional weapons, cannot be regarded as a substitute for all-out warfare with nuclear weapons was spectacularly demonstrated during the Berlin crisis in 1961. The then President Kennedy, in his television address made in the summer of 1961, implied that the United States had a choice of fighting either a nuclear war or a war with conventional weapons, over the status of Berlin. He opted, the then President Kennedy implied, for a war with conventional weapons. The then President Kennedy implemented his option for a limited war over the status of Berlin by calling up a million or so reservists and by bolstering the United States garrison in Berlin by adding foot soldiers flown from the United States. The result of the Kennedy speech and its implementation were the erection of a wall between the Eastern and Western parts of Berlin, the announcement of a rearmament drive by the then Soviet Premier Khrushchev, and subsequently the resumption of atomic testing by the Soviet Union. Implicit in these moves by the Soviet Union was the assumption that, if a war over the status of Berlin were to break out, it would invariably develop into an all-out nuclear war. This by now historical example can well be taken as a test case in which the military stratagem of limited warfare was exploded when the test of historical reality was applied to it.

This proof of the historical unreality of the limited war stratagem did not have any effect, however, on the range and direction of military planning by the Kennedy administration. In this case, the Kennedy administration appears to have labored under the assumption that the disproof of a given assumption in a singular case does not necessarily invalidate the assumption as such. Under other circumstances, the military planners in Washington appear to think, the proposition of limited warfare conducted with conventional weapons might well prove applicable. Limited warfare is at present put to a test in Vietnam, where United States military personnel and equipment are used to bolster the forces employed by the government of South Vietnam against the Vietnamese insurgents. The engagement of United States military personnel in South Vietnam can be continued, within the range of limited warfare, only so long as other nations which claim an interest in the political situation in South Vietnam permit the war to remain limited. In other words, the decisison to conduct a war within a limited range does not rest with the United States Government alone, but has to be made by the United States Government with the implicit consent of other interested governments. The limited war proposition thus remains beyond the sole control of the United States Government. A decision, by governments other than that of the United States, to take part in the Vietnamese conflict and not to limit its participation to the use of conventional weapons, will, of necessity, turn a limited war, fought with conventional weapons, into an unlimited war, fought with nuclear weapons.

The very take-off of Kissinger's military stratagem, the experience of the Korean War, belies his thesis. Kissinger's entire range of argument is keyed to the proposition that the overall United States military planning at the time preceding the Korean War was based on the expectation of the need of fighting an unlimited nuclear war. That expectation did not materialize at once, and, therefore, the United States military leaders were left without an adequate military stratagem in the conduct of the Korean War. What Kissinger left out is the latent danger, which prevailed during the conduct of the Korean War, of its escalation into an all-out nuclear war. This latent danger became acute at the time when the Communist Chinese military force entered the conflict.

When the Chinese sent in their military force to fight in Korea, they gave expression to their acute interest in the outcome of the war. At that point the United States military planners were about to transform the war fought with conventional weapons into a nuclear war. Reports circulated at that time, and recently confirmed, show that only the quick intervention by the then Prime Minister of Britain, Clement Atlee, (later Lord Atlee) dissuaded the then United States President, Harry Truman, from using atom bombs in the further conduct of the Korean War. The decision not to drop atom bombs in Korea predetermined the indecisiveness of the outcome of the war. The outcome demonstrates that the use of conventional weapons cannot enable a nuclear power to win a war in a traditional sense.

The reason why a nuclear power is unable to win a war with conventional weapons lies in the realization of the likelihood of nuclear retaliation by another nuclear power which has an interest in the outcome of a given conflict. In the case of the Korean War, the prospect of the Soviet Union's siding with China and entering the conflict with Korea, with the use of atomic weapons, is a case in point. Neither, for that matter, would the use of atomic weapons by either the United States or the Soviet Union in the Korean War have brought about a decision in the conventional sense. Korea would have been reduced to ashes in the process.

Thus, neither a war fought with conventional weapons by any of the nuclear powers, in the presence of other nuclear powers, nor a war in which the use of nuclear weapons by one power is answered by the use of nuclear weapons by another nuclear power, can be won in the manner in which wars have been won in the past. At best, limited wars, fought with conventional weapons by a nuclear power against a non-nuclear power, can, in the presence of other nuclear powers whose interests are involved in the conflict, result in the reattainment of the *status quo ante*.

That was exactly the situation which resulted in Korea at the termination of hostilities. It was stated at that time by several commentators, in and out of uniform, in the United States, that, for the first time in its modern history did the United States military forces stop short of winning a military victory. The stopping short of military victory was mentioned with regret by the United States commentators, since it did not conform to United States military tradition. It certainly did not so conform, and for the good reason that the development and operational readiness of atomic weapons had made an end of all traditional strategic concepts, in regard to both the conduct and termination of a war.

The attempt of Kissinger to reintroduce pre-nuclear strategic concepts in the nuclear age presents an ahistorical proposition. This ahistorical proposition cannot replace the strategic considerations which a nuclear power must take into account in the presence of other nuclear powers. The attempt to revive pre-nuclear concepts in a nuclear age, if it is aimed at the replacement of strategic concepts of the nuclear age, can lead only to disastrous illusions, as the cases of Korea, Berlin and most recently Vietnam well demonstrate.

The application of Kissinger's concept of limited warfare with conventional weapons can at best result in supplementing the stratagems of nuclear war with those of a non-nuclear war. The application of this strategy is very limited, however, since, as has been pointed out above, it is predicated upon the consent of other nuclear powers to refrain from using nuclear weapons. Such consent can be had only to a point, and no nuclear power will inform another nuclear power beforehand of the point at which it will apply nuclear weapons. Thus, a so-called "limited" war with conventional weapons of a nuclear power is bound to be a war in which the threat of the transformation of the limited war with the use of conventional weapons into an unlimited war, with nuclear weapons, will ever be present.

A situation similar to that of the Korean War has come to prevail in regard to the war in Vietnam. The potential threat of the use of atomic weapons by the United States, as well as China and the Soviet Union, precludes a resolution of that conflict on military grounds. A political solution of the Vietnam conflict has become imperative.

As far as the actual political resolution of the Vietnam conflict is concerned, the United States will have to admit that South Vietnam had been engaged in a civil war. The presumption of the Johnson Administration that the fighting in South Vietnam was merely caused by an invasion of South Vietnam by North Vietnam armies appears to be untenable. The reason why United States officials were reluctant to admit the civil war character of the fighting in South Vietnam is because they did not want to grant the South Vietnamese rebels, the Viet Cong, the status of a belligerent.

In the above stated connection, the conspiracy theory of history, to which many influential people inside and outside the government in the United States subscribe, came in handy. That theory does not conceive of the possibility of a genuine civil war as an expression of deep rooted maladjustments, in any given country. It is in line with that kind of prejudgement which makes the United States government deny the legitimacy of the claims of the rebels in South Vietnam. That predjudgement is further in line with any stand the United States administration is likely to take, were a civil war to break out in any other country of the world. And, it is this kind of prejudgment which makes the outbreak of other Vietnams, with subsequent United States intervention in other trouble spots of the world, not unlikely.

The likelihood of such development can only be considered as being tempered by the increasing unpopularity of any further involvement in foreign civil wars by the United States electorate. The United States electorate had been sobered by the punishment the United States military forces had to take in Korea as well as in South Vietnam. More than half of the postwar years after World War II have been years of war for the United States population, in which the Korean and Vietnam conflicts stand out most prominently. That experience should be considered as enough of a chastening factor, as far as a lighthearted embarking by any United States administration in other military adventures abroad is concerned. President Nixon has remarked recently that he detects the revival of an isolationist mood in the United States. If by isolationism Mr. Nixon means a growing distaste for possible United States military adventures abroad, he is likely to have taken the correct pulse of American public opinion.

The test that the United States side is willing to settle the Vietnam conflict on political grounds will come at the point when the United States side of the Paris peace conference will realize the necessity of discussing substantive matters of a political settlement with the representatives of the South Vietnamese rebels, the Viet Cong. It is the South Vietnamese, the Viet Cong, whom the United States military forces have been fighting all along in South Vietnam and without whose consent, a political settlement of the Vietnam conflict cannot be had.

Counterinsurgency, the military doctrine which had been advanced by United States military strategists in the fighting in Vietnam has not stood the test on the battlefield. Aside from the fact that insurgents always show a higher morale than counterinsurgents, since the latter regard a war but as a police action while the first are bent on fighting for a cause, there are strictly military matters to be considered. There are distinct strategic and tactical limitations which are attached to the counterinsurgency. Counterinsurgency has to be placed within the context of the fighting strength characterized by firepower and manpower. Are those factors of firepower and manpower insufficient to attain military victory over the insurgents, counterinsurgency cannot become fully effective. Counterinsurgency is to be specifically understood as a follow-up pacification move, after victory in the field has been won over the insurgents. If military victory is unattainable, counterinsurgency cannot be made to serve as a substitute for it.

Out of fear to have the Vietnam conflict escalate to the point of having to employ atomic weapons, the Johnson Administration abstained from providing sufficient firepower and manpower in order to defeat the insurgents in South Vietnam militarily. That condition predetermined the military indecisiveness of United States war activity in Vietnam. In addition, the more or less vocal opposition to the further escalation of the war in Vietnam on the part of the United States electorate, as well as their political representatives in Congress, has precluded further military escalation of the conflict after about five hundred thousand United States military personnel had been committed to the fighting in Vietnam. Former President Lyndon Johnson, who had staked his position as President of the United States on a military victory in Vietnam, had come to realize that such a victory is unobtainable, if United States military commitments in Vietnam is not to be further escalated. Mr. Johnson took the consequences and withdrew from active political life. Whether the United States war planners in the Pentagon have learned the lesson of the limitations of counterinsurgency strategy and tactics from the debacle of United States military forces in Vietnam remains to be seen.

The Vietnam War also exploded a particular operational device which had been perfected for that conflict by Herman Kahn. Kahn, in his book entitled *On Escalation,* tried to present the factor of military escalation of an armed conflict as an open-end proposition. In other words, he asserted, he is able to demonstrate how military escalation of an armed conflict could become calculable. In various variants, Kahn tries to shows how military escalation of an armed conflict proceeds step by step in expectation of desired results. What is concluded in the above stated deliberations of Kahn is that the effects of any military action, and any military action linked to an escalation in particular, remain predictable. And at that point Kahn has proven to be wrong. Just the opposite is the case, any military action, and in particular a military action linked to escalation, has to be judged unpredictable in terms of its effects. The unpredictability of an escalated military action, in particular, is rooted in the inability of one adversary to know exactly how the effects of the military escalation are appraised by the other adversary.

The adversary trying escalation is bound to remain in the dark about its effects, as far as that effect registers or does not register, with the other adversary. Before the final termination of hostilities, it is almost impossible to tell, and in particular, to tell in short term intervals, what effect a military action of one adversary has on the other adversary. Escalation of military activity, if pursued step by step, is likely to lead into a blind alley. In leading into a blind alley, step by step escalation is eventually likely to lead to more and more uncontrollable military actions. Such uncontrollable military actions can, in the end, if one of the adversaries is in the possession of atomic weapons, imperceptibly lead to an atomic war.

That the Johnson Administration suddenly reversed itself and tried de-escalation in the Vietnam conflict, can well be explained by its growing realization that a further step-up in escalation could lead to a point of no return, in terms of a possible transformation of a so-called limited war into an unlimited war in which atomic weapons were to be applied. It took the uncommon persuasiveness of the former Secretary of Defense Clark Clifford to convince the Johnson Administration that in escalating the United States military activities in Vietnam, it had embarked upon a course with uncalculable consequences. The point which Clifford made for de-escalation is also a point which could be made to demonstrate the strategic and tactical inoperativeness of the escalation device as it had been propagated by Kahn. Kahn, however, could claim to have provided a safety catch in the propagation of his escalation device. He did not exclude atomic war from his open-ended escalation strategy. In that regard, Kahn can well be considered consistent, since he has built his reputation on making atomic war palatable to the United States military planners as well as the lunatic fringe of the American public.

When it comes to basic, local military strategems, which underlie the United States military planning, a distinction has to be made between the period in which the United States had a monopoly of nuclear weapons and the period in which that monopoly in the manufacture of nuclear weapons was lost. While the United States had that monopoly, the focal United States strategem consisted of the threat of massive retaliation by the United States, addressed to any non-nuclear power. No matter how powerful an initial thrust on the United States with non-nuclear weapons might have been, massive retaliation with nuclear weapons by the United States would have dwarfed any damage which such an initial thrust, with non-nuclear weapons, could have wrought upon the United States. Such prospects, it could then have been cogently argued, would have made the initiation of any armed conflict by a non-nuclear power on a nuclear power unthinkable, in terms of a rationally conceived military strategy.

The temptation, in turn, of a nuclear power, such as the United States, to initiate a war against a non-nuclear power, like the Soviet Union, at a time when the latter did not possess nuclear weapons, was great. Until the late forties, the United States, being in sole possession of the atomic bomb, conceivably could have done irreparable damage to the Soviet Union by starting a war against that country. An initial massive thrust by the United States nuclear bombs would have made it extremely unlikely for the Soviet Union to retaliate in a manner which would have turned the scales of such a war in favor of the Soviet Union. It is very unlikely, in brief, that the Soviet Union would have had the chance of a comeback in that kind of a war.

The theory that a country upon which an atomic assault has been visited could, in the absence of atomic weapons for a counterthrust, fight on in a so-called 'broken-back' stage, can be considered acceptable only to a limited extent. In the so-called 'broken-back' stage, a country which had been made subject to atomic assaults upon its territory and population could do no more, in the absence of nuclear weapons of its own, than to salvage some part of its population and territory from the ruin of the rest of the country. Thus, a nucleus for eventual recovery could be preserved. The military outcome of that kind of war, in which a country in possession of nuclear weapons is pinned against a country which does not have nuclear weapons, can be considered predetermined from the very beginning.

There is no way for a non-nuclear power to win a war against a nuclear power, except perhaps when the non-nuclear power knows the place where the nuclear weapons of the nuclear power are manufactured and stored. In such case, the non-nuclear power could attempt to destroy these places and thus eliminate the nuclear superiority of the nuclear power. Even with the limited range of the manufacture of nuclear weapons in the middle and late forties, and the limited number of nuclear weapons in the possession of the United States at that time, it is highly unlikely that the Soviet intelligence had sufficient specific knowledge of the exact places in the United States where nuclear weapons were manufactured and stored.

It is even more unlikely that, at that time, the military forces of the Soviet Union, and in particular, its manned bombers, had the capability of reaching the United States to unload their bombs on specific targets. The United States military strategists at that time could have discounted, and probably did discount, the possibility of the destruction of United States manufacturing facilities and storage places of nuclear weapons by manned Soviet bombers. For all practical purposes, the nuclear striking power of the United States, at the time when it had a monopoly in the manufacture and possession of nuclear weapons, was as good as invulnerable.

With an indubitable military advantage as nuclear military power, the United States did not go to war against the Soviet Union, which was a non-nuclear power up to the end of the forties. The reason for this is that the government and people of the United States realized that a war against the Soviet Union, then a recent ally of the United States in the war against German and Italian Fascism and against Japanese militarism, was not in the national interest of the United States. In arriving at this decision, the United States administration was pursuing the political course which has become traditional in the period of the existence of national states. National states, since they had come into existence about five hundred years ago, went to war when their respective governments regarded war as a means of advancing or defending the national interests of their particular national state. Wars actually were started in the period of national states because a state considered itself directly threatened by the military forces of another national state. Such a threat could and did exist only when military forces of a national state were actually mobilized.

In that period, the mobilization of military forces was the result of a decision to go to war. The decision itself was not made on the basis of the existence and presence of military forces in the country of a potential adversary, because any such country was in a state of military demobilization prior to an actual outbreak of hostilities. To be sure, the government of any country which contemplated war on another country considered the military potential of its adversary. But a military potential was not considered identical with the military forces and equipment which existed before war broke out. In the long history of national states, mobilization of military forces and equipment constituted a move from non-mobilized status to mobilized status.

Under present conditions, however, the situation can be characterized as a status of continuous mobilization of the armed forces and equipment of the major military powers. So far this state of continuous mobilization of the military forces and equipment of the major powers, with the United States and the Soviet Union in the lead, has not been followed by an actual outbreak of hostilities. However, should hostilities between the two major military powers, the United States and the Soviet Union, break out, the war would have to be fought in its decisive stage by the military forces and equipment which were present in the state of continuous mobilization.

Any addition of manpower and of non-nuclear equipment, after the outbreak of hostilities and after the decisive blows by the nuclear weapons of the major protagonists of military power, the United States and the Soviet Union, have been struck, could be of little moment.

Moreover, the state of continuous mobilization makes the outbreak of hostilities an instantaneous proposition. The only act which would transform the military forces and the military equipment of the two major protagonists, the United States and the Soviet Union, from a latent state into a state of acute warfare would literally be the pushing of a button.

This pushing of a button will unleash missile driven nuclear attacks, which will within hours reduce each of the two major powers to a status of military powerlessness. The danger of such a course of events is ever hanging over the respective countries as long as an unauthorized, an accidental pushing of the button cannot be entirely ruled out. Some additonal safeguards, it is reported by the *New York Post* on February 26, 1969, had been taken against unauthorized and accidental pushing of the buttons by the Kennedy Administration. In a book published in March, 1969 by Norman Moss entitled *The Men Who Play God,* it is stated that the Kennedy Administration instituted remote control locks on all nuclear weapons. Norman Moss informs that the locks can be worked only by radio messages which would be sent to military officers along with the order to fire. The officers handling the weapons directly do not, Moss asserts, have the combination.

Moss further relates that the system was planned initially only for the weapons under joint control in NATO countries, but the Kennedy Administration in 1962 extended it to weapons in American military services as well. Moss further relates that the military "resented the electronic lock as a slur on their reliability and integrity. They felt that the present controls were tight enough." The move, Moss further relates, was also resented by some Congressmen, who had proposed the special locks for NATO weapons only. Before this, Moss states, a two key system was used in NATO countries to launch a bomb. One was worn around the neck of an officer of the host country, the other by an American officer on the base. Whatever the safeguards against the unauthorized and accidental pushing of the button might be, the turning of the potential danger of mutual annihilation into an actual danger is more likely to come in a premeditated manner. This premeditated manner is fed by the type of unrealistic strategems which are at present current in the United States.

When the period in which the United States possessed a monopoly of nuclear weapons came to an end with the acquisition of nuclear weapons by the Soviet Union, the strategy which applied as long as only one of the two major protagonists of military power in the world was in possession of nuclear weapons had to be revised, if not abandoned. The posing of the threat of massive retaliation by the nuclear power against the non-nuclear power had effectively demonstrated that in a war between a nuclear and a non-nuclear power, the former power had a good chance of winning such a war.

With the acquisition of nuclear power by the other of the two major military powers in the world, the threat of massive retaliation, if it were to continue to play a role in military strategy, no longer could have the same meaning which it had while only one of the two major military protagonists in the world possessed nuclear weapons. Were the term *massive retaliation* to continue in use in the period when both major military protagonists in the world had acquired nuclear weapons, it could apply only to the sequence of nuclear annihilation.

In continuing to refer to massive retaliation in the period when both major military protagonists in the world had acquired nuclear weapons, one could only mean a reference to the factor of which of the two major military protagonists in the world were to precede in rendering the other militarily powerless. This very proposition of massive military retaliation has thus lost any particular meaning. Either of the two major military protagonists in the world could effectively threaten the other with massive retaliation, which, in effect, would eliminate the factor of massive retaliation as a means of winning a war.

With the loss of the American monopoly in the manufacture and stockpiling of nuclear weapons, United States military strategists replaced the proposition of massive retaliation, which was a valid strategic factor at the time when the United States was the only nuclear power, with a variety of strategic propositions, which were to meet the changed position of the United States in a world in which the other major military protagonist, the Soviet Union, had also become a nuclear power.

The basic strategic proposition, which was to replace the proposition of massive retaliation, was named "counterforce." The very name of the new proposition indicates that it was not meant to serve as an overwhelming threat of annihilation directed at an adversary of the United States. The name "counterforce" rather indicates that this strategic factor was meant as a means of getting even with an adversary. In this sense, the proposition of counterforce can well be regarded as a realistic strategic adjustment to the changed position of the United States, from that of a power with a monopoly of nuclear weapons to that of a power which has to parry the nuclear weapon capability of another power.

The reliance upon counterforce as a strategic proposition signified, by implication, that what it can be expected to accomplish is most likely a draw. Yet, in a situation in which the two major adversaries are in possession of nuclear weapons, the application of the strategy of counterforce can, in all likelihood, accomplish a draw which will be characterized by total destruction of both sides. Were this to take place – and the odds are very much on the side of such an outcome of a war in which two nuclear powers were to use their nuclear striking power to the utmost – there is no question any more of winning the war in any traditional sense.

What the application of the counterforce proposition amounts to in the stated situation is but an assurance that the adversary will not be able to destroy the United States as a nation without being penalized by having to face its own destruction as a nation. It is this interpretation of the counterforce proposition which has to be placed above all the subsidiary strategic propositions, which have been subsequently derived from it.

These subsequently derived devices can well be regarded as merely built-in propositions which are to fit within the range of the basic factor of counterforce. Within the range of the counterforce proposition, a discussion arose in regard to the factor of first strike and second strike. The entrance of the first and second strike propositions is quite relevant to the counterforce proposition.

The discussion of the subsidiary propositions, of first and second strike, can well be regarded as a discussion of operational means by which the counterforce proposition can be effectuated. The first strike proposition is closely related to the proposition of preventive war. Actually, the carrying out of any first strike proposition can be easily dressed up as a preventive war move. Preventive war can be considered one which is aimed at forcing the potential adversary either to abstain from pursuing a certain national, political aim or at compelling him to take a certain political action by way of declaring and making war on the potential adversary.

As an example of a preventive war conducted in the past, the case of the Anglo-French War against Russia in 1855-56, the so-called Crimean War, can be cited. The war was aimed at preventing Russia from taking over Turkish territory, in particular the Dardanelles, in the wake of the disintegration of the Turkish Empire. As another example of preventive war, the war of Japan against Russia in 1904-5 can be cited. That war aimed at preventing Russia from taking over Chinese territory, in particular Korea, in the wake of the disintegration of the Chinese Empire. These preventive wars, and others which could be cited, met with success, because the countries which had started the preventive wars were militarily better equipped and employed a superior strategy than the countries which they had attacked.

A preventive war assumes, however, an entirely different character in the age of nuclear weapons. A preventive war in which the first strike proposition is applied by a nuclear power cannot be expected to force the attacked country to refrain from taking any particular move, since the result of a preventive war by a nuclear power can only be the destruction of the attacked country and the elimination of that country as a political entity on the international scene. In case the country which is attacked by a nuclear power engaged in a preventive war is itself a nuclear power, it can be expected to use its nuclear weapons to punish the aggressor and, depending upon the swiftness and accuracy of the return blow, to inflict irreparable damage on the attacker. This return blow by a nuclear power attacked by another nuclear power, in a so-called "preventive war", is known as the second strike.

The issue in this case boils down to the query: How effective can one expect the first strike and the second strike moves to be, and which strike can guarantee greater overall destruction of the adversary, in the shortest possible time? In most recent United States discussion of strategic matters, the second strike proposition has been emphasized over the first strike proposition. The argument in this case runs as follows: The more and more nuclear weapons and their means of delivery the missiles are stockpiled, the greater is the likelihood that a sufficient number of nuclear weapons and their means of delivery will be preserved after a first strike by another nuclear power has been absorbed. Thus, the country which has absorbed the first strike will be able to destroy the power which has delivered the first strike as a military and political entity by a second strike, the argument concludes.

A counterargument to this view could show that the increase in the number of nuclear weapons, as well as the increased hitting power and precision of those weapons, plus the increase in the means of delivery, the missiles, as far as their number, their speed and precision are concerned, will, as time passes, increase the likelihood that the first strike will become more and more effective. Thus, by way of this counterargument, it can be maintained that the effectiveness of the return blow, the second strike, will be reduced more and more, as time passes. Were this counterargument to be accepted, the issue of preventive war could be expected to gain ascendancy.

The acceptance of the argument that the first strike will, as time passes, gain in effectiveness over the second strike, might lead to the inference that the second strike, delivered by the country which has absorbed a first strike, will not prove sufficient to destroy the country which has delivered the first strike as a military and political entity. Such a line of argument could be used in support of choosing a first strike strategy over a second strike strategy.

A further counter-argument could cite, however, that with the overkill nuclear capacity of both major protagonists ever increasing, even a small portion of the overkill left to the country which had absorbed a first strike might still be enough to destroy the first striker by way of a second strike. The acceptance of this line of argument could then be cited in support of a continuous reliance on second strike strategy.

The first and second strike strategies and their respective impact have become the subject of an elaborate discussion. Herman Kahn, in his book *On Thermonuclear War,* has attempted to calculate the degrees of devastation which either a first or a second strike is likely to inflict. In mathematical terms, there is, of course, an almost infinitesimal number of the conceivable ranges of devastation. Kahn has applied his mathematical ingenuity to the presentation of a wide variety of degrees of devastation. In doing so, he has applied what is generally called operational analysis to the fullest possible degree. As an operational analyst in the sphere of military strategy, Kahn has excelled many others. Operational analysts construct an imaginary situation and then argue within the range of that situation. An operational analyst, if he is pledged to remain within the scope of an operational analysis, does not have to submit the imaginary situation he construes to the test of empirical reality. An operational analyst can consider his task accomplished when he has completed the construction of a model.

Such a model, the way it is posited by the operational analyst, is not constructed by any reference to actual conditions prevailing in a given sphere, but to contrived conditions. It is not likely that any of the wide ranges of operational models which Kahn conceived, in regard to the degrees of devastation which a country subjected to nuclear attack could absorb, will ever be given a chance to stand a test of actual conditions. Kahn's configurations can, therefore, be imbued with an air of authenticity only as long as peace is preserved.

In conducting his operational analysis, Kahn is out to convince people in and out of the government that survival on a comparatively large scale is possible in the course of a thermonuclear exchange. A specific impact of the Kahn type of operational analysis may be seen in the creation of the impression, on wide sections of the United States population, that civil defense measures, and, in particular shelters, can be regarded as potent safeguards against nuclear devastation. In line with the fostering of the stated illusion, are the views expressed by Edward Teller, the developer of the United States hydrogen bomb. In a book entitled *The Legacy of Hiroshima,* Teller tries to make the case for the entire United States population to go living underground. That prospect had been duly rebuked among others of note by a prominent United States scientist, Harrison Brown.

A variant in the discussion of first and second strike propositions pertains to the factor of the graduation of either of the two strikes. That discussion has been generated by a book of Richard Frykland entitled *100 Million Lives; A Maximum Survival in a Nuclear War.* The Frykland thesis has become fashionable among some strategic planners in the United States. The line of argumentation advanced by Frykland amounts to a proposal to attempt to limit the impact of the United States nuclear striking force attack by directing it to strike only against military objectives and military forces, the civilian population not to be a target of attack. Whether such a strategic directive can be effectively carried out is open to question. The possibility of aiming the nuclear attacks has not reached such precision as would be required for the effective implementation of the stated directive. The development of effective nuclear strategy in the foreseeable future is more likely to be in the direction of accumulating greater stockpiles of nuclear weapons and missiles, so as to increase the probability of hitting the desired target at a cost of hitting a greater number of undesirable targets. The factor of precision in reaching the right targets can be expected to conform to the probability principle, which is based on the expectation that a certain target is more likely to be hit, if the number of attempts to reach the target is to be multiplied, unless the other side communicates and lets one know how one's image of oneself looks to the other.

Now, as far as military strategy is concerned, it must be considered as an incontrovertible tenet that its evolvement is preconditioned by the ability of one side not to let the other side know what the one side considers the image of the other side to be. To apply this to the case at issue, it can be considered as an unalterable factor of Soviet strategic thinking not to let the United States military strategists know what impression the United States strategic image of itself makes on the Soviet military strategists. A more familiar term in the stated connection is the word *posture*. The United States military strategists, one can thus say, are preoccupied with presenting the United States military posture to the world. The Soviet Union military strategists are not likely to tell their United States counterparts what they think of the United States military posture, and thus the United States military strategists will not know it as long as peace is preserved.

To bring up the factor of deterrence in the stated context, one can well argue that one can never establish with any degree of certainty that what one side considers a deterrent is actually playing that role as far as the other side is concerned. To make it more explicit, the United States military strategists who speak of, and actually invoke, a variety of deterrents in devising military strategy can never learn whether any of the deterrents actually is a deterrent to the other side. One could argue, with a certain degree of conviction, that none of the devices which one side intends to be deterrents are considered, by the other side, to be deterrents. Conversely, if peace is preserved under the given conditions, there are factors other than the intended deterrents which restrain one side from waging war on the other side.

In the history of international relations in the period of existence of national states, the military strength of a particular country did not play the role of a deterrent. What deterred a country from going to war was a self-deterrent or a self-restraint born of a country's consideration for its particular national interest. To take an example from recent history, one can cite the no-war policy of the Soviet Union immediately following the cessation of hostilities in World War II and the subsequent withdrawal of United States troops from Europe. Militarily, it is conceivable that the Soviet Union could have overrun Western Europe at that time, but it did not do so for political reasons. The Soviet leaders did not consider the overrunning of Western Europe by Soviet military might to serve the long-term national interests of the Soviet state.

One could bring up the counter-argument that the possession of the atom bomb by the United States deterred the Soviet Union from invading Western Europe. But this counter-argument does not appear to be potent, since, technologically considered, the few atom bombs which could have been dropped at that time on Soviet targets could not by themselves have decided the outcome of the presumptive war of the Soviet Union against Western Europe. Moreover – and here the illusory aspect of the deterrent proposition enters the picture – Stalin and his close military advisors were not impressed by the military impact of the atomic bomb, as United States top military personnel learned at the Potsdam Conference. The image of the posture of the United States as the sole possessor of the atom bomb had not been effectively communicated to the Russians, whose military strategists, from Stalin down, continued to think of the United States military image in terms of conventional weapons.

The danger of the reliance on illusory propositions in devising and applying strategy can best be illustrated by a reference to the aspect of a pre-emptive war. One must clearly recognize the difference between a pre-emptive war and a preventive war. The latter is a war which is started by one country in an effort to have the other country meet the political demands made by the attacking country. The decision to start a preventive war is usually based, and in the past was based, on objective considerations, in which the burden and the risks of fighting a war were weighed against the national benefits which reasonably could be expected from winning such a war. A pre-emptive war is a war which is started by one country because, in the opinion of the military decision makers, another country can be expected to start a war. A pre-emptive war is to be viewed as a more strictly military matter than a preventive war, which can be considered as more deeply rooted in political considerations. A pre-emptive war is thus but a war which is aimed to pre-empting the impending military blow by another country. What makes a pre-emptive war a rather risky undertaking is, first of all, the difficulty of assessing the factor of the impending attack by another country. The

116

extent to which a military blow by another country may be considered as impending depends very much upon subjective considerations. It depends upon the impression which measures of military preparedness of one country make upon the military decision makers in another country. What one military observer might regard as an indication of an impending military blow might not be regarded as such by another.

When intense partisanship enters the picture, matters which, upon calmer consideration, might not be regarded as indicating an impending blow, can well come to be regarded as such. The proposition of pre-emptive war can be extended even further; in such a case, one would not have to look for indications of an impending blow. One could argue that a given long-term military strategy of any country, must, in the end, lead to an attempt to strike the first blow. A pre-emptive war could then be decided upon in answer to such long-term expectations. This can be considered as the theory of pre-emptive war in the pre-nuclear age, when full scale destruction of the country of the potential belligerents was not at issue. In the nuclear stage, when the wholesale devastation of any country which is subjected to atomic attacks is at issue, a decision to start a pre-emptive war comes to be rooted in much more intensified fears than the ones which prevailed in the pre-nuclear age. Therefore, the danger that a pre-emptive war will break out is much greater in the nuclear age than it was in the pre-nuclear age.

The yardstick by which subjective considerations come to be judged is the factor of credibility. Credibility, to be sure, is itself a subjective proposition. Thus, subjective propositions other than credibility, such as the basic proposition of deterrent, are, in turn, related to the aspect of credibility. Such a correlation of subjective factors does not make for greater objectivity. Just the opposite is the case. The correlation of subjective factors makes for still greater subjectivity and thus for greater unreliability. In this connection, one must ask how one can make sure that an intended deterrent is made credible to the other side. The answer is that one cannot make it sure. What impression an intended deterrent can be expected to make on the other side must be left open to conjecture. As far as United States strategic planning is concerned, however, it is not left open to conjecture. What then occurs is that the United States side imputes credibility to the other side. But such imputation is not verifiable. If strategic planning is continued on the basis of the imputed credibility, it might and, in all probability, will lead to entirely unexpected results. Imputed credibility is hardly distinguishable from credulity, and credulity can hardly be considered a reliable guide for any kind of planning, least of all strategic planning.

With respect to strategic planning in the Soviet Union, one can make the general statement that the strategic planners of the Soviet Union have recognized that nuclear weapons have ushered in a new era in the technology of warfare. This was not the case until Stalin's death. The creation of special nuclear weapons units in the organizational pattern of the Soviet military forces indicates that a revamping of the entire composition of the Soviet armed forces has been undertaken since Premier Khrushchev had come to head the Soviet Government. This revamping has not been undertaken to the exclusion of the traditional armed forces, such as the army, navy, and air force. What has happened is that the nuclear fighting force has been added to the existing traditional armed forces. Subsequently, the planned activities of the nuclear fighting force came to be coordinated with the planned activities of the traditional armed forces.

In regard to the matter of first and second nuclear strikes, it can be assumed that the pros and cons of the power of the first and second strike, and of the opting for or against an emphasis on first or second strike, are still being debated in the Soviet Union, as they are in the United States. It can also be assumed that the Soviet military strategists adhere more directly to the assessment of technological factors and prospective trends in technological development in working out strategic propositions, than do the United States strategic planners. Such an assumption can be backed up by the knowledge that subjective considerations do not play an important part in Soviet planning in general and, therefore, cannot be expected to play any important role in strategic planning. It would be wrong, however, to carry this assumption so far as to imply that Soviet strategic planners entirely disregard the subjective aspects of United States strategic planners. They would be unrealistic if they were to pay no attention at all to the subjective aspects of United States strategic planning.

One can be sure that the strategic planners in the Soviet Union know what is said in the United States about deterrent, posture, credibility, and not the least, about pre-emptive strike. It is likely that the presence of subjective aspects in United States strategic planning enters an additional factor of uncertainty into the principles of Soviet strategic planning. Were the Soviet planners to try to answer the subjective propositions of United States strategic planning with subjective propositions of their own, the correlation of United States strategic plans with Soviet strategic plans would become a much more conjectural factor than it is today. Uncertainties about the effectiveness of the applicability of each other's strategic plans would become confounded. A decision to move from preparedness for war to actual warfare could, in such a case, be made on much more tenuous grounds than is the case at present.

Special consideration must be given to the role of the powers allied with each of the major military protagonists in the world, the United

118

States and the Soviet Union. The NATO Alliance up to recently could be regarded as a geomilitary extension of United States power. Until recently, the strategy of the European partners of the NATO Alliance had beeen determined in Washington. The role assigned to the major powers of the NATO Alliance in Europe was to serve as a forward launching ground for United States nuclear weapons and as a potential shock absorber of troops, which could be expected to advance from Eastern Europe to Western Europe. There took place, however, recently, some variations in the positions of the three major European powers in the NATO Alliance, Britain, France and West Germany.

Britain has for some time been in the possession of nuclear weapons of her own. Hence, Britain had both military detachments with nuclear weapons under the control of the United States military command, and British military installations with nuclear weapons over which the British exercised control. The decision of the United States government, to which the British government, headed at the time by Harold Macmillan, acceded, to provide Britain with Polaris submarines instead of manned Skybolt bombers, did not affect the aforementioned division between the British and United States commands in Britain. It did, however, change somewhat the strategic posture of the British forces under British command. The Polaris-based missiles can be considered as less vulnerable to first and second strikes of an attacking force than the manned Skybolt bombers.

The British Labor government, headed by Harold Wilson, had been veering in the direction of giving up its own nuclear striking force in favor of a complete dependance of British military strategy on the United States nuclear umbrella. Such a policy on the part of the British Labor government could well have contributed to a lessening of restraint on the part of United States nuclear military strategists. The Foreign Secretary of the present Conservative government appears to be veering away from the idea of placing Britain more firmly under a United States nuclear umbrella. Mr. Home went on record in placing the British government's increasing reliance on agreements between the United States and the Soviet Union, to have the danger of the outbreak of an atomic war reduced.

As far as France is concerned, the situation is somewhat different. Until recently, France was not in possession of nuclear weapons. The agreement between France and the United States, prior to the accession of the DeGaulle Government, contained a provision similar to that which governs the use of United States atomic weapons to be launched from Britain. The French goverment was to be informed about the prospective and actual use of nuclear weapons launched from United States bases on French soil.

119

After the ascendancy of the DeGaulle regime, the French government insisted that, unless it was given a veto power over the use of nuclear weapons to be launched by the United States from French bases, it would not permit the United States to use French bases. As a result of this demand of the French government, the United States nuclear weapons and the means of their delivery were withdrawn from France.

Subsequently, DeGaulle rejected the United States offer to supply France with Polaris submarines. DeGaulle had embarked on a course to establish France as a nuclear power which will make its own strategic decisions in regard to the use of nuclear weapons. The attainment of DeGaulle's goal, the establishment in France of an independent nuclear striking force, the so-called Force de Frappe, can in turn, not fail to have a restraining effect on the United States nuclear military strategy in regard to Europe.

In the face of these developments in Europe, the spokesman for United States military strategy, the Secretary of Defense in the Kennedy Administration and subsequently the Johnson Administration, McNamara, had tried to reaffirm the United States insistence on a uniform NATO nuclear strategy, laid down by the administration in Washington. The Secretary of State of the Kennedy Administration and subsequently, the Johnson Administration, Dean Rusk, at a meeting of the NATO powers in Athens, introduced in turn, the idea of a new military strategy for the European NATO allies of the United States. This strategy was to make the European NATO powers increase their conventional forces. The then Secretary of State's revival of the emphasis on conventional forces was in line with the strategic concept accepted by the Kennedy Administration, the introduction of the proposition of limited war as it is spelled out in Kissinger's book, *Nuclear Weapons and Foreign Policy,* as well as in the book of Maxwell D. Taylor *The Uncertain Trumpet.*

Neither McNamara's proposition of a centralized nuclear strategy nor Rusk's proposition of a greater reliance on conventional forces by the European powers has found much favor with the governments of the European NATO powers. The two major Western allies of the United States, England and France, expressed opposition to McNamara's announced proposal, not only because their acceptance would imply continued European submission to United States strategic military decisions, but also because the principal European partners of the United States regarded these new concepts as inherently unworkable.

The strategic and political posture of the official Washington strategists, which has encountered opposition by its European allies, according to Cyrus Sulzberger's column in the *New York Times* of July 8, 1962, is based on the acceptance of the strategy which provides that no cities be bombed, a strategy spelled out in a book by Frykland entitled *One Hundred Million Lives*. This strategy calls for hitting Soviet military installations first with nuclear bombs. An attempt would thus be made to spare the civilian population of the cities in this first strike.

In this case, the Western European allies of the United States would be expected mainly to employ conventional forces in the first phase of a prospective nuclear war against the Soviet Union. This first phase would be accompanied by a warning that unless the Soviet Union spares the cities and the civilian population of the United States and its Western allies, the second phase of the United States nuclear strike would be directed against civilian targets in the Soviet Union.

The proponents of this nuclear strategy insist that they have sufficient information on the locations of Soviet military installations, in particular of the missile sites, to expect the Soviet authorities to adhere to the proposed unwritten gentlemen's agreement not to undertake any nuclear bombing of United States and Western allied cities, under threat of annihilation of the Soviet civilian population by a second phase strike. Although Sulzberger's presentation does not specifically state this, what such a nuclear bombing policy implies is the expectation that the Soviet Union will surrender after their military forces, in particular, their nuclear striking force, have been destroyed in the first phase of a United States nuclear strike.

Should the Soviet Union not surrender after the first phase of the United States nuclear strike, the second phase of the United States nuclear strike, directed at civilian centers of the Soviet Union, is to follow. This second phase of the nuclear strike against the Soviet Union and its allies would be supported by Polaris and Poseidon missile submarines stationed in European waters. In the execution of that plan, several United States missile carrying submarines have subsequently been placed at the disposal of the Western allies of the United States, notably in British, Italian and Turkish waters.

The objection of the European partners to this United States nuclear bombing policy was based on the reluctance to accept the notion that it is either technologically or geographically possible to bomb military installations without hitting centers of the civilian population. It can be assumed that the representatives of the United States allies in Europe further question whether the United States has complete knowledge of the location of all military installations, and in particular, of the missile launching sites in the Soviet Union. Nor have the Western allies of the United States conceded that it is possible to launch with assured precision an attack on those military installations in the Soviet Union whose location is known to the United States.

On these grounds, the European allies, it can be assumed, do not expect that the surrender of the Soviet Union could be had after the first phase of a nuclear strike. The incredulity of the European allies of the United States is presumably heightened by their distrust of the United States expectation that the Soviet Union could be pressured into accepting any kind of an unwritten gentlemen's agreement to refrain from bombing United States and Western European cities in the initial phase of a nuclear war. Were the Western European powers (against their better judgment) to accept the United States government's position on the no-city strike bombing strategy, the representatives of the Western European governments could argue that their cities and their civilian population would be subjected to the threat of being wiped out before the European arm of the NATO nuclear striking force could have a chance to undertake the unrestricted bombing of the Soviet Union.

Thus the representatives of the Western European powers could well maintain that their acceptance of the no-city bombing strategy in the first phase of a nuclear war might well turn the cities and the civilian population of Western Europe into pawns in the supreme military contest of the two foremost world military powers. The non-acceptance of the no-city bombing strategy of the United States is likely to be accompanied by the rejection of an increased reliance on conventional arms and troops by the Western European allies of the United States.

Aside from considerations of the military ineffectiveness of such moves, the Western allies of the United States are also likely to shy away from the economic burden which the maintenance of a larger conventional military force could thrust upon them. Furthermore, an increase in the standing army constitutes a touchy political problem in any of the Western European countries.

As far as the overall strategic position of the Atlantic Alliance is concerned, the withdrawal of France from full partnership in that Alliance has considerably weakened the defensive as well as the offensive position of the Alliance. The withdrawal of France from active participation in the defensive and offensive strategy of the Atlantic Alliance has left West Germany in an overexposed strategic position. Even with France remaining a full-fledged partner in the Atlantic Alliance, it had been cogently argued, that West Germany as well as France do not present a sufficiently extended landspan for defensive and offensive military operations. It was argued, in that connection, that Spain would have to be included in the Western landspan to lend the military forces of the Western powers greater maneuverability. The establishment of United States military bases in Spain is in line with the above stated argument.

With the withdrawal of France from active participation in the Atlantic Alliance the landspan in Western Europe, to be used for defensive and offensive military operations, has been reduced to sub-marginal levels. What this means is that the landspan of Western Europe has, in terms of defensive and offensive military operations, were it to be effected by conventional weapons, become inoperative. It should be mentioned in the stated connection that the addition to the Atlantic Alliance of the Benelux countries, Belgium, Holland and Luxembourg, as well as Norway and Denmark, does not add to the core of the military terrain for which West Germany and France were geographically suited to serve. The Benelux countries in addition to Norway and Denmark can be used but for military flank movements. Such flank movements could not, however, prove effective in a military sense, if the center, – the core of the military terrain, – to which the Benelux countries as well as Norway and Denmark could serve but as adjuncts, – were not to prove adequate in geographical and military terms.

A flank which is to support an insufficient strategic mainland is of little use. In that connection one can say that the withdrawal of France from active participation in the Atlantic military Alliance has left the whole Alliance hanging, so to speak, in the air, in strategic military terms; Italy, still an active member of the Atlantic Alliance, can in no way take the place of France in the effectuation of the Western military Alliance. Italy forms but an underbelly of the strategic terrain of Western Europe, as far as its geographic and strategic position is concerned. Militarily, Italian armed forces can but serve as supporting units, if a war in Western Europe is to break out. Such supporting military moves would be of little strategic impact, were the main strategic terrain in Western Europe not be of sufficient range. This, however, is certainly not the case, if French territory is to be kept off limits for strategic operations of the Atlantic Alliance.

What goes for Italy is even more so relevant as far as Greece and Turkey are concerned, which are also members of the Atlantic Alliance. The supporting role of Greece and Turkey could be termed peripheral in military terms, even if France had remained an active member of the Atlantic Alliance. With France withdrawing as an active member of the Western military Alliance and the mainland of Western Europe becoming indefensible, in terms of conventional weapons, the role of Greece and Turkey as strategic terrains assume a highly questionable character in regard to their possible military effectiveness.

The precarious strategic posture of the Atlantic military Alliance came to be highlighted during the aftermath of the events in Czechoslovakia of August, 1968. The active members of the Atlantic Alliance conducted military maneuvers in January 1969 in the proximity of the Czechoslovak border of Western Germany. The maneuvers were conducted in the expectation of a presumed invasion of Western Germany by Warsaw Pact armies. It was argued in high Western circles that if the Warsaw Pact powers found it incumbent upon themselves to intervene militarily in Czechoslovakia, they could find it also incumbent upon themselves to intervence militarily in Western Europe. What this line of argumentation leaves out is the political and strategic context which prompted the intervention of the Warsaw Pact powers in Czechoslovakia. Such constellation of factors, it should be pointed out, does not exist and is not likely to come into existence in the relations of the Warsaw Pact powers and the Western powers, which constitute the Atlantic Alliance.

In intervening in Czechoslovakia, the Eastern European powers were defending a strategic status quo. An intervention of the Warsaw Pact powers in Western Europe would, on the other hand, present a violation of a strategic status quo. Such a development would amount to a radical departure from the political and strategic concepts on the basis of which the Warsaw Pact powers have been operating all through the period following World War II. There is no sign that such a radical departure from the strategic concepts which bind the Warsaw Pact powers has ever been under consideration.

What was revealed, however, in the course of the military maneuvers conducted by the active participants of the Atlantic Alliance at the West German Czechoslovak border, was the reaffirming of the realization among responsible leaders of the Western powers that West Germany cannot be defended by conventional weapons. In terms of conventional weapons, the then British Minister of Defense Healey contended the Soviet Union has an overwhelming power in men and material. Hence, the only war which could be fought in which West Germany were to face the Soviet Union and other Warsaw Pact powers would be a nuclear war, Healey declared. In making that statement the then British Minister of Defense Healey echoed General Eisenhower, who at the time when he was President of the United States made it clear that, if a war were to break out in Western Europe, it would have to be a nuclear war. The Healey and Eisenhower statements can well be regarded as a reference which is applicable to all the militarily active powers of the Atlantic Alliance. If such is to be the case, Western Europe, as far as it adheres to the Atlantic Alliance, is faced with the prospect of complete extinction within a single hour after the nuclear holocaust breaks out.

In that connection the declarations of former Soviet Premier Khrushchev have to be brought back to mind. Khrushchev declared that the Soviet Union had sufficient nuclear fire power to erase Germany and Britain from the map of Europe almost instantaneously. One is not to take these declarations of Khrushchev as empty boasts. Furthermore, if the Soviet Union had the nuclear capability to wipe West Germany and England off the map of Europe within minutes when Krushchev was in office, it has even more such capability now. The application of United States nuclear power in retaliation to the strike of the Soviet Union in Western Europe would not be able to undo the havoc wrought by Soviet thermonuclear power in Western Europe. No matter how the nuclear exchange, if and when it starts in Europe, is subsequently to affect the Soviet Union and the United States, Western Europe, as a populated region within the range of the active participants of the Atlantic Alliance will certainly cease to exist.

In the stated context, the reliance of the NATO military planners on what they call tactical atomic weapons appears to be an unrealistic policy. It constitutes but one more demonstration of the United States led reliance on the second strike strategy. It is highly unlikely that the Soviet Union has a strategic plan short of all-out atomic warfare, should any war in which atomic weapons are to be used break out in Western Europe. That such is the case can well be inferred from the insistence on the part of the Soviet negotiators at a recent session of the Soviet Union and United States talks on the reduction of offensive and defensive weapons, that all atomic weapons stationed in Western Europe should be categorized as offensive strategic weapons. The United States negotiators refused to waive the distinction between tactical and strategic atomic weapons in regard to the United States and NATO war plans for Western Europe. Such a distinction in regard to the possible execution of United States and NATO war plans for Western Europe could only be maintained, however, if the Soviet Union and the Warsaw Pact powers would also agree to adhere and execute such a distinction, which, as it has been demonstrated here, is not the case.

The stated prospective nightmare could be banned through negotiation and signing of an all European security pact. Such a pact could ban war as an instrument of policy on the whole of the European continent. The former French President De Gaulle's call for a Europe from Calais to the Urals could be seen as an invitation to a move in the above stated direction. Europe which for centuries had remained a powder keg and which had become the military terrain in the two most devastating wars in history, World War I and World War II, is best suited to become the first pacified continent of the globe. Within a framework of an all European security pact, there would be no place for an Atlantic military Alliance, nor would there be any need for any Warsaw Pact agreements. The banning of war as an instrument of policy could find Western and Eastern Europe in a common bond pledged to maintain overall European security. Within the stated framework, aggression of any European state, whether in Eastern Europe or in Western Europe, against each other, will come to be banned. Collective European security would come to serve as a dependent shield for keeping war out of the European continent.

As far as the military strategy of the Soviet Union in regard to its East European allies is concerned, one can assume that the strategy for the Warsaw Pact powers is drawn by the military planners of the Soviet Union in consultation with its East European allies. It can be assumed that strategic planning in the Soviet Union is coordinated with strategic planning in the East European countries allied with the Soviet Union. As far as it is known in the West, none of the East European countries allied with the Soviet Union has any nuclear capability. The Soviet forces stationed in any of the East European countries presumably include troops equipped with nuclear arms. It is not known whether and to what extent the Eastern European nations have any say in regard to the use of these arms.

The coordination of the military policy of the Soviet Union with that of the other Eastern European countries was demonstrated in the Fall of 1962, when the military forces of the Soviet bloc countries in Europe were alerted to the possible danger of an outbreak of hostilities over the status of Berlin. The coordination of the military strategy of the Soviet Union with that of its East European allies constitutes of necessity a coordination of a nuclear strategy with a strategy in the use of conventional weapons. The military policy of the Soviet Union itself has not given an indication that it has abandoned its reliance on conventional military weapons. But there appears to be a greater organizational division between the forces equipped for the use of nuclear weapons and the forces not equipped for the use of nuclear weapons than in the West.

The strategic posture of the Warsaw Pact powers has come into bold relief by the course of events which transpired in Czechoslovakia at the end of August 1968. Reference is made here to the military intervention of Soviet, Polish, Hungarian, East German and Bulgarian military units in Czechoslovakia. Had Czechoslovakia dropped out of the Soviet Political orbit, the whole strategic framework of the Warsaw Pact Alliance would have become militarily unhinged, since geographically Czechoslovakia occupies a key strategic position within the defense perimeter of the Warsaw Pact powers. It is in that context that the decision made by the Warsaw Pact powers to intervene militarily in Czechoslovakia is to be understood. To counter and even prevent any possible future jitters which Warsaw Pact powers and NATO powers could come to experience in their relations to each other, a reduction of the international tension in Europe is to be of necessity pursued. Such reduction of tension could be attained through a negotiation and signing of a non-aggression treaty between the Warsaw Pact powers and NATO powers. The negotiation and the signing of an all European security agreement would constitute a step in the above stated direction.

The way for a discussion of an all European security agreement has been eased by the conclusion in August, 1970 of a non-aggression treaty between The Federal Republic of Germany, led by Chancellor Willy Brandt and the government of the Soviet Union as represented by Premier Aleksei Kosygin. The signing of that treaty has not merely military strategic importance, it has wide political implications as well. From a military strategic as well as a political point of view the signing of the non-aggression treaty between West Germany and the Soviet Union actually completes the cycle of the development which has been inaugurated by the military stratagem devised and effected for France by De Gaulle. France under De Gaulle's direction withdrew from playing the role of a potential avant-garde of the use of United States atomic weapons stationed in Europe. In signing of the non-aggression treaty with the Soviet Union, the Federal Republic of Germany signifies a halt to the cultivation of a revanche policy for the effectuation of which the territory of West Germany was to serve as a place d'armes. Thus the Federal Republic of Germany, even with the United States atomic weapons deployed on its territory, has opted for a European political stratagem, instead of serving as a European vanguard of the effectuation of the United States military strategy in its relation to the Soviet Union. That option was strengthened by the signing of a joint declaration of the Federal Republic of Germany and the Republic of Poland, which recognizes the Oder-Neisse border between those two countries. By that joint declaration the Federal Republic of Germany renounces any claims to the reacquisition of the former German territories which at present constitute the Western part of the Polish state. Thus, the Oder-Neisse border of the Polish state has come to be legitimized by the consent of the government of the Federal Republic of Germany.

As far as the alignment of non-European powers is concerned, the alignment of countries of the Near East Asian countries, as well as North African countries, has first to be taken into consideration. Some of those countries, such as Turkey, Iran and Pakistan, form part of a Cento Alliance which is formally allied with Great Britain and in which the United States takes part as an observer. On the whole, the Cento Alliance can be regarded as an extension of the military arm of the Atlantic Alliance into the Near East territory. This extension of the Atlantic Alliance into Near Eastern territory is wrought with contradictions. Some of the Near Eastern countries such as Iraq have severed their relationship with the Cento Alliance. Others of the member states of the Cento Alliance are dragging their feet, as far as active participation in the working out of strategic plans is concerned.

As a counterpart of the Near Eastern military alliance, which is expected to collaborate with the leading powers of the Atlantic Alliance, the realignment of some other Near Eastern countries and some North African countries with the Soviet Union can be cited. The Near Eastern states such as Iraq, Syria and South Yemen, as well as the North African states, Egypt and Algeria, have formed a more or less military alliance with the Soviet Union which supplies those countries with military equipment. This alliance of some Near Eastern and some North African countries with the Soviet Union enables the Soviet Union to extend the radius of operations of its naval arm to the Mediterranean basin.

In that regard an age old ambition of the Russian state has been realized. For nearly two centuries, Russian diplomacy had tried to secure a strategic foothold in the Mediterranean. During the era preceding the Napoleonic wars, Russian armies had crossed the Alps under the generalship of Suvorov and entered Northern Italy. That successful campaign was started during the reign of Catherine II with the aim of countering French and British influence in Western and Southern Europe. The stated campaign was called off by Paul I, the son of Catherine II, without the securing of any permanent political and military rights for Russia in the region South of the Alps. During the Napoleonic campaigns, a Russian expeditionary force landed in Naples in Southern Italy and effected the exit of the regime of Napoleon's brother-in-law Marshall Joachim Murat, who had been installed as the ruler of the Kingdom of Naples and Sicily. Again no permanent political and military arrangements in the Southern part of Italy were effected in the wake of the successful military operations of Russian forces in that part of the world.

France and England had, on their part, succeeded in keeping Russia out of an effective control of the Dardanelles, the waterway which guards the links between the Black Sea and the Mediterranean. The so-called Crimean War was sprung on Russia in the middle of the 19th century by France and Britain for the very reason of making it politically impossible for Russia to wrest control over the Dardanelles from the weakened Ottoman Empire. Though the Crimean War was not transformed into an all-out war and was fought within the range of a limited war, the blows which the French and British expeditionary corps in the Crimea were able to deliver at the Russian army and navy in the Crimean conflict were sufficient to effect an international agreement which forestalled political and military control of the straits of the Dardanelles by Russia. Turkey was left with the right to exercise control over the movement of commercial and military vessels from the Black

128

Sea into the Mediterranean and vice versa.

It should be further noted that the military assistance which the Russian Empire had given the Balkan nations of Roumania, Serbia and Bulgaria, in their struggles against the Ottoman sovereignty over those countries in two wars in the 19th century, could also be interpreted as a move on the part of Russia to gain political and military access to the Mediterranean. Again, Russia did not capitalize, in terms of any political and military advantage, from the gains which were made with the assistance of its military forces by any of the Balkan countries. Roumania, Serbia, Bulgaria and Montenegro eventually gained their independence from Turkey with the assistance of Russia. The Mediterranean basin remained, however, closed to Russia in the political and military sense after the stated Balkan states had gained their independence.

That situation continued to prevail after World War I. It was one of the aims of Imperial Russia in that war to gain control over the Dardanelles. Even after the overthrow of the Czarist regime the foreign minister of the provisional Russian Republican government Melyokoff reaffirmed Russian aspirations to assume control over the straits of the Dardanelles in the wake of an expected victory of the Western allies. Yet, when Russia after the Soviet takeover dropped out as an active combatant at the closing phase of World War I, the regulations governing the passage of vessels through the Dardanelles came again to be vested in the hands of the Turkish administration. When, after the end of World War II, Stalin wanted to have the matter of the passage through the Dardanelles to be opened for discussion, Churchill was instrumental in blocking that move.

It is only through its diplomatic and military collaboration with some Arab states in the Near East and North Africa, that the Soviet government has been able to some extent to circumvent the effects of blocking of its right to exercise control over the passage of its vessels through the Dardanelles. It is to be understood in that connection, that Turkey by itself would not have been strong enough to deter either Imperial Russia or Soviet Russia to exercise effective control without the active backing of the Western powers. England as well as France are among the signatory powers which keep effective control over the passage of vessels through the straits of the Dardanelles in Turkish hands. Other Western powers, notably the United States, acceded to the effectuation of that regulation. The political and military collaboration of the Soviet Union with the Arab states in the Near East and North Africa did not result in the formalization of the establishment of Soviet military bases in the Mediterranean. For all practical purposes, however, the Soviet Union has gained some freedom of movement for its commercial and military vessels in the Mediterranean, as long as a general war in that area does not break out. Whether Turkey would have the power to effect a closing of the straits of the Dardanelles to Russian vessels, in case of a general war in that area, with active Soviet Russian participation, remains to be seen.

In the above stated strategic context, the military position of the State of Israel becomes a rather perplexed matter. Israel is militarily caught in a vise between the arraignment of Western and Eastern naval power in the Mediterranean. As the Soviet fleet is arraigned against the Sixth United States fleet, the British, French and Italian fleets in the Mediterranean are reduced to an auxiliary position in regard to the United States naval force. The land arm of the Soviet fleet operating in the Mediterranean is formed by the Arab states in the Near East and North Africa with whom the Soviet Union maintains an informal alliance. The land arm of the United States Sixth fleet and its auxiliary British, French and Italian fleets is, in turn, represented by the European Mediterranean countries which are part of the Atlantic Alliance, such as England, France, Italy, Greece and Turkey. Again Israel is caught in a vise between the respective land arms of the Soviet navy and the United States navy with the addition of its Atlantic Alliance partners in the Mediterranean.

It will require very skillful maneuvering on the part of the leadership of the State of Israel to retain its integrity in the face of a potential big power confrontation in that area. A non-aggression pact between all powers, big and small, with interests in the Mediterranean basin, strengthened by a specific ban on the employment of nuclear weapons, could well diffuse the tension in that region. Were that to take place, a peaceful growth of the State of Israel, as well as a peaceful development of the Arab states of that region, could well be assured.

As far as the alignment of non-European countries in the Far East is concerned, the so-called SEATO powers constitute the military arm of the United States in the Pacific region. The non-European full members of the SEATO alliance are small powers, such as Australia, New Zealand, the Philippines, Thailand and Pakistan, which cannot be expected to challenge the strategic plans of the United States. These small powers, which constitute the active membership of the SEATO alliance can thus be considered as mere geographical extensions of the United States military power. Pakistan, it should be noted, has refused to take an active part in the SEATO alliance.

Of late, the territorial waters of some of the active members of the SEATO alliance have been used as a basis for a display of United States military power in the Pacific. Such is the case in Thailand, into whose territory United States marines were moved as a show of force a few years ago. The actual United States military activities in the

South Pacific are conducted with the direct assistance of conventional forces of some of the SEATO powers. Such was the case in connection with the conflict in Laos in its earlier phase and is now the case in connection with the conflict in South Vietnam which of late has spread to Cambodia and Laos. Whether the active members of the SEATO alliance of the United States can be considered a sizeable addition to the military power of the United States, even if all the military forces of the SEATO powers were to be brought into play, is questionable. The military power of all the SEATO countries put together is negligible in comparison with the preponderant military power of the United States. In case of a major military conflict in which the United States might become involved, the SEATO allies can, for the most part, be expected to serve as but bases for United States military operations.

The other Pacific power with a sizeable military potential of its own is the Peoples Republic of China. As to the past record of the Peoples Republic of China pertaining to its international relationship the following is to be noticed. The responsible leaders of the Peoples Republic of China have gone on record declaring that they would not be the first to use atomic weapons in any international conflict. That kind of declaration has also been made by the official spokesmen of the Soviet Union. The official representatives of the Peoples Republic of China have not gone on record, however, in declaring that wars in the post World War II period have lost the character of inevitability as it has been proclaimed by the leaders of the Soviet Union. The difference between the leadership of the Peoples Republic of China and the leadership of the Soviet Union lies in the above-stated respect on an ideological plane. The leadership of the Peoples Republic of China, as stated in the document by the heir apparent of Mao Tse Tung, Lin Piao, sees the future of wars in the period ahead as wars in which the rural population of underdeveloped countries were to strive to free themselves of oppression in their own countries. The tactic to be used in the uprising of the oppressed rural population will, according to Lin Piao, be that of guerrilla warfare. In assigning the uprisings of the rural population and guerilla war tactics a preponderant role in the warfare which lies ahead, the leadership of the Peoples Republic of China differs in its world outlook with the leaderschip of the Soviet Union. The leadership of the Soviet Union has not denied that uprisings of the rural population in underdeveloped countries with the use of guerrilla tactics will occur in the years ahead. It has not gone on record, however, in assigning to those uprisings a major characteristic in the prospect of warfare in the years ahead. To put it differently, the uprisings of the rural population with the use of guerrilla tactics are considered but incidental factors in the perspective of future warfare, as viewed by the leadership of the Soviet Union.

On its part, the leadership of the Peoples Republic of China considers the peasant uprisings with the use of guerrilla tactics as essential characteristics of prospective warfare. In assigning peasant uprisings with the use of guerrilla tactics a preponderant role in future warfare, the leaders of the Peoples Republic of China are no doubt influenced by their own experience. The weathering of the Kuomintang counter revolution in the caves of Yenan and the victorious march from Yenan, which led to the establishment of the Peoples Republic of China, appears to the Chinese leadership as a prototype of the peasant uprisings with the use of guerrilla tactics which they consider to be the wave of the future in warfare. Both the leadership of the Peoples Republic of China and the Soviet leadership use the name of wars of liberation in referring to peasant uprisings and the use of guerrilla tactics. Where the leadership of the Peoples Republic of China and the leadership of the Soviet Union differ is in the assaying of the impact of the wars of liberation for the historical period ahead.

The leadership of the Soviet Union does not assign to wars of liberation a major role in the warfare which lies ahead. That stand on the part of the Soviet leaderschip is influenced no doubt by the experience of Russia in World War I and World War II. Those two World Wars were in the main wars between industrialized countries. As far as Imperial Russia's part in World War I is concerned, its armies were in the main armies of peasants. The peasant character of the army did not, however, have much of a social significance of its own as long as the Czarist army remained intact and the serving in the army retained for many soldiers the character of involuntary servitude. Only after the dissolution of the Czarist army, when the ideological character of the war turned from an imperialist to a civil war, did the part played by the peasant composition of the Bolshevik army play to a certain degree a role of its own, in the sense that it came to express the social aspirations of the fighting men. In the latter respect the fledgling Red army of peasants can, to some extent, be compared with the army of peasants which brought about the establishment of the Peoples Republic of China. Nonetheless, even in that period which immediately followed the dissolution of the Czarist army in World War I, the industrial workers constituted an important section of the fledgling Red army. So it was more of an alliance of peasants and workers which characterized the composition of the fledgling Red army. It was, at any rate, much more of an alliance of peasants and workers than was the case with the Yenan army which successfully undertook the conquest of Kuomintang China.

As far as World War II is concerned, it was fought at the time when almost half of the population of the Soviet Union lived in urban areas. The Soviet Army therefore consisted at that time to a much higher degree of industrial workers as had been the case in the first World War and its immediate aftermath. Neither the social composition of the Soviet Army in World War II nor its tactics could be characterized as a peasant army employing guerrilla tactics. It is this army in which industrial workers constituted a major part, and in which guerrilla tactics, such as forays of partisans operating behind Nazi lines, played a subsidiary role, which continues to serve as a prototype of any army which could be called upon to fight a future war in the eyes of the leaders of the Soviet Union.

Taking off from the ideological and strategic divergence which characterizes the different outlooks on the future of warfare by the leaders of the Peoples Republic of China and the leaders of the Soviet Union, one could try to assess what roles each of the two countries are likely to play in their relationship to each other, were a major war to break out. It should be noted that a mutual assistance treaty between the Peoples Republic of China and the Soviet Union, which was signed after World War II, has not been abrogated. Whether it will be put into effect and under what conditions, if the Soviet Union were to find itself involved in a major war in which atomic weapons are to be employed, is difficult to tell.

What could conceivably happen is the possibility that the Peoples Republic of China would not immediately enter such a conflict but would try to sit it out, as long as possible. One should admit, however, that if the conjectured major conflagration of world proportions were to involve the use of atomic weapons, the sitting out time, if that were to be attempted by the Peoples Republic of China, could be only of an extremely short duration.

PART II:

THE CONSEQUENCES OF THE DIALECTICAL
TURN IN MILITARY TECHNOLOGY

Chapter 5

DEMILITARIZATION

The strategic plans which have been presented in the preceding chapter can well be brought under a common denominator. That denominator can be identified as the means of preparedness for death. *Neither* of the strategic variations which have been spelled out in the preceding chapter can be regarded as a strategic device which could bring victory to either of the two major protagonists of military power in the world today, the United States and the Soviet Union. In view of the over-kill capacity possessed by either of the two chief protagonists of military power in the world, the relative strategic advantage or disadvantage which either the United States or the Soviet Union may possess at one or the other stage in the continuous arms race does not really matter. The maximum application of all the military power at the disposal of the two protagonists will leave both countries in a shambles.

Such prospects will not, however, deter the two protagonists from claiming military superiority over each other at different stages in the continuous arms race. Nor will such claims deter either of the two protagonists from attempting to consider a preventive war or its counterpart, a pre-emptive strike, as a means of bringing about a military decision. As time passes, preventive war by way of a pre-emptive attack, as its counterpart, will constitute an ever increasing temptation. The military strength accumulated in the past is likely to become increasingly dim, while the military strength added in the present by either of the two protagonists will, by comparison, shine brighter for the particular protagonist who scores a temporary advantage over the other.

The present military posture of the United States vis-à-vis the Soviet Union will be presented here as the case at issue. Authoritative sources in the United States now contend that the United States has an overall missile and bomb superiority over the Soviet Union. Such a contention has, in turn, led the United States strategists to believe that a military victory over the Soviet Union is possible. Such a belief can well be turned into an expectation that a preventive war, presented as a pre-emptive strike, might bring about a quick military victory over the Soviet Union. Though far from being a realistic appraisal of the military strength of the United States vis-à-vis the Soviet Union, it can nonetheless be made to form the basis on which United States authorities reach military decisions. Were such military decisions made on the basis of an unrealistic estimate of the comparative military strength of the United States and the Soviet Union, the result could well be catastrophic for the United States as well as for the Soviet Union.

In a sense, the expectation that a quick and not too costly victory can be had over the Soviet Union reminds one of the expectation of the Hitler high command. Hitler gave his generals the impression that a quick and rather cheap military victory over the Soviet Union was easily obtainable. Hitler and his generals vastly underestimated the staying power and the military combat potential of the Soviet Union. This underestimation of the Soviet resistance was not limited to Hitler and his generals, however. Western military authorities, the United States military strategists in particular, succumbed to the same belief that a quick and easy military victory over the Soviet Union was in the cards. The marginal military help, in terms of military supplies as well as in terms of the assignment of military priority to secondary Western fronts in Europe, can well be regarded as an indication that some military circles in the United States and highly influential sources in Britain had settled for but a token assistance to Soviet military forces, in expectation of their quick collapse.

There came a rude awakening, not only on the part of Hitler and his generals, but also on the part of the responsible military strategists and commanders of the West, when the Soviet forces showed themselves superior to the Hitlerian forces. With the presence of nuclear weapons and missiles today, a rude awakening of some United States strategists to the unexpected intensity of Soviet counter blows could cost the United States and its allies more than the price of the expected victory over the Soviet Union. The stakes are much higher today; they involve more than military defeat. The very physical existence of the United States and the Western allies is at stake, and no person in a responsible position in the United States and in the countries of its Western allies should undertake to gamble with that kind of outcome in view.

One should not consider the Soviet Union entirely immune to the idea of preventive war or its counterpart, the pre-emptive strike. The basis for such a decision to engage in a preventive war or in its counterpart, the pre-emptive strike, would be likely to be made in the Soviet Union more in desperation than out of military arrogance. Should the Soviet military strategists become convinced that a preventive war on the part of the United States becomes more and more likely as the armament race progresses, they might assign top priority to the timing of a preventive war. In their attempt to specify the proper time for a pre-emptive blow, the Soviet strategists will become engaged in a guessing game with United States military strategists. A preventive war could then start because each side presumes to have outguessed the other side in regard to the proper timing of such war from the point of view of either of the two contestants – frightening prostect indeed.

The contention has been advanced that the present arms race between the major protagonists has resulted in a stalemate and that the stalemate, as such, can be taken as a guarantee for the preservation of peace. No country, this argument runs, will undertake to wage war on any other country when it is sure that such an undertaking will lead to its own destruction. This argumentation has been developed into a theory of the so-called "balance of terror". From a psychological point of view, the proposition of a balance of terror must be considered a misconception. No people, from the responsible leaders down to the common man and woman, will consent to live indefinitely in the expectation that their country, since it cannot prevent its wholesale destruction if a major conflict were to break out, consider itself defenseless. Each side will continue to contend that any expectation of such disaster pertains but to a temporary situation, which, in due time, can be remedied.

Not so long ago, during the last two years of the Eisenhower Administration, some United States military analysts contended that the Soviet Union had reached military superiority over the United States in its mass production of missiles. The missile gap proposition had become, so to speak, military doctrine of the armchair strategists in the United States. Whether there actually was a missile gap or not between the Soviet Union and the United States during the second term of office of the Eisenhower Administration is beyond the point. Even if the United States had lagged behind the Soviet Union in missile design and production, the total United States striking capacity, considering the use of all kinds of weapons, could not have been considered inferior to that of the Soviet Union at that time. Nonetheless, the missile gap proposition was considered to be a basic factor and shaped United States military opinion and mass psychology. Remedial action was called for.

Remedial action was taken during the first year of the Kennedy Administration by the official United States proclamation that the missile gap proposition, as it had been advanced during the last years of the Eisenhower Administration, had been a myth. The shoe is on the other foot, the authoritative spokesmen of the Kennedy Administration contended. Not the United States but the Soviet Union had a missile gap, declared the people in high office in the early years of the Kennedy Administration. With that contention, it appears, the military superiority of the United States has been regained, at least as far as the feelings of the United States armchair strategists and of the United States public are concerned. One cannot expect that the authoritative military spokesmen of either side will admit the existence of a lasting balance of military power between the two sides. Were such an admission made, there would

139

be no basis for the continuation of the arms race. Spokesmen for the Soviet government have, in their turn, maintained all along during the premiership of Nikita Khrushchev that the Soviet Union has military superiority over the United States in terms of striking capacity.

The alleged superiority in arms in the arms race of one power over another, be it the United States or the Soviet Union, constitutes a major roadblock in the path of prospective disarmament. It is the same roadblock which paradoxically, in turn, makes complete and total disarmament the only realistic way out of the vicious circle in which one side tries to outdo the other in the quality and quantity of the arms it possesses. Only if complete and total diarmament is effected will the basis on which either side can continue to claim alleged military superiority be removed. While we may expect that the question of armed superiority can be removed, should complete and total disarmament be attained, the phasing of moves towards disarmament will continue to be hampered by the allegation of arms superiority.

Here we have an almost insurmountable problem. With the allegation of arms superiority as a major factor in the continuation of the arms race, we can hardly expect that either of the two major protagonists, the United States or the Soviet Union, will either directly or indirectly admit that any suggested stage of disarmament can be regarded as a point at which equality in arms has been reached.

At the present stage of official disarmament negotiations, some writers have attempted to provide a conceptual framework into which a disarmament plan could be channeled. Among their works is a book by Amitai Etzione called *The Hard Way to Peace, A New Strategy* which is worth mentioning. Etzione suggests that the phasing of disarmament moves start with the discarding of conventional weapons. The discarding of nuclear weaponry and rockets is, in Etzione's plan, the final phase of disarmament. Etzione's approach does not present any real advance over the officially conducted disarmament negotiations, since it does not remove the basis on which one party to the negotiations claims superiority in arms over another party. It does not really matter what kind of weapons are discarded at an early or late stage of disarmament, because the way disarmament negotiations are officially conducted today, it will be possible for any party to the prospective disarmament to claim either arms superiority or arms inferiority at any suggested phase of disarmament.

The only way in which this apparent contradiction in the conduct of disarmament negotiations could be removed is by providing a systematic correlation between armament and disarmament plans. Disarmament — and that is a major proposition which has to be made to register in official and non-official circles — does not mean picking military equipment at random and turning it into a junk pool. Disarmament must be considered a strategic countermove aimed at the elimination of armament. Within such an approach to disarmament, it becomes imperative to correlate the strategic propositions on which the arms policy is based with strategic propositions on the basis of which disarmament is to be undertaken.

In spelling out an approach which relates a strategy of disarmament moves to a strategy of armament moves, one must first consider the various types of military conflict which the strategy of the major protagonists of military power in the world today have devised. In that connection, the so-called limited war proposition, in which conventional weapons are to be used, must first be separated from the proposition of an unlimited war, in which nuclear weapons are to be employed.

In countering the strategic moves which provide for arming for a so-called limited war and, in turn, for an unlimited war, it appears reasonable to suggest that separate disarmament plans be drawn up for each of the two types of possible wars. When the question arises as to what kind of weapons are to be slated for elimination first, and what kind of weapons are to be eliminated last, the question of the escalation of a limited war into an unlimited war, must be taken up. It stands to reason that a limited war can easily be escalated into an unlimited war. The elimination of nuclear weapons must, therefore, be given priority over the elimination of non-nuclear, conventional weapons.

Such a decision will not, however, eliminate many vexing questions which have to be tackled. The ban on the testing of new and more powerful nuclear weapons can well be regarded as a reasonable preliminary step in a move towards nuclear disarmament. A voluntary reciprocal test ban agreement between the Soviet Union and the United States was in effect for several years up to 1961. The reciprocal nuclear test ban agreement put a technological ceiling, so to speak, on the development of those weapons. The lifting of that ceiling, first by the Soviet Union in 1961, and subsequently by the United States in 1962, resulted in quite noticeable advances in the technology of weapons and, in particular, in the technology of nuclear weapons. The Soviet Union, during the 1961–62 nuclear test perfected weapons which increased the destructive power of a single nuclear bomb manifold. This increase in the size and the destructive power of nuclear bombs, which the Soviet tests demonstrated, makes a saturation attack on any adversary of the Soviet Union easier to attain.

Considering that the Soviet Union has available a quantity of missiles of adequate delivery power, the supplying of those missiles with nuclear bombs of greater size and destructive power than those which had been available to the Soviet Union before the tests of 1961 reduces the chances that Soviet Union bomb-laden missiles will miss their targets on the territory of the adversary. The time in which the Soviet Union can complete a saturation attack on a potential adversary has, in turn, been greatly reduced by the Soviet tests.

The United States nuclear tests conducted in 1962 appear to demonstrate a technological advance of a different range as compared with the one attained by the Soviet Union in its 1961-62 nuclear weapons test. The United States appears to have perfected, on an experimental basis, nuclear weapons which could be used in outer space. The United States tests of 1962 thus advanced the possible use of nuclear weapons in a qualitative manner. The qualitative advance perfected in the United States 1962 tests can be considered close to a technological breakthrough.

The use of outer space as a nuclear weapons delivery sphere could well upset all the strategic considerations which have been brought up in regard to the conduct of a possible war in which nuclear weapons were not to be used in outer space. If greater perfection of nuclear weapons for use in outer space is effected, it might well be possible to use the outer space vehicles, in which astronauts have circled the earth, as nuclear delivery devices. Should that take place, strategic concepts entirely different from those which have been devised up to the present would have to be formulated.

Were that to be the case, the countermoves aimed at the elimination of outer space weapons would also have to be revised to fit the new strategic concepts keyed to outer space warfare. Without prejudging the specific strategic concepts which were to guide the conduct of warfare in which outer space delivery vehicles were to be used, one can definitely say, that the total destruction of any country through an attack by such vehicles will become an absolute certainty. The time limit within such destruction could be effected will, in turn, be reduced from days and hours to minutes and seconds. The Soviet Union, it should be realized, could match the aforementioned United States advance in any subsequent series of nuclear tests which it undertakes. As far as outer space delivery vehicles are concerned, the Soviet Union is not inferior to the United States in capabilities, as it is well known.

In 1963, a nuclear test ban agreement was put into effect which binds the Soviet Union, the United States and other signatory powers to refrain from testing nuclear bombs on the surface of the earth, in the air and in the water. Underground tests are excluded from the agreement. In 1964 a reciprocal agreement between the Soviet Union and the United States was arrived at, according to which the production of fissionable material is to be suspended. There is, furthermore, a reciprocal agreement in effect between the Soviet Union and the United States which binds the two parties not to use outer space vehicles for military oper-

142

ations, though experimentation with weapons in outer space is permitted. All those agreements are but steps in the direction of a comprehensive disarmament agreement.

In the meantime, the armament race, except for the stated limited restraining aspects, goes on. Great prominence is being given at present to an anti-missile defense system. An authoritative spokesman for the Soviet Union maintains that the Soviet Union has perfected an anti-missile missile which has been incorporated into its defense system. Some United States authorities have expressed doubts as to the validity of the Soviet claim to the possession of an adequate anti-missile defense. The United States, in its turn, is at present conducting a series of tests in the development and functioning of the anti-missile missile. The successful completion of an anti-missile missile test recently has been given prominence by the United States authorities. Regardless of the present stage of the development of anti-missile defenses, either in the Soviet Union or the United States, one can reasonably expect that, in due time, both the United States and the Soviet Union will be in possession of a fully developed anti-missile missile defense system.

The question arises, in the forementioned connection, whether the establishment of a system of anti-missile missile defense can by itself be regarded as another aspect of a technological breakthrough. The answer, it appears, must be in the negative. The argument in this case can be pursued in terms of an analogy with the development of anti-aircraft guns. The experience with anti-aircraft equipment does not show that the firing of anti-aircraft guns has substantially reduced the effectiveness of bombing by aircraft. Conceivably, if the number and the location of the anti-aircraft guns were to be multiplied, the operation of bomber planes could be more substantially obstructed than it has actually been in the past. It seems doubtful, however, that a vast multiplication of anti-aircraft guns and their location would have resulted in a proportionate increase in the downing of aircraft bombers. Aside from this, there is a limit to which resources can be used for specific defensive weapons engaged in neutralizing the effects of specific offensive weapons.

Additional difficulties have to be considered in regard to the possible effectiveness of anti-missiles. The range of accuracy and precision required of an anti-missile missile is of a much higher degree than that required of an anti-aircraft gun. To hit a missile in flight without the knowledge of where the missile took off and to what target the missile is directed becomes a rather accidental proposition. The accidental nature of the effective employment of anti-missile missiles is not reduced by the steady course which a missile can be expected to pursue after it is launched, because the launchers of the anti-missile missile have great difficulty knowing the exact course of the missile before it can be made the target

143

of anti-missile missiles. The only way to launch an anti-missile missile in a comparatively effective form is to launch it in the direction of the missile launching sites of the adversary. This would have to be the aim regardless of whether or not the particular missile launching sites were in operation at a given time.

If a missile were actually launched from a missile launching site, the possibility of hitting it and of rendering it ineffective would become rather slight. The only way to increase the probability that an anti-missile missile will hit a missile in flight and make it inoperative is through a manifold multiplication of anti-missile missiles. Should such manifold multiplication of anti-missile missiles be effected, then those anti-missile missiles could even be fired at random. The expectation would be in such case that a massive launching of anti-missile missiles could possibly hit a flying missile at which it was not specifically directed by sheer coincidence.

Such a way of anti-missile missile operations, however, must be regarded as much too wasteful. Such wastefulness could not be considered acceptable, either in regard to the totality of the resources which any country has at its disposal in the conduct of a war, or, more specifically, in regard to the quantitative relationship of resources allocated to a given weapon (in this case, the missile), as compared with the respective counter weapon (in this case, the anti-missile missile).

The installation of an effective anti-missile missile defense system is, therefore, prohibitive in terms of a proportional allocation of resources for all types of weapons and counter weapons. Under those circumstances, the perfection and installation of an anti-missile missile defense system is definitely not going to result in a qualitative change in the strategy of the conduct of a war in which bomb-laden missiles are to be employed. The installation and employment of anti-missile missiles on a non-massive scale could and, in all likelihood, will lead to but the addition of one aspect which will require special consideration in the application of the strategic concepts which are to govern the employment and discarding of bomb-laden missiles. The installation of anti-missile missiles, on a non-massive scale, will thus become an added factor in the strategy to be applied in the armament race, as well as in the stategy to be applied in the disarmament drive. A drastic change in the basic concepts of armament as well as a fundamental change in the basic propositions relating to disarmament will not be required in this context.

From what has been said here, one can deduce that the continued experimentation with the anti-missile missiles, and the subsequent installation of an anti-missile missile defense system on a non-massive basis will not interfere with the continuation of the present disarmament negotiations. Such a development, if kept within the range of a non-mas-

144

sive scale, will not require the formulation of an entirely new basis for disarmament measures.

Should, however, a decision be made to install anti-missile missiles on a massive scale, such move could well be regarded as a decision favoring further escalation of the arms race. Were that to come to be the case, future disarmament negotiators will be confronted with another hurdle which will be difficult to surmount. That hurdle could well be interpreted as a psychological block created in the minds of United States disarmament negotiators against partaking in any meaningful disarmament negotiations. The false sense of security which the massive deployment of anti-missile missiles could result in can be seen as the creation of a Maginot line psychosis on the part of the United States disarmament negotiators.

The Maginot line psychosis nourished by a sense of false security is likely to be heightened by the expectation on the part of the United States negotiators that the short range rockets supplied with atomic warheads, which are to be attached to the anti-missile missiles, could deliver a blast at the incoming long range rockets of the adversary and prevent those enemy rockets from hitting the targets in the populated United States areas. The precision of those short range rockets has not been tested however. It could well happen that some of the short range rockets of the adversary could bring about an atomic explosion in the air, which could ricochet and hit back the population area which the short range defense rockets were supposed to protect and, furthermore, envelop the population area in a radioactive belt. It can futher be expected that in a massive attack by long range rockets a great many short range defense rockets would not be able to head off many of the incoming long range rockets at all. For, to cause a total devastation in a delimited population area, it is enough for one or two of the long range incoming rockets to get through. And, this is not only a possibility, but a high probability, which has to be taken into consideration.

In the above stated connection the strategic planners of the installation of an anti-missile missiles system and their supporters might do well to listen to an expert scientist. A well known Professor of Radiation Physics at the University of Pittsburgh, Ernest J. Sternglass, had the following to say in a letter published in *The New York Times* on February 19, 1969: " . . . all that an enemy has to do in order to defeat the purpose of the anti-missile system is to aim his missiles 25, 50 to 100 miles upwind from the Sprint and Sentinal sites located near our population centers", Professor Sternglass warns. He further proceeds to spell out the maleffects of the operational deficiency of the anti-missile missiles. "By using a large number of small warheads detonated near the ground, whose radioactive debris descends in a matter of minutes to hours rather than months or years, he can insure that heavy fallout will descent on our population". Professor Sternglass concludes his letter published in *The New York Times* with the following somber observation: "The widespread installation of nuclear tipped anti-missiles and the resulting need to multiply offensive warheads will greatly increase the total amount of local and worldwide fallout ... The ABM system may well increase rather than decrease the danger to the biological survival of our nation and all mankind". Whether those somber observations of an expert scientist will lead the strategic planners in the Pentagon tot reconsider their plan for the installation of anti-missile missiles remains to be seen.

Opposition to the plan to install an anti-missile missile system has in the meantime been growing in the United States. Close to a majority of United States Senators expressed their opposition to any deployment of anti-missile missiles. Senator Edward M. Kennedy, the only surviving brother of the assassinated President John F. Kennedy and the assassinated Senator Robert F. Kennedy, has addressed at the end of January, 1969 a letter to the Secretary of Defense, Melvin R. Laird, in which the Senator protested, "that it would be a political folly and a serious technical mistake for the United States to commit billions of dollars to build a yet unproved missile defense system." In his accompanying public statement on the issue, Senator Edward Kennedy proposed that the Administration impose a freeze on the construction of sites of anti-missile missiles, named Sentinel, while it conducts a National Security Council Review into the desirability of deploying a missile defense system. "Such a freeze", Senator Kennedy continues his protesting letter, "would make a definite contribution to the cause of world peace, would reassure the nation that our national defense programs are more rational and would heighten the possibility that we would be able to deal more effectively with our domestic needs". Kennedy's protest against the installation of an anti-missile missiles defense system was echoed in the United States Senate Foreign Relations Committee, which under the Chairmanship of Senator Fulbright provided the hard core of the resistance to the manufacture and installation of the Sentinel missile anti-missiles system. It has been reliably reported that the offices of United States Senators and Congressmen in Washington, D. C. had been flooded with letters from their constituents, who are protesting the designation of sites for the installation of anti-missile missiles close to populated areas.

In response to the above stated considerations, President Nixon made on March 14, 1969 a statement in which he conveyed a modified plan of anti-missile missiles installation. Anti-ballistic missiles renamed Safeguard, President Nixon stated, will not be installed to protect population centers. A massive Soviet missile attack, the President related, can inflict upon the United States population centers "unacceptable losses", regardless as to whether anti-missile missiles are installed in close proximity to population centers or not. Therefore, President Nixon declared the plan to install anti-ballistic missiles close to population centers has to be abandoned. The installation of anti-missile missiles, President Nixon coninued in his statement, is to be limited to the protection of emplaced missiles.

This limitation places Mr. Nixon on record in trying to preserve the United States second strike capability. In opting for the installation of anti-ballistic missiles as a second strike strategy, Mr. Nixon opted for the utilization for the anti-missile missiles system as an instrument of defense. Thus, for the time being, the transformation of anti-ballistic missiles into an instrumentality of offense has been precluded. In keeping the anti-ballistic missiles as a weapon of defense, Mr. Nixon kept in line with the Soviet's position on the use of anti-ballistic missiles. The reports circulating in the West about the alleged deployment of anti-ballistic missiles in the Soviet Union have not alleged that the Soviet Union is engaged in a massive deployment of anti-ballistic missiles, which would lay the basis for an intensification of a drive to install more offensive weapons by the United States and subsequently by the Soviet Union as well. Whether the Soviet Union has actually deployed anti-ballistic missiles on its territory is not definitely known in the West. That a massive deployment of anti-ballistic missiles in the United States would have forced the Soviet Union to take tactical and strategic countermeasures could hardly be doubted. What would have resulted, if the United States would have persisted in deploying anti-ballistic missiles on a large scale, would have been an acceleration of the arms race on the part of the Soviet Union. That acceleration would have come, in turn, to result in a considerable increase in offensive as well as defensive weapons and in particular, missiles and anti-missiles in the United States. President Nixon's declaration of self-restraint in regard to the installation of anti-ballistic missiles in the United States is not likely to aggravate the situation as far the current disarmament negotiations between the Soviet Union and the United States are concerned.

Whether the $6 billion dollars to cover the cost of two anti-missile sites were to be approved by Congress when Mr. Nixon supported that proposal was not certain at the time when that proposal was submitted. The funding of Mr. Niixon's proposal won Senate approval only by a majority of one vote. The total costs of manufacture and installation of anti-ballistic missiles in an attempt to protect all United States based missiles can be counted to be in excess of $200 billion dollars. Mr. Nixon seems to pursue the policy of serving Congress the bitter pill of the total costs of anti-ballistic missiles by having it administered in small doses. For action by the United States Congress in 1971 there is proposed an addition to the two already approved anti-missile sites of two other anti-missile sites.

It is to be noticed that there is a mood of reappraisal of the alleged need to increase armament expenditures prevalent in the United States Congress. The military industrial complex, it appears to the United States legislators, has become a self-perpetuating phenomenon in the economy of the United States, it should be noted. That complex pertains to a ready collaboration between the military procurement agency and the producers of military hardware. With a steady flow of orders from the procurement offices to the manufacturers of military hardware the military industrial complex finds its economic situation secure. Such security which cannot be readily had in the market of civilian goods is highly valued by the leaders of those enterprises who again and again are assured of new military procurement orders.

The largest United States corporation led by such giants as General Motors and General Electric are assured of the bulk of the military procurement orders. In such a way those corporations are cushioned against any ups and downs in the operation of their enterprises. Though nominally pledged to an operation on the basis of a cost plus proposition the factor of costs remains open-ended in the context. Costs for new types of weapons based on new designs are not calculable within set bounds. The possibility of overcalculating costs and thus reaping officially disallowed surplus profits is wide open. Not excluded, is, however, also the possibility of undercalculation of the costs on the part of a defense contractor in an attempt to land a contract in competitive bidding.

As of late a gross undercalculation has come to affect one of the major aviation construction companies in the United States, the Lockheed Corporation. Only a redemption by United States funds saved that huge business enterprise from bankruptcy for the time being. Some major industries which are not directly engaged in the manufacture of war goods do also partake in government subsidies. Such is the case with United States railroads which carry military materiel and personnel on orders of the Defense Department. Whether the civilian economy would be able to function properly, if and when government spending is substantially reduced is by no means certain. It is in particular by no means certain in the minds of those business executives who are kept in business or assisted in their business operations by monies spent by the Defense Department. Nor are labor leaders free from fearing that workers will become unemployed as a result of a cutback in armament production.

That such fears on the part of the business leaders and labor leaders have some substance to it can be seen from the reduced profit margins and the reduced employment figures which in 1969 and 1970 were in part due to the leveling off of armament orders and government subsidies connected with it. Cutbacks in research and development funds pertaining to defense goods production in the last two years has, in its turn, resulted in bringing about substantial unemployment among people trained in engineering and scientific skills. A basic restructuring of the civilian economy will be required, if and when the sector of the United States economy geared to the production of war goods comes to be substantially reduced.

Former President Eisenhower's warning in his parting statement, about the dangers of the growing demand of the military-industrial complex, has come to be heeded at present by many United States legislators. At present the realization seems to be dawning upon United States Congressmen and Senators, that an increase in spending for armaments does not necessarily enhance United States security. There is the additional factor of the over rapid technological development as far as military hardware is concerned. It should be kept in mind that billions of dollars are expended yearly on research into new weapons development. More than two thirds of all research in the United States is at present weaponry research which is financed by the United States government. That vast expenditure bears fruit. There is a continuous stream of new technological devices to be used in various arms, flowing from the government financed laboratories. That a technological device which could be used in a weapons development program is new does not necessarily make it more effective.

The cost effectiveness device to be applied to weapons which had been instituted by the former Secretary of Defense Robert McNamara was not sufficiently broad in range to be really effective. In its limited range the cost effectiveness device, instituted by McNamara, concentrated in the main on the cost of material used in the production of weapons, which came to be related to the price which the weapon producing company charged to the government. As far as the effectiveness of a weapon is concerned, it would have to correlate the degree of destructiveness the weapon is likely to cause and the cost of the weapon. The degree of destructiveness is, however, a correlate not only of the cost of the weapon, but also of the degree of the precision in weapon performance minus the counter performance of the weapons and the anti-weapons of the adversary. Those are, however, factors which are largely uncalculable. It is in that sense, that the cost studies instituted by Mc Namara and probably continued after his departure from the Pentagon are to be termed as largely marginal in their effect.

It can be said, in particular, in regard to the rapid and self-contained development of military technology, that its irrational, anti-human ends are defying comprehension in rational human terms. Even advancing military technology comes to play the role of a Frankenstein, which, if unchecked, will devour the humans which are creating the monster.

Rapid technological advancement is, however, not limited to the sphere of weapon development. Technological development in not strictly military spheres, could, however, also be put to use for military purposes. Reference in the stated connection is made here in regard to the use of the lower reaches of outer space for military purposes. The lower reaches of outer space are not subject to an agreed upon ban on using outer space for military purposes. President Nixon in his February 14, 1969 statement, on the limitation of the deployment of anti-ballistic missiles in the United States, stated that the Soviet Union is perfecting the use of weapons in what the President referred to as a semi-orbital range, which is but another wording for a reference to the lower reaches of outer space. No doubt, the United States is also experimenting with the use of the lower reaches of outer space for military purposes.

Recently a news item in United States papers referred to the military aspects in the operation of the satellite communications system as it is being developed in the United States. This is but one aspect of the experimentation in the United States with the military use of the lower reaches of outer space. In the stated connection an article published in the *New York Post* on March 9, 1971 is of interest. The stated article asserts that "flight paths of two recently launched Soviet satellites (Cosmos 349 and Cosmos 397) indicate a new test of the system to knock out unfriendly space vehicles". Confirmation of that assertion has not been forthcoming.

The lower reaches of outer space could as well be used as operating stations in the directing and redirecting of rockets with nuclear warheads. That the mounting and manning of such operating stations in the lower reaches of the outer space is not a fantasy can be gathered from the success of the exchange of astronauts in manning rockets in outer space. That spectacular feat, to which the world had been treated in January, 1969, was performed by Soviet astronauts who replaced each other in manning their respective rockets in outer space.

The stated spectacular feat had brought nearer the practicality of operating and manning platforms in outer space. That achievement has come to be demonstrated by Soviet cosmonauts in June 1971. It is certainly not too farfetched to suggest that the whole array of rockets as means of delivery of nuclear weapons could be made more effective, were it possible to establish a number of operating platforms in outer space. Since that stage has been reached, the practicality of a redirection of delivery instruments of nuclear weapons from platforms circling the globe at a rate superseding supersonic speed has come to be within reach. Hence total destruction of any country subjected to that kind of redirected and controlled nuclear attack could conceivably be achieved with almost complete certainty within seconds.

Were the practicality of placing operating platforms in outer space for the redirection of atomic weapons to be fully established, it appears to be highly probable that the lower reaches of outer space will come to be used for military purposes. The latest exploit of United States astronauts who circled and landed on the moon in March 1969 and February 1971 constitute an additional demonstration that the United States is able to make its own weighty contribution to the conquest of outer space. That the United States advances in the exploration of operational means in the reaches of outer space could have as much of a military implication, as does the exploration of operational advances in outer space by the astronauts of the Soviet Union, goes without saying. The ejection of one rocket by another rocket, to cite one of the most spectacular feats of astronautical navigation performed in March 1969 by three United States astronauts, can well lend itself to a specific military application. A rocket with multiple atomic warheads could be attached and subsequently ejected from another rocket, which after the ejection of the rocket with nuclear warheads, could continue its course, possibly for reloading, – in other words reattachment of another rocket with atomic warheads, – to be dropped on the adversary from outer space.

With the constant advance in the exploration of the operational means in conquering the vista of outer space, the temptation will increase to use not only the lower reaches of outer space, but the higher reaches of outer space as well, for military purposes. It appears unthinkable that a country threatened with complete annihilation, which has the capacity to use the lower as well as the higher reaches of outer space for military purposes, will refrain from doing so, even if it violates an agreed upon ban on such utilization.

Were the outer space to be used for military purposes, the role of landbased rockets would be greatly reduced. Even if all landbased rockets with nuclear warheads were either to be used up or destroyed by the respective adversaries, there still would remain the possibility of using rockets in outer space to deliver a coup de grâce to the adversary on its territory. In that respect the second strike proposition might acquire ominous proportions.

It looks very much, however, as if the second strike proposition will come to rate more and more as an unreality and not only in connection with the possible utilization of outer space for the launching of atom laden missiles. The supplying of missiles with multiple warheads, the stage for which has been at present set, can well be rated as inaugurating the super-overkill period of military technology. While in the overkill period the military planners could count on a margin of misses in the first strike phase and could, therefore, consider that there will be a chance to apply a second strike to undo the misses of the first strike. No such possibility will come to be present, if all ballistic missiles were to be supplied with multiple warheads. The massive launching of missiles with multiple warheads will leave no room for misses. The total destruction of the nation subjected to a massive attack by missiles with multiple warheads, its material and human resources, will become a complete certainty at the first strike. There will, therefore, be no material basis in existence in the nation subjected to a massive nuclear attack with multiple warheads for any comeback at all. It is in that connection that the idea of a pre-emptive first strike will be left as the only rational strategy to be opted by a nuclear power.

It is in that connection that the offering of the antiballistic missiles, the so-called Safeguard, as a bargaining item in the present strategic arms limitation talks between the United States and the Soviet Union, appears to make little sense. What is at stake in the deployment of ballistic missiles with multiple warheads is the vulnerability of the entire technological defense apparatus of any nation which becomes subject to a massive ballistic attack with multiple warheads. That this kind of ominous prospect has dawned upon some military technologists in the United States has come to the fore in recent public utterances. In an educational television program, televised by the Eastern educational network in New York on March 1, 1970, leading military technologists in the United States, among them Jerome Wiesner, former science adviser to the late President John Kennedy and at present President of the Massachusetts Institute of Technology, openly admitted that the entire defense apparatus established on the soil of United States is about to become obsolete in the not too distant future.

In the light of that prospect, the fate of the Safeguard anti-missile missile which has become a major pro-administration propaganda item in the last few years, comes to be deprived of any significance, it assumes the character of so much hot air. What the Safeguard anti-missile missile is supposed to protect, the leading United States technologists, who took part in the above specified televised debate, maintain, is not practicable. It is not practicable because what it is supposed to protect is going to lose its military-technological effectiveness. It is an illusion that a military-technologically outdated weapon can be protected even if the anti-missile device as such would be proven to be effective, the televised debate has brought out. In the light of the stated television debate, the missile as well as the anti-missile missile device could be expected to disintegrate in a tangle of radioactive debris were they to become subject to a massive attack by missiles with multiple warheads.

From the above cited statements, it can be concluded, that all the advanced military equipment which has come to be installed since the first atomic bombs were manufactured, have not provided for any military security at all for any nation equipped with atomic weapons. That stark realization has not yet sufficiently dawned upon the governments and the peoples concerned. Whether the governments and the peoples of the countries concerned, in particular in the two major atomically equipped nations, the United States and the Soviet Union, would be able to act rationally, when they do come to realize that they have bought decreasing military security, one cannot be certain. Total atomic mobilization, which was ushered in with the dawning of the age of atomic weapons, has come to result in a total military insecurity, a truly dialectical development of monstrous proportions.

Were a rational conclusion to be drawn from this paradoxical development, it would call for a total atomic demobilization. As far as the present disarmament negotiations are concerned, they appear to be within the range of trading off tokens against tokens of armament. Only an aroused public opinion in all nations possessing atomic weapons could bring about the enlargement of the scope of disarmament negotiations to an extent which is called for by the present stage of advanced nuclear military technology.

Those leading United States technologists who are aware that the total atomic military equipment is becoming obsolete and will have to be scrapped have come up with a substitute. Since land based missiles cannot be considered as having the capacity to protect any country in an atomic onslaught on it with multiple warheads, atomic military installations have to be removed from a nation's soil; they have to be moved to the high seas. The same leading United States military technologists who took part in the above cited educational television program on March 1, 1970 have made the suggestion that the entire atomic striking force of the United States, if it is to retain any effectiveness, is, in the near future, to come to consist of two to three dozen missile bearing submarines, which on their part are to be supplied with multiple warheads. Those submarine based missiles with multiple warheads, to be called Poseidon in the United States, are to replace the submarine based missiles with single warheads which had been named Polaris in the United States. In line with that suggestion Poseidon tests have been carried out in the United States. It can, therefore, be expected that missile launching submarines with multiple nuclear warheads will soon be made operational in the United States. The Poseidon tests are but follow-up tests of multiple warheads which are to be attached to land based missiles. The replacement of single warheads with multiple warheads in all land based missiles in the United States is planned for the near future.

The Soviet Union, as far as it is known in the West, has for some time conducted tests of multiple warheads on its territory and on the high seas. Short of re-equipment of all of its land based missiles and its missile launching submarines with multiple warheads, the military technologists and strategists of the Soviet Union continue to depend on oversized atomic bombs. The Soviet military technologists and planners do not appear to be entirely sold on the idea of fragmentization of nuclear bombs, they appear to be leaning more toward the strategy of delivering a Sunday punch, to use a slang, with their oversized atomic weapons with the intention of a total knockout of the adversary. As a reflection of that position, the spokesmen for the military strategists and military planners of the Soviet Union did not accept a distinction between strategic and tactical atomic weapons at the 1970 sessions of the Strategic Arms Limitation Talks (SALT), conducted by the Soviet Union and the United States. The Soviet Union negotiators wanted the so-called United States tactical atomic weapons stationed in Europe included in any possible agreement on the limitation of offensive weapons to be negotiated between the Soviet Union and the United States.

Implicit in that position of the Soviet Union negotiators is the expectation on their part that the range of devastation wrought by what United States strategists and planners call either strategic or tactical weapons could not be made distinguishable. The United States negotiators refused to waive the distinction between strategic and tactical atomic weapons stationed in Western Europe. As a result, the Soviet Union negotiators refused to discuss further the matter of limitation of offensive atomic weapons. The Soviet Union negotiators suggested the discussions of an agreement on the limitation of the number of anti-missile missile sites and installations which it had been agreed upon to regard as defensive weapons. That was a negotiating position which the United States had taken in the first phase of negotiations on the limitation of offensive and defensive weapons. According to later information the Soviet Union and the United States negotiators at the Strategic Arms Limitation Talks (SALT) agreed to take up the matter of the limitation of offensive strategic weapons at the next scheduled session in Helsinki, Finland in the summer of 1971. It is the understanding that an agreement on the limitation of defensive weapons is to precede the taking up the matter of the limitation of offensive weapons.

In a sense, the installation of missiles with multiple warheads on the soil of the United States as well as the supplying of missile launching submarines with multiple warheads present a contradictory development from a military technological point of view. In the opinion of leading United States military technologists, among them the above cited Jerome Wiesner, former science advisor of the late President Kennedy, the installation of missiles with multiple warheads on the soil of the United States is a self-defeating undertaking. It is self-defeating since it constitutes an open invitation to other atomic powers, and in particular to the Soviet Union, to go ahead with the deployment of missiles with multiple warheads – on their territory. The equipping of another atomic power with missiles with multiple warheads nullifies the advantage gained by the atomic power which had first installed such missiles. The atomic power which first installed missiles with multiple warheads on its territory becomes for all practical purposes a sitting duck, so to speak, for the second atomic power which undertakes to install missiles with multiple warheads on its territory. The words sitting duck can be justly applied in the stated connection because, when two atomic powers are supplied with missiles carrying multiple warheads, there is no strategy left for either side other that the one of striking a pre-empted blow on the other side.

To escape the inescapable dilemma leading United States foremost technologists, among them once more Jerome Wiesner, have come to place their reliance on the submarine based missiles with multiple warheads called Poseidon. In the view of Wiesner and some of his leading fellow technologists, the submarine based Poseidon missiles roaming the high seas could not easily be detected and could, therefore, not be automatically made sitting ducks. The above cited military technologists do not maintain that the submarine based missiles with multiple warheads are completely invulnerable. Some of the submarines with multiple warheads could become targets of missile launching submarines with either single or multiple warheads of an adversary, leading United States military technologists are willing to concede.

As to the aspect of damage which the missile launching submarines with multiple warheads could inflict upon a prospective adversary, the above cited United States military technologists, have not been very specific about that matter. The tactics which the submarine based Poseidon missiles with multiple warheads could be expected to apply are those of a hit and run range. Where such hit and run tactics to be applied only by about two dozen or so submarines, as envisioned by the above cited leading United States foremost military technologists, such tactics could not bring about the total destruction of an adversary. Were the adversary of the United States, presumably the Soviet Union, to have missile launching submarines with multiple warheads of its own, it could make its missile submarines with multiple warheads launch attacks on the territory of the United States. Again, such attacks by two dozen or so submarines could not result in a total destruction of the United States as a military power. Only the construction and deployment of several hundred missile launching submarines with multiple warheads by each of the two foremost atomic powers, the United States and the Soviet Union, and the putting of those submarines into operation could lead to the inflicting of an unacceptable damage by each adversary upon the other. If that were to be the case, the situation would approach the overkill scenario which was characteristic of the time when land based missiles with one atomic warhead had been installed. It is that scenario which had been reached at the time when a simple overkill situation prevailed. It was the scenario which was in effect before the super-overkill situation came to be reached, as a result of the installation of missiles with multiple warheads. One can be sure, that, with advancement and proliferation of military technology left unchecked, the overkill situation of the missile launching submarines with multiple warheads will be followed by another super-overkill arraignment of the two foremost atomic super-powers, the United States and the Soviet Union. It is that situation, let us recall, with which one was confronted when the super-overkill situation came to be reached with attachment of multiple warheads to land based missiles.

The only way to escape the destabilization effects of the advance of atomic technology is to place new devices pertaining to atomic weapons and means of their delivery under the control of a joint commission of signatories to any agreement on the limitation of the manufacture and deployment of offensive and defensive weapons. Only an experimental testing of new military technological devices is to be regarded permissible under such an agreement. Manufacture and installation of new military technological devices is, on its part, not to be undertaken without approval of the stated joint commission. Short of the establishment of the above-stated controls, any agreement arrived at by atomic powers in regard to the restriction of the manufacture and installation of atomic weapons will but result in the testing, manufacture and installation of more potent weapons than the ones which had been covered by an agreement arrived at. With a view of the just stated perspective any dicussion and adoption of an arms limitations agreement pertaining to atomic weapons will have to be rated as an exercise in futility. Any new proposals and any new possible agreements on arms limitation pertaining to atomic weapons will, moreover, continue to be an exercise in futility unless the just stated approach, in terms of an establishment of an international control agency over the manufacture and installation of new types of atomic weapons, becomes a reality.

In spite of the above stated consideration the United States official military technologists and strategists continue to operate on the basis of a second strike strategy. Embedded in the second strike strategy is the so-called deterrent doctrine. The second strike military strategic approach professed by the United States war planners presumes, moreover, that the political and military strategists of the Soviet Union also subscribe to that kind of approach. There is little evidence, however, available to support

156

such a presumption on the part of the United States political and military strategists. Evidence to the contrary can be gathered from what is known in the West about the Soviet Union's strategic military posture. The Soviet Union's military and strategic planners appear to emphasize dependence upon oversized atomic warheads and oversized missiles. They do, in turn, appear to deemphasize and to some extent disregard middle sized and small scale atomic weapons and means of their delivery. As far as the dependence of the Soviet Union on oversized atomic weapons and means of their delivery is concerned, the latest United States intelligence information, announced in United States papers, as well as on the radio and television at the beginning of March, 1971, appears to support the above stated military posture of the Soviet Union. The stated intelligence information was to the effect that the Soviet Union is engaged in digging holes for larger missiles than the ones in which missiles presently installed in the Soviet Union had been placed.

As a pendant, the deemphasis on the supply of medium sized and small scale weapons in the atomic arsenal of the Soviet Union is supported by the information published by the United States nuclear scientist Lapp in the News of the Week Sunday edition of *The New York Times* as of March 14, 1971. Lapp reports, as far as the information available in the West is concerned, the Soviet Union has not embarked on providing their missile borne atomic warheads with multiple independently targeted warheads. Instead, according to Lapp, the Soviet Union has come to be engaged in providing their missiles with multiple warheads to be used for strikes at random. It thus comes to look very much that the military technologists and strategists of the Soviet Union are sold on the idea of a Sunday Punch, meaning that they are committed to a strategy of one strike with employment of all atomic weapons available in an attempt to effect a knock-out blow of total devastation upon the adversary. There is one additional reason to be noticed why the Sunday Punch scenario forces itself upon the thinking of the strategists of the Soviet Union. Such reasoning is to be considered but as a follow-up of the pledge of the political leaders of the Soviet Union, not to be the first to use atomic weapons and thus refrain from initiating an atomic war. The United States, on its part, as it is reported on March 8, 1971 in the West German journal *Der Spiegel,* has up to the March, 1971 session of the limitation of strategic arms between the United States and the Soviet Union refused to make such a pledge.

Under such circumstances, the military and political strategists of the Soviet Union have to make plans for a contingency that they would have to unleash their entire atomic arsenal in answer to a United States first strike. In such a contingency, there would be no time left for the Soviet Union to employ any other strategy than that of a supreme blow.

157

It just wouldn't make sense under the stated contingency conditions to use any other strategy than the unloading of the entire atomic arsenal at its disposal at once in an all-out strike.

By contrast, the scenario to which the United States military technologists and strategists continue to cling to is based on the assumption that only a part and preferably a minor part of the total United States atomic arsenal is to be used at the initial first strike. The expectation on the part of United States military technologists and strategists is that a follow-up political maneuvering could ensue. A major feature of the maneuvering scenario is to be the demand for capitulation addressed to the other side on the threat of succeeding blows by atomic weapons unused in the first strike.

The United States military technologists and strategists have so far not demonstrated that they have taken into account that their reliance on the first and second strike strategies could and possibly would put the United States in a disadvantageous position. In the absence of a commitment to first and second strike strategies on the part of the political and military leaders of the Soviet Union, the United States could and probably would find itself in a knock-out situation in a nuclear confrontation with the Soviet Union were the Soviet Union to unload its entire atomic arsenal in answer to the first strike on the part of the United States in initiating an atomic war. In doing some rethinking, in view of the above stated contingency, the United States political and military strategists might have to shift from a strategy of two strikes to a one strike strategy. Were such reversal of the strategy to be effected on the part of the United States planners, the United States scenario for a nuclear confrontation with the Soviet Union would have to place an increased reliance on the pre-emptive blow. Were that to be the case, the United States strategists might have second thoughts as to whether it would not be to the advantage of the United States to extend a no first strike pledge to the Soviet Union.

Were, however, a pledge of no first strike not to be forthcoming from the United States, the Soviet Union, on its part, would have to consider whether it is not to the advantage of its military strategic scenario to renounce its pledge of no initial first strike atomic blow. Thus, the Soviet Union would then also come to depend increasingly on a pre-emptive first strike strategy with the employment of all its atomic arsenal in that strike.

Thus, the stage were to be set with both, the United States and the Soviet Union, speaking metaphorically, looking down into each other's gun barrel. With the terror of the expectation of a first strike to the horror of having to push the button for an all-out assault by atomic weapons, there will be little choice left. This kind of counterposition is certainly not to result in a deterrent for either side. On the contrary, the temptation to strike a pre-emptive blow by one side on the other will be continuously increasing.

The response available to the adversary upon whom the pre-emptive strike of total devastating proportions were to come to be visited would be the unloading of its own crippled arsenal upon the other side. That crippled return strike was to come to rate as the only strike, the country which had become subjected to an initial pre-emptive strike of total devastating proportions could possibly be able to deliver. Such a contingency would reaffirm the inefficacy of the second strike strategy. In the stated contingency, the total devastation wrought on the victim of the first pre-emptive strike could not conceivably undo the crippling damage sustained by the first strike. The reaction strike of the assaulted country in answer to a pre-emptive strike by the other side could only be a spite strike, a strike short of total devastation.

In view of the magnitude of the just stated problem the scope of the discussion at past disarmament conferences appears to be much too narrow. Let us state, for instance, the range of the discussion pertaining to the underground atomic test ban at the 17 Nations Disarmament Conference in Geneva. An agreement on a ban of the testing of underground nuclear devices has so far been held up by the problems of detection and inspection. A few years ago, a seismic device had been perfected, in the form of boxes placed on the territory of any given country; this device could have been used as an instrumentality for detection. The United States representative at the 17 Nations Disarmament Conference has maintained that the detection by the stated seismic boxes cannot be considered foolproof, and that by shaking or otherwise deliberately manipulating the seismic boxes could be made unreliable as a detection device. Further disagreements arose over the question of the number of boxes which should be placed on a given country's territory and the location of those boxes in a given country. The Soviet Union, on its part, was willing to accept international control of the seismic boxes to be placed on its territory. In addition, the then Soviet Premier Khrushchev had agreed to have three regular annual inspections of the seismic boxes made on the territory of the Soviet Union. No agreement on the ban of testing underground nuclear devices has so far been reached.

Mistrust by one party of the other party, in this case the mistrust by the United States government of the government of the Soviet Union, is not going to make matters easier, as far as the progress in disarmament negotiations is concerned. The mistrust of the good will of the government of the Soviet Union by the government of the United States has more recently come to the fore when the perfection of a new device to detect underground nuclear tests has been announced. That device was to make it feasible to detect underground nuclear testing around the globe by a testing device placed outside the territory of the testing country. Were the applicability and effectiveness of such a device to be demonstrated, the need to place detection inspectors on the territory of the country conducting underground tests would become superfluous. The United States representative at the 17 Nations Disarmament Conference, at which the perfection of this detection device had been announced, was not moved, however, to give it any serious consideration. The question can be raised in that connection as to whether the resistance of the United States representative at the disarmament conference does not constitute a deliberate effort to have the disarmament negotiations on the matter of banning underground atomic tests stalled. The freezing of the position of the United States representative at the 17 Nations Disarmament Conference by continuing to insist on sending inspectors to the territory of the testing country comes to look very much as but an excuse to have the disarmament talks on that issue to be deferred ad infinitum.

It should be kept in mind, however, that the continuation of the present ban on tests of nuclear weapons, even if underground tests remain excluded, does constitute an important preliminary step in the furtherance of disarmament, though by itself it does not constitute disarmament but rather a slowing down of the armament race. To attain real disarmament, successful negotiations on the destruction of stockpiled nuclear weapons, of means of their delivery and of their manufacturing facilities, have to be effected.

If a reasonable basis for a disarmament agreement is to be attained some hurdles in regard to the above stated matter have to be overcome. While it would be comparatively easy to define a stockpile of nuclear weapons, the verification of its existence and its subsequent destruction constitute a problem. The Soviet Union has been insisting on verification by non-Russians only of the destruction of a given stockpile; it has refused to submit the part of the stockpile, not subject to immediate destruction, to an inspection by non-Russians. Evasion of the agreed upon destruction of given amounts of nuclear weapons could be effected, it should be realized, by moving a given stockpile from one place to another, after the phase of the destruction of the nuclear weapons has begun. To make such evasion effective, the particular party would have only to underdeclare the amount of nuclear weapons at its disposal at the time agreement to destroy all existing stockpiles is reached. Were such an evasion to take place, it would be impossible for any non-native inspector to verify the amount of the remaining stockpile after subsequent phases of destruction of existing stockpiles had been completed.

160

Only by permitting foreign inspectors to roam freely over the country on whose territory stockpiles of nuclear weapons were to be destroyed could the underdeclared and moved stockpiles possibly be detected.

It does not seem likely, however, that any country will permit non-native inspectors to move freely about its territory, in an effort to detect hidden stockpiles of nuclear weapons. It stands to reason, therefore, that a certain degree of trust has to be established between the negotiating powers, if they are to use a workable agreement on the destruction of existing stockpiles of nuclear weapons. A quick succession of moves which were to lead to the destruction of the entire stockpile of nuclear weapons on the territory of the signatory powers, followed by one single inspection designed to spot any undestroyed nuclear weapons, could provide a basis for an agreement acceptable to all prospective signatories. Thus the question of whether the inspector is likely to become an informer on all retained nuclear striking power of the suspected signatory, regardless of whether the stockpile be legitimate or illegitimate, within the range of the given disarmament treaty, would not arise. Here again the atmosphere of mutual suspicion and recrimination so far has extended its cold breath to the negotiating table.

Further complications have arisen when the problem of the destruction of the means of delivery of nuclear weapons has come up for discussion. In this case, it is not only the equipment, the missiles and the bomber planes which must be destroyed, but also the launching sites of missiles. The moving of launching sites could be made subject to evasion. Moreover, the reduction of delivery equipment on one site with a subsequent increase in the delivery equipment of another site could also constitute an evasion. A disarmament plan pertaining to delivery equipment and its geographic location must be subject to phasing in which the quantity of the delivery equipment and the particular location of the delivery equipment are to constitute specific units.

The priority to be allocated to the specific units could be determined on the basis of strategic considerations. Delivery units in locations which are closer to each other, as far as the territories of two signatories are concerned, could be considered subject to elimination on first priority. The assigning of first priority to the elimination of delivery units closest to each other's territory of the signatories can well be explained by the need to reduce the most acute danger of attack on each other's territory.

It could, however, be argued in the above stated connection, that the speed of delivery in regard to the distances at which delivery could be effected, is almost instantaneous, and that, therefore, it does not really matter where, geographically, a certain concentration of delivery vehicles is situated at a given time. With that in mind, the presence of United States delivery equipment in Western Europe could not be considered as substantially strengthening the United States strategic posture vis-à-vis the Soviet Union.

What the presence of United States delivery equipment means to the Soviet Union, in turn, is that the Russians must match their delivery equipment apportioned for use in Western Europe with the delivery equipment the United States has in Europe, as well as with the delivery equipment the United States has on United States territory. It presents, therefore, a need for greater dispersion of delivery equipment as well as a need for greater diversification of delivery equipment on the part of the Soviet Union vis-à-vis the United States.

Not excluded in this connection is the factor that European powers could increase their delivery equipment as well as the sites of their locations as time passes on. President De Gaulle's efforts to establish a French nuclear striking force is a step in this direction. De Gaulle was bidding for an independent French nuclear striking force; Britain continues to possess nuclear weapons of its own. The use of those weapons will not in all likelihood be placed under direct United States high command. Any move in the direction of an establishment of an European striking force independent of the United States high command will make disarmament in the nuclear, as well as in the non-nuclear sphere, a more complex problem.

As far as the dispersal of delivery equipment of nuclear weapons is concerned, the missile launching sites in the Soviet Union and the nations allied with it in Eatern Europe are comparatively less dispersed than the missile launching sites on the territory of its opponents, which include the United States and its West European allies. The greater dispersal of the missile launching sites of the opponents of the Soviet Union is due to the geographical distance between the United States territory and the territory of its West European allies, as compared with the geographical proximity of the Soviet Union to its East European allies. A growing independence of the West European striking forces will add weight to the bearing of the factor of geographical distance between the United States and the territory of its Western allies. The comparative compactness of the missile launching sites in the West European countries themselves cannot be considered as a factor compensating for the distance between the territory of the United States and that of its West European allies.

The Soviet Union's comparative strategic plans have to take into consideration the overall striking power of the United States and its Western allies. Nuclear saturation bombing of the United States and its Western allies presents, for geographical reasons, a more difficult task for the Soviet Union than the saturation bombing of the Soviet Union and its East European allies, which has to be worked out by the United States strategists in concert with the strategists of its West European allies. The disadvantage of the Soviet Union and its East European allies vis-à-vis the United States and its respective West European allies in regard to the relative compactness and dispersal of the missile launching sites has increased with the planned substitution of missile launching sites on the territories of the countries of Western Europe with submarine-based Polaris and Poseidon missiles on the shores of those countries.

The Soviet negotiators at the 17 Nations Disarmament Conference in Geneva, have insisted on the elimination of the United States bases on the territory of the European powers in the first phase of the elimination of the delivery equipment. With the substitution of seaborne Polaris and Poseidon missiles for launching sites on the territory of the West European countries, the matter of territorial bases for use by delivery equipment of atomic weapons appears to have assumed a new dimension. The Soviet negotiators have included the removal of seaborne-based Polaris and Poseidon missiles from the shores of the European NATO countries in their demand for the elimination of United States bases in West European countries.

At all stages and phases of disarmament negotiations, the factor of real comparative advantage and disadvantage to one prospective signatory power over another is always present. It is a highly intricate problem which has to be solved at each succeeding phase of the disarmament negotiations. What appears to be an advantage or disadvantage to one side cannot always be squared with what appears to be an advantage or disadvantage to the other side. Real and apparent advantages and disadvantages have to be differentiated from imaginary or unreal advantages and disadvantages. Those hurdles will not be easily surmounted.

The Soviet Government has, so far, not been willing to permit inspection on its territory of nuclear bombs and means of their delivery, which were to be kept intact in the initial phases of the effectuation of a disarmament agreement. The Soviet negotiators so far have been willing to allow inspectors from foreign countries only to verify the destruction of the quantity of bombs and delivery equipment destroyed at each specified stage of disarmament. The Soviet Government is also willing to permit inspectors from foreign countries on its soil to verify the effectuation of the final phase of the destruction of all nuclear bombs and of all delivery equipment. United States negotiators continue to insist on inspection and verification of the destroyed and undestroyed bombs and delivery equipment at each stage of disarmament.

Special problems arise in connection with the disarmament phase dealing with the dismantling of the facilities for the manufacture of nuclear weapons and means of their delivery. The verification that the specific facilities in specified localities are destroyed in the specified time is not an issue. The Soviet negotiators are willing to permit inspection and verification of the part of the facilities slated for destruction at a given stage of disarmament. They are reluctant, however, to submit to inspection and verification of the part of the manufacturing facilities of nuclear weapons and means of their delivery which is to be kept intact at a given stage of disarmament. The United States negotiators insist, in their turn, on the inspection and verification of both the destroyed and the undestroyed facilities of manufacturing nuclear weapons and means of their delivery. The inspection factor in the case of the manufacturing facilities of nuclear weapons and means of their delivery assumes an aspect which is different from the one which pertains to the proposed destruction of existing nuclear stockpiles and means of their delivery. In the case of the latter, evasion could take place, for the most part by way of moving the nuclear stockpiles and means of their delivery which have been made subject to destruction at a given phase and a given time of disarmament to another place, in violation of the specific disarmament provision.

It has been suggested by Professor Sohn of Harvard University, that specific regions are to be devised within the territory of each signatory power on which random inspection is to be undertaken. Such a form of inspection would prevent the disarmament inspectors from roaming all over the country of the signatory powers. It would thus negate to some extent the presumption of the Soviet negotiators that, by opening Soviet territory to unrestricted inspection by disarmament inspectors, they lay themselves open to spying. This plan of regional inspection has, however, been rejected by the Soviet Union in the reiteration of the spying charge. Whether any compromise proposal on the respective inspection and verification acceptable to both parties, could be evolved remains to be seen.

A further problem arises in connection with the destruction of manufacturing facilities of nuclear weapons and means of their delivery. It pertains to the retention of the relevant production devices. If the formulas and blueprints for the re-establishment of the production facilities of the nuclear bombs and means of their delivery are retained by the respective signatory powers, what guarantee is there that a unilateral rearmament will not take place on the slightest provocation? This possibility will have to be countered by a perpetual system of inspection. The inherent difficulty in laying down the rules for such inspection is that formulas and manufacturing facilities for the production of non-war products can easily be transformed into formulas and facilities geared to the production of war goods. The question whether even an intricate system of inspection could cope with that kind of problem remains to be answered.

Some relief in regard to the aforementioned problem-complex could be provided by the internationalization of nuclear development programs and space research plans. The international agency for the peaceful uses of atomic energy, as well as the agreement between the United States and the Soviet Union on joint space exploration programs, constitute steps in this direction. The widening of this sphere of internationalization of scientific and technological progress might well lighten the task of perpetual inspection of the territory of the signatory powers, a task which otherwise might become unmanageable.

The phase of disarmament which is related to conventional weapons presents a qualitatively different problem, compared with the phase of disarmament in terms of nuclear weapons and means of their delivery. Disarmament, as far as it involves non-nuclear weapons and means of their delivery, are matters of differing dimensions. The introduction of nuclear weapons can be considered as the extension of the Second Industrial Revolution to the sphere of warfare. Nuclear weapons and means of their delivery constitute the automatic equipment, as it applies to the preparation and conduct of war in the era of self-propelling equipment. The latter constitutes the major characteristic of the Second Industrial Revolution. The automatic equipment involved in the existence and possible application of nuclear weapons has removed man from direct contact with the means of making war and with their application.

When one says that all that is necessary to start a nuclear war is to push a button, one is pointedly expressing what can be expected to take place the second when the war is to be made to start. The push button proposition can well be extended to cover the entire range of the conduct of a war in which nuclear weapons are to be delivered by way of missiles. All that is required of those who are in charge of launching missiles supplied with nuclear warheads is that they push buttons or turn a switch. Nor will the party on the receiving side, at which the missile is directed, be expected to undertake any action in which premeditated human ingenuity and resourcefulness are to be involved. Human activity, in terms of purposeful activity, will be as much removed from the receiving end of the bomb-laden missile as it is from the launching site of the missile. The effect of the landing of the bomb-laden missiles will be predetermined wholly by technological factors.

The human element is in this case predestined to play a merely passive role. The human, under these conditions, is doomed to physical extinction. Whether he will face that prospect in a contemplative mood or with a sense of horror, does not really matter, as far as the cessation of his physical existence is concerned. The war in the age of automation is to be conducted by robots, identified as bomb-laden missiles, to which the human being, if he does not do away with those robots, has no choice but to submit. The human being will have to submit in reaction to a pushed button, in expectation of a quick death, were he not to demonstrate sufficient imagination and ingenuity to dispose of the robots before they start spreading death.

Disarmament measures in regard to the nuclear and missile aspects of warfare, conversely, require a special kind of approach. An example of the kind of disarmament approach suitable to the technological aspects of nuclear weapons and missiles can be seen in the perfection of the seismic device in box form, which could be used for the detection of underground atomic blasts. Such a technologically self-enforceable detection device is in full accord with the automated aspect of nuclear and missile warfare. Self-enforceable detection devices in regard to other aspects of nuclear and missile disarmament, can be expected to be in the offing. Human monitoring, however, of even the most efficient self-controlling devices, cannot possibly be fully eliminated. Even if mutual suspicion and recrimination, fed by the Cold War, were to be eliminated, there still would remain the need of agreement on the human factors involved in the operation of self-enforceable disarmament devices.

When it comes to the application of conventional weapons, we are back in the period of the First Industrial Revolution, in the wake of which the worker became the tenderer of the machine. Conversely, the soldier became the tenderer of the machine-weapon, such as, for instance, the sub-machine gun. The tending of the non-automated machine and of the non-automated machine-weapon did not dispose of the continuous human activity, as far as the employment of the machine and the application of the machine-weapon is concerned. Nor was the technological effectiveness of the non-automated machine-weapons such as to make a defense against a non-automated machine-weapon ineffectual. Human ingenuity and resourcefulness could have been and were made to bear on attempts to escape death and destruction by non-automated weapons. Wars in the age of non-automated weapons could still be won and lost. The limited destructiveness of non-automated machine-weapons permitted the conduct of wars as means of attaining national political ends.

Disarmament measures in the age of pre-nuclear and pre-missile warfare were different from those which are to be taken in the age of nuclear and missile warfare. Disarmament measures in the pre-nuclear and pre-missile era could be confined to the quantitative limitations on the manufacture and retention of weapons. Disarmament in the pre-nuclear and pre-missile age, moreover, was not meant to effect a change from a warfare state to a non-warfare state, because a warfare state in terms of an accelerated mass production of weapons in peacetime did not exist in the pre-nuclear and pre-missile state of warfare. Disarmament measures in the pre-nuclear and the pre-missile age were but meant to reduce the possibility of the outbreak of a war.

The experience with measures to limit the amount of weapons in the period from the end of World War I to the beginning of World War II demonstrates the ineffectiveness of such measures in preventing the outbreak of a war. It can even be argued that disarmament measures, such as the limitation of the number of warships by an international treaty, did not even delay the outbreak of World War II, nor did they effect any restraints on the use of naval vessels in that war. Nor did reductions of land-based weapons imposed by one country upon another, which constituted an arms limitation measure, prove effective. A case in point is the arms limitation forced upon Germany by the victorious powers and written into the Versailles Treaty. When Germany considered it politically expedient, it violated the arms limitation clause of the Versailles Treaty and embarked on the rearmament which led straight to World War II.

Since arms limitation did not play any decisive role in the prevention of war in the pre-nuclear and pre-missile age, it certainly cannot be expected to play an important role in the age of nuclear and missile warfare. Neither the limitation of nuclear weapons and missiles nor the limitation of non-nuclear weapons can by itself prevent the outbreak of a war. Only the elimination of nuclear as well as non-nuclear weapons as a means of mass destruction can lead to the abandonment of war as a means of national policy.

The argument that, the limitation and subsequent elmination of nuclear weapons and missiles from the armories of the countries which at present possess them can be considered as a fully adequate measure for the prevention and outbreak of nuclear and missile warfare, can be easily punctured. It can be punctured with the counter argument that any country which has knowledge of the production of hydrogen weapons and missiles can be expected to avail itself of that knowledge, in case it becomes engaged in a war in which, initially, no nuclear weapons and missiles were employed. No country knowing of the production of nuclear weapons and missiles can be expected to commit itself to go down to defeat before it makes use of nuclear weapons and missiles.

A war between the present nuclear powers which, if it were to start with the employment of weapons of the pre-nuclear and pre-missile age, will of necessity turn into a nuclear missile war. This contingency requires a qualitative change in the approach to disarmament. Neither a division of the scope of disarmament into two separate compartments, one of nuclear weapons and missiles, and the other of pre-nuclear and pre-missile weapons, will do. Nor will a limitation of either nuclear weapons and missiles, or a limitation of pre-nuclear and pre-missile weapons do. The only effective way to banish war as an instrument of national policy in the relationship of the present nuclear powers to each other lies in the direction of the elimination of both types of weapons, the nuclear weapons and their means of delivery, as well as the pre-nuclear weapons.

Preliminary to, but not as a substitute for, disarmament, some forms of disengagement could well be tried. The plan of the former Polish

Foreign Minister Rapacki for the denuclearization of Central Europe as well as the realization of plans for the denuclearization of the South American and Pacific areas could well contribute to a lessening of tensions between East and West. The signing of a non-aggression pact between the NATO powers and the Warsaw Pact countries could as well contribute to the reduction of the charged atmosphere. In that kind of uncharged atmosphere, disarmament negotiations could be conducted more successfully than they have been so far.

Wars, to draw a general conclusion, have been with humanity for a long time. By devising the maxim *homo homines lupus est,* Thomas Hobbes implied that the conduct of wars is inherent in human nature. Human nature, however, contrary to Hobbes, is subject to change, and warlike instincts, if they did prevail in the past, can be channelized into worthwhile peaceful pursuits. Such a change, of course, will not take place by itself; it will have to be directed. As far as European culture and its transplantation to the Americas is concerned, war continues to be an inherent part of the Western cultural heritage. Popular nationalism, which since the Industrial Revolution has replaced the aristocratic monarchical nationalism of the period of the Commercial Revolution, has but broadened and deepened the national roots of the apotheosis of wars. The United States can serve as a good example of this. United States nationalism has its very roots in the Revolutionary War, which led to the political independence of the United States.

The traumatic experience of the Civil War, to cite another major armed United States conflict, was the price the United States had to pay for the removal of slavery as a bar to its industrialization and to its subsequent gaining of economic independence. Expansion of the United States from a peripheral coastal state to a continental power with overseas possessions was largely made possible by way of a series of wars which are generally regarded in the United States as the road to the acquisition of national power. Participation of the United States in World War I and World War II continues to be acclaimed in the United States as the basis for the emergence of the United States as a foremost world power.

The national historical consciousness of the American people is deeply rooted in the apotheosis of war. It should be granted that the feudal trappings of the exaltation of warfare, which have been carried over to a great extent from the period of the Commercial Revolution to the period of the Industrial Revolution in monarchical European states, is not present in the United States. The United States as a bourgeois state par excellence has created the most bourgeois army. The United States army, as far as its officers' corps is concerned, has since the Revolutionary War consisted of business people and those who subscribe to business interests. The business interests to which the United States officer corps subscribed since the Revolutionary War, were, as far as the war service of those officers is concerned, projected into a national scope. The United States officer corps' adherence to business interests since the Revolutionary War is, in turn, responsible for the subordination of the role of the United States Army to the role of the United States civilian authorities. At no time in all the history of the United States was a determined effort made to have military rule substituted for civilian government.

Unlike South America, wherein the officer corps continues to be keyed not only to anti-industrial but anti-commercial interests as well, the United States officer corps has at all times of its existence been thoroughly rooted in its dedication to commercial and, subsequently, industrial interests. The preponderance of anti-commercial and anti-industrial land-owning interests in South American countries makes, in turn, for identification of military and civilian power. In that sense one is presented in South America with a feudal heritage. The wedding of civilian and military power was one of the major characteristics of the land-owning society in the early patrimonial and late patrimonial monarchical age. The difference between the early patrimonial and late patrimonial monarchical age is to be seen in the apparently greater centralization of the wedded civilian and military power in the two respective periods.

As far as South America is concerned, the monarchical trimmings of the late patrimonial, monarchical age have been discarded as far as the officer corps of those armies are concerned. The social basis for the existence of the officer corps in South America, in terms of dedication to the interests of immobile wealth, represented by land, continues, however, to be present there, as it did in the early patrimonial and the late patrimonial monarchical Europe. What is further of interest in regard to the anti-commercial and anti-industrial character of the South American officer corps is that it is not geared to national expansion; it confines itself to the preservation of the social status quo within given national boundaries. In that sense, the attitude of the South American officer corps is defensive and unlike the attitude of the officer corps of the European armies which for the most part served aggressive monarchical interests.

A digression into the mentality of the South American officer corps was undertaken here to demonstrate the fundamental difference between the bourgeois character of the North American officer corps and the non-bourgeois character of the South American officer corps. This comparative characterization is meant to prove that one can hardly expect the North American officer corps to turn to the mentality of the South

169

American officer corps. We can expect that the submission of military authority to civilian authority in the United States will remain intact. Nor can one expect the United States officer corps to continue to harbor expansionist tendencies to the extent of presenting a challenge to civilian rule, were the civilian authority to forsake expansionist tendencies in favor of a concerted effort of national United States development.

American society and economy does offer a sufficient absorption capacity for all the United States officers, high and low, now serving in the United States military establishment to land socially desirable and economically rewarding positions in civilian life. Therefore, one cannot expect any widespread resentment among the United States officer corps, were a large scale program of demilitarization to take effect in the United States. One of the reasons for the supremacy of military over civilian rule in South America, it should be kept in mind, is that its officer corps has extremely limited opportunities to secure socially desirable and economically rewarding positions in civilian life.

As far as the Soviet Union is concerned, its citizenry could not have escaped the impact of wars on its national consciousness. The very existence of the Soviet Union as a national state is rooted in its winning the Civil War which followed the October Revolution. Nor can the wars of the pre-Soviet period be fully erased from the national consciousness of the Soviet people. The growth of the Muscovite state from a feudal dukedom to a world power was made possible by a series of victorious wars. By subduing the recalcitrant feudal lords, the boyars, Czar Ivan IV, nicknamed by the feudal lords "the Terrible," consolidated the Russian monarchical state. In the times of the Emperor Peter I, called "the Great," and the Empress Catherine II, also called "the Great," Russia became a major European power. Those two monarchs had enlarged the national territory of the Russian state by reducing the military power of Sweden and Turkey, respectively. Russia had, furthermore, become the preponderant power in continental Europe by playing a major role in the defeat of the Napoleonic armies. Soviet Russia, in turn, has emerged as a leading world power as a result of taking a leading role in the defeat of Nazi Germany.

As far as the Soviet officer corps is concerned, it is rooted in socialist as well as in national traditions. The feudal trimmings of the Czarist officer corps are eliminated. Those feudal trimmings were rooted in the preponderance of the landowning Russian gentry in the officer corps. That gentry no longer exists, since land has become national property. It cannot be assumed that the Soviet Russian officer corps serves any propertied interests, because propertied interests, whether in terms of land or any other property which could serve as a basis of personal enrichment, does not exist in the Soviet Union.

It can be assumed, nonetheless, that the Soviet Russian officer corps does have group interests of its own. It is questionable, however, whether the specific group interest of the Soviet officer corps is sufficiently distinct to set it against other group interests in the Soviet Union, such as for instance the interests of managers of state enterprises. Even the group interests of the top echelon of the Soviet officer corps, which includes the marshals of the Soviet Union and the top administrative officers of the defense establishment, can hardly be regarded as group interests which sets that group fully apart from the group interests of the top managers of Soviet industry and agriculture.

The possibility that the Soviet officer corps will assume power is institutionally foredoomed by the presence of the Communist Party control on all levels of the Soviet military establishment. The so-called "political guidance officers," as well as party cells on all levels of military formations, provides a sufficient guarantee that civilian control will prevail over military control. As long as the Communist Party remains intact and its political arm in the military forces continues to be present, military rule does not have any chance to supplant civilian rule in the Soviet Union. Thus, the execution of a vast demilitarization program, with a vast reduction of the officer corps, cannot be expected to run into any effective opposition from the Soviet officer corps.

What will be needed, however, in the United States and the countries allied with it, as well as in the Soviet Union and the countries allied with it, is the institution of a vast program of re-education. The history of the respective countries will have to be rewritten. The apotheosis of war will have to be supplanted with an apotheosis of peace. National grandeur to be attained by military victories will have to be replaced in the rewritten history books by national grandeur attained by peaceful attainments.

The hero worship of heads of states as war leaders, and of generals leading armies to victory, will have to be replaced by the exaltation of those who perform deeds of valor in advancing culture, science, and technology in the respective countries. The heroes of the demilitarized societies and economies of the United States and its allies, as well as of the Soviet Union and its allies, are to be epitomized by the hero worship of their respective astronauts. In this kind of hero worship, the conquest of outer space, divested of its military implications, is to symbolize the culmination of the advancement of the horizon of all mankind in its cultural, scientific and technological aspects. It is in that direction that a peaceful world is to be expected to move after the curse of war will have been lifted from mankind.

As far as the United States is concerned, the discontinuation of the cult of violence is to be put on the agenda of a warless world. The public awareness of the permeation of violence, as one of the main features of the American way of life, has come into the open in connection with the recent political assassinations in the United States. The gunning down of political leaders as represented by President John F. Kennedy, as well as the leader of the Negro resistance movement Martin Luther King, and the candidate for the nomination to the office of the President of the United States, Senator Robert F. Kennedy, along with the assassination of a number of civil rights activists, has focused United States public opinion on the issue of violence.

Recently the public awareness of the permeation of violence in the United States has found its expression in the public discussion of weapon licensing legislation pertaining to gun permits for private citizens. The opposition to a strict limitation to the issuing of gun permits and mandatory registration of guns owned by private citizens is led by the United States National Rifle Association, a private group counting many thousands of members. That group had sprung up during the Civil War. The leadership of that group maintains that it carries out a provision of the United States Constitution which guarantees the bearing of arms to all United States citizens. The said constitutional provision can well be regarded as an upshot of the Revolutionary War, which was fought for United States political independence.

In that sense, United States history is not different from the history of most countries, and European countries in particular, which came into being through the application of armed force. As far as the United States is concerned, application of armed force was repeated on several occasions, in United States history. United States authorities came close to applying genocide methods in killing the native population of America, the American Indians. The preservation of the union of the states coupled with the issue of retention versus abolishment of Negro slavery was decided in the United States by force of arms. The enlargement of United States territory was in many instances attained through the application of armed force. The war with Mexico, more than one hundred years ago, constitutes but one of the glaring instances among United States conquests.

The establishment of the United States as a world power, which started with the United States armed conflict with Spain over Spanish colonial possessions, was also brought about through armed force. United States armed intervention in Cuba at the end of the 19th century and the Phillipines, former Spanish colonies, can be cited in the stated context. And, last, but not least, United States armed participation in World War I and World War II, which resulted in establishing the United States as a predominant world power, is to be kept firmly in mind. Such historical events will not easily be erased from the consciousness of the American people.

The difficulty of banning violence as an instrument of national policy will continue to be enhanced by the cult of violence in everyday living in the United States. The cult of violence expressed in innumerable books of high and low calibre has assumed the intensity of a torrent in the United States publishing field. Reference to but just a few recent publications extolling violence can present a telling point. The fanfare about Truman Capote's book *In Cold Blood,* as well as the publication of a volume entitled *The Confessions of Nat Turner* by William Styron, which both became best sellers overnight, shows the wide appeal which the violent solution of problems appears to offer to a great many of the readers of such books in the United States. The portrayal of the solution by way of violence of the issue of individual social and economic maladjustment, as in the case of the book of Capote *In Cold Blood,* and the resolution by way of violence of individual social and economic oppression and exploitation, as in the case of Styron's book, *The Confessions of Nat Turner,* is most likely to be regarded by the vast majority of the readers of those books as the proper way of squaring social and economic accounts.

There should be little doubt, however, too, that the authors of the stated books were betting on public acceptance of violence as a laudable way to solve problems, in making the main characters of the two books appear as spontaneous perpetuators of violence who are to be absolved of any social and economic responsibility for their acts of violence. The main characters of the two stated books were no doubt drawn in a way as to elicit sympathy for their violent acts by the readers. The very writing of these books, as well as many others of the same type of book, can well be considered as an attempt to demonstrate that means of non-violent resolution of conflicts are not available. The writing of those books as well as the writing of other books of the same type is further aimed, it could well be concluded, at cutting short or even avoiding any discussion which could lead to a realization that other than violent means are available to solve social and economic conflicts.

Moreover, more recently, in the wake of the assassinations of Martin Luther King and Robert F. Kennedy, books which extoll violence have come to gain added prominence. Any book which presents violence as an habitual way to solve social and economic conflicts, is sure to be prominently reviewed. Any book on the general theme of violence linked to supposedly innate aggressive instincts of man such as Konrad Lorenz' book entitled *On Aggression* has a good chance to become a best seller.

There is nothing of the soulsearching and groping, nothing of the social consciousness of Dostoyevsky's heroes that is brought out in the fictionalized offerings of Capote and Styron and in the more generalized presentation of Lorenz, the latter aiming at abstractions. Violence is taken for granted by these authors, violence is made to appear ingrained in human nature. Not the perpetuation of violence is considered to be accidental, but the abstentation from the perpetuation of violence is implied to be accidental. One is not acting in accord with human nature, if one abstains from the application of violence, one, conversely, acts fully in accord with human nature if one permits one's violence to erupt. That is the philosophy of violence as a way of life which lurks behind the yarns out of which the stories told by Capote and Styron and the generalizations offered by Lorenz came to be woven.

On a lower literary level, one has to turn one's attention to the flood of mysteries and detective stories which inundate the market of books in the United States. Among the writers of mysteries and detective stories which excell in the extolling of violence, Mickey Spillane has to be prominently mentioned. His books which came to be popular since World War II extoll sadistic traits in which violence comes to be presented in exhibitionist terms for the satisfaction of most perverse tastes. One could summarize the philosophy which underlies Spillane's writing by putting it into the following formula: the more violence, the more confounded violence, – the more perverted pleasure. One could link the approach used by Spillane and many less talented writers of mysteries and detective stories, who subscribe to Spillane's philosophy, to the violence which came to be acceptable in the United States when it became a co-belligerent in World War II. Naturally, the social and economic as well as political issues which underlied the application of violence by United States armed forces and those who were the co-belligerents of the United States in World War II are not mentioned in Spillane's mysteries and detective stories and those of Spillane's ilk of writers. The underlying issues are being suppressed.

The suppression of the underlying political, social and economic issues, which underlied the fighting spirit and morale of the belligerents fighting against Hitler and his armies, could lead but to the putting of the violence of the anti-Hitler armies and the pro-Hitler armies on an identical plane. That such was the premeditated aim of Spillane and of his fellow writers of the Spillane type of writing can hardly be proven. What could be shown, however, is that neither Spillane nor his fellow writers of the Spillane type of writing were not unsympathetic to the above stated conclusion. What could further be demonstrated is that any fighting man's morale among those who fought against Hitler's armies was likely to be lowered by reading Spillane's books and those of his fellow writers of the same type. The cause for which violence was applied by the anti-Hitlerite armies could not in any way be tied to the perpetuation of violence for violence's sake, which glares from the pages of Spillane's books and those of his fellow writers of the same type of writing.

Moreover, it can be well argued, that the demoralizing character of the Spillane type of books is not limited to a low calibre literature. Books by United States writers of a higher calibre, which specifically dealt with war themes related to World War II, show a similar disdain for ascending above the level of war scenes and a philosophizing about war merely as a means of applying brute force. It would be proper to characterize three books with World War II themes with a wide audience, which constitute a comparatively higher level of writing than the Spillane type of books, as presenting war, no matter what kind of war, as a means of working off violence by the combatants. Those three books are, Norman Mailer's *The Naked and the Dead,* Irwin Shaw's *The Young Lions,* and James Jones *From Here to Eternity.* Norman Mailer's volume is a more pretentious book than either the Shaw and the James volume. The pretension of Mailer's book lies in his attempt to reach ideological heights. Those attempts, on the part of Mailer, end, however, in failure, since he is placing anti-fascist and fascist ideas on an undifferentiated ideological plane.

With the re-igniting of the Cold War after World War II, to descend again to a lower type of writing, the mystery and detective story writers started to key their expositions of acts of violence to spy activities. The king of the mystery and detective story writers who rose to fame with his Cold War spy stories was Ian Fleming. As a former member of the British Intelligence Service, he keyed his mysteries and detective stories to the shift of British as well as United States intelligence services to Cold War pursuits. Though Fleming himself was a Britisher, and his publishing career originated in England, he was soon adopted by United States readers who had become even more conditioned by Cold War policies than did the British readers. The conditioning of the readership of mysteries and detective stories in the United States by Cold War policies resulted in Fleming's finding many admirers of his spy stories imagining vicarious participation in the operation of a web of United States intelligence agencies and those of its allies. The phenomenal success of those spy stories in the United States, as far as the number of readers is concerned, cannot, in turn, have failed to make many of those readers conclude that a resolution of Cold War aims could only be attained on a violent plane.

What is further to be realized is that the philosophy behind those spy mysteries and detective stories was, and still does, constitutes in the eyes of their readers, the only feasible contact between the two sides in the Cold War. The above stated contact is made to appear to the readers as but one of deception, cheating and in the end, perpetuation of violence. Both sides, in an effort to outwit each other, are presented by Ian Fleming

175

as operating on a subhuman level. Thus by accepting the notion that the only form of permissible contact between the Western and Eastern powers is one on a subhuman level, the readers of the Fleming type stories, greatly contributed to the perpetuation of the Cold War. One could, conversely, take it as a sign that a thaw has taken place in the conduct of the Cold War, that the popularity of the spy mysteries and detective stories, which had their background in the Cold War, has more recently somewhat declined. A sizeable reduction, and in the end, a cessation of the vogue in writing and reading of spy mysteries and detective stories linked to the Cold War, can only be expected, however, if the Cold War as such will come to be terminated in political terms.

As far as the movies are concerned, the factor of violence has been recently rekindled in the course of the fighting of the war in Vietnam. The movie *The Green Berets,* based on the book of the same title by Robin Moore, is supposed to present the elite of the counter-insurgency troops trained for the war in Vietnam. The insurgency and counter-insurgency issues are not presented either in the book or in the movie in any realistic manner. The presentation in the movie as well as in the book boils down to the contrivance of means of perpetuation of violence as a way of putting the contrived opponent to death. What the conflict is all about, one would not expect to be informed in the movie or in the book, from which it is made. It is a degrading of the whole counter-insurgency fight to a subhuman level, which emerges from the movie as well as from the book.

Last, but not least, it has to be added, violence permeates most of the television programs in the United States. Were one to turn on, in quick succession, one after another of the many television programs offered at any of the television stations in the United States, at various times of the day, one is most likely to see drawn guns either directed at the viewer or directed by one actor at another. Some of the television features which dramatize violence are called Westerns. The Westerns deal with rough manners which were prevalent in the sparsely settled Western frontier towns in the United States in the second half of the 19th century. Those, so-called Westerns, are supposed to have a historical background. In the sense that violence had a place in United States history, the claim that Westerns are realistic portrayals of life in sparsely settled Western parts of the United States cannot be wholly refuted. It should be pointed out, however, that the settlement of the sparsely populated Western parts of the United States was not undertaken in order to make violence an accepted way of life. After all, those who moved West did so in an effort to better themselves economically and, in the process, came to be involved in developing that part of the United States. The flare-up of violent outbreaks and their frequency are to be regarded as but incidental factors. The makers and promoters of the features of the Westerns on the television screen make it appear, however, as if the entire Westward movement of the people of the United States was undertaken, in order to grant the exercise of violence a free play.

Strangely enough those features of the Westerns which are shown on the television screen are generally regarded as features well suited for the edification and entertainment of the young. The simplicistic form of storytelling in those features of the Westerns is not, to be sure, beyond the level of comprehension of the very young. However, the use of the simplicistic framework of the features of the Westerns on the television screen as a means of demonstrating that any conflict can be resolved by violence, and only by violence, constitutes a deliberate misrepresentation and cannot but mislead the young viewers as well as their elders.

Another example of the demonstration of overkill on the television screen can be seen in the making and promoting of adventure stories or science-fiction presentations which are made to culminate in violence. One of such programs called "Batman" has been enjoying the widest popularity among youngsters. The program has been offered in the early evening hours and many parents report that they cannot get their children to go to bed before they have seen the current sequel of the "Batman" feature on the television screen. What is lamentable in regard to those features is that the inquisitiveness and the daring spirit of the young in regard to adventures and mysteries of science is exploited in order to submit the youngsters to the shock of a violent resolution of unsolved problems. The problem or problems in those features are presented to make the actors act out in violence. It is not violence which is treated in those features as an incidental factor, it is the problem or problems which are presented as factors incidental to violence. Violence becomes the necessary ingredient, problem complexes are brought up as disposable schemes. In that kind of context, cause and effect come to be perverted, and the youngsters are left with the taste of sour grapes in their mouths, since they are made to conclude that, short of violence, no adventure and no scientific endeavor could possibly succeed.

Many television features which attract the young and the old are but re-enactments of crimes or blueprints for crimes. Those pure and simple crime stories are but a counterpart of the mysteries and detective stories which are put into print. Since the television medium is less susceptible to argumentation than a book, the crime stories presented on the television screen are much cruder than those appearing in printed form. Yet, even in their crude form, the pure and simple crime features on television are potent enough to condition millions of viewers to the acceptance of violence as an habitual way of life. The reversal of that trend, the disclaiming of violence as a way of life and as a means of artistic expression, will no doubt present formidable difficulties, even if violence were to be outlawed as a means of resolving international conflicts.

As far as the Soviet Union is concerned, the display of violence for the sake of making violence palatable is not considered justifiable in terms of artistic standards by any means of artistic expression in that country. Violence is treated as an anti-social expression of human maladjustment. The probing below the surface of violent expressions of human behavior is considered sine qua non in any form of artistic expression of violence. Crime is considered a social phenomenon, an individual caught in the vise of social maladjustment is not encouraged by any artistic means to seek an easy way out through the committing of an act of violence. If violence is permitted to erupt in any means of artistic expression, it is not made subject to extolling and approval. Hence, violence is not allowed to become a portrayal of a way of life of the people of the Soviet Union.

The only context in which violence is portrayed as a positive factor in the Soviet Union is the violence which is committed in acts of war. In wars fought for the defense of the country, the committing of violence against adversaries and the victimization of humans by the committing of violence against adversaries in warfare, are presented as historically necessary events. In the stated context, violence is placed on a socially elevated plane. Acts of violence against adversaries in a war of the defense of the country are presented as deeds of valor. The submission to the acts of violence in a war of the defense of the country is, in turn, portrayed as a form of supreme human sacrifice.

A war in rightful defense of a country can always be regarded as an effort to stop a war. In the stated regard, a war of the defense of a country is but a war for the attainment of peace. Within that kind of perspective, the committing of violence can be considered as an act aimed at stopping violence. Only in the stated framework is it considered justified for any artistic expression in the Soviet Union to engage in the glorification of war. There will be no need, however, to continue that artistic practice in a warless world.

Chapter 6

ECONOMIC MOBILIZATION FOR PEACE

In the previous chapter, the argument centered on the military aspects of disarmament. In the present chapter, the economic aspects of disarmament will be dealt with. Since the degree of armament in peacetime has reached unprecedented proportions, it stands to reason that the economic aspect of arming in peacetime has also reached unprecedented proportions. It has been stated in this exposition that, in relation to the military aspect of armament in peacetime, a stage of actual military mobilization has been reached. Conversely, the statement can be made here that the economic aspect of armament in peacetime has reached the stage of actual economic mobilization. This general statement, regardless of whether it applies to the military or the economic aspect of actual mobilization, reflects the real state of affairs.

Neither in the strictly military nor in the economic sense can a substantial addition to the present actual stage of mobilization be expected, were a war to break out, in which rockets carrying nuclear bombs were to be used. The military forces, as well as the economic resources which are at present mobilized, will have to serve as "forces in being," should a nuclear war, geared to a saturation attack by nuclear bomb-carrying rockets, take place.

In this context, it might be useful to take a brief retrospective look as to what role the economic aspect of arming played in the past. In such a way we can gain a historical perspective, which, in turn, will make it possible to realize the uniqueness of the economic aspect of mobilization in peacetime with which one is confronted today.

Since the period of the Industrial Revolution, a standing army in peacetime was considered as no more than an auxiliary police force, which was kept for the most part, to assist in the maintenance of the internal social and political order in a given country. The maintenance of such a force, from an economic point of view, was for the most part limited to the operation of an ordinance department. The ordinance department within a given army setup provided the military personnel with weapons. The latter were, for the most part, manufactured in government-owned production installations. As the Industrial Revolution progressed, and heavy equipment, such as iron ships and cannon, were added to the armory of the industrialized nations, the production of these types of equipment was farmed out, i.e., assigned for production to production establishments owned by civilians.

One can well maintain that the expansion of shipbuilding, as well as the growth of the coal and steel industries in the industrialized nations, was greatly assisted by orders coming from the military establishment of the industrialized nations. However, no industrialized nation ever reached a stage in peacetime which could have been called a state of full economic mobilization, in regard to the privately owned shipyards, the coal and steel companies, and the given production establishments which used steel as raw material.

A state of full economic mobilization on a continuous basis, in particular, was not necessary in the age of pre-nuclear weapons, since there was always time to convert to maximum production of military equipment after war had been declared. Unless a war came to an end in a matter of weeks, the full impact of economic mobilization, which came into effect after the outbreak of hostilities, could not make itself felt before several months of the war had elapsed. As far as the United States is concerned, it had not even reached the stage of full economic mobilization when World War I terminated. Full economic mobilization in World War II was reached in the second year of active United States participation. For once, there was no need to depend entirely upon the military forces, military equipment, and mobilized economic resources, to the extent to which those were available at the very beginning of the outbreak of hostilities, since the threat of almost instantaneous annihilation through a thermonuclear exchange was not present.

In the pre-nuclear age, it had also been customary to count upon economic compensation on the part of the vanquished for the damages incurred upon the victor. This kind of economic compensation must be considered as a holdover from the conduct of warfare in the pre-industrial age. In the pre-industrial age, to cite but the Thirty Years War, which took place from 1618-1648, one of the commanders of the contesting forces, Wallenstein, generalized the economic practice of the conduct of pre-industrial warfare, by providing the maxim that war must feed war. What Wallenstein meant is that the fighting forces had to be supplied by the civilian population, and that the civilian population of a territory occupied by a fighting force had to provide that force with provisions and other economic essentials required for the maintenance of troops and the conduct of a war. In addition, the vanquished party was expected to provide what was called a contribution, as a kind of ransom, which was to protect the vanquished party from total destruction by the victorious side.

In a way, the Revolutionary War in the United States under the leadership of General George Washington was partially conducted in its economic aspects, on a pre-industrial basis, as far as the supplying of the troops of the Revolutionary Army is concerned. The billeting of the forces of the Revolutionary Army and the requisitioning of provisions and other items, needed for the conduct of the war, did not differ, in its essential part, from the pattern of the pre-industrial wars which had been conducted in Europe. As far as the issuing of bonds and the contracting of foreign loans is concerned, the Continental Congress and the Revolutionary Army led by Washington adhered to the economic aspects of warfare as they had come into practice during the period of the advanced stage of the Commercial Revolution.

The last time the matter of compensation for damages inflicted upon the territory of the victorious powers has been applied on a grand scale was at the termination of World War I. The misfiring of the grand scheme of so-called reparations can well serve as a patent example that this carry-over of the postmedieval economic practice does not have much of a place under contemporary economic conditions. As the well-known British economist, John Maynard Keynes, had predicted in his book, *Economic Consequences of the Peace,* the transfer of raw material and industrial equipment, as well as of monetary funds from the vanquished country, in this case Germany, to the major victorious powers, in this case England and France, led to economic consequences which were to prove undesirable for the victorious powers.

What actually did happen in the attempt to carry out the economic clauses of the Versailles Treaty was a strengthening of the German economy, accompanied by a comparative weakening of the economies of Britain and France. With funds supplied by United States investors in bonds, German municipal utilities and German corporate industrial plants became modernized, while the industrial plant of Britain and France became relatively obsolescent. The modernization of the German plants made it feasible for the Germans to carry out the part of the reparation clause of the Versailles Treaty which called for the payment of indemnities to Britain and France. This execution of the reparation clauses by Germany was greatly facilitated through the financial assistance of that other major victorious power, the United States. On balance, Germany got more out of the United States investments in Germany than it turned over in reparations to Britain and France. In the end, the United States came to hold the bag. When full scale preparations for World War II and actual outbreak of that war took place, Germany defaulted on all United States loans.

The lesson of the misfiring of the reparation scheme instituted against Germany and in favor of Britain and France after World War I is that national economies are interdependent and that war damages, inflicted upon any country, cannot be undone by penalizing the vanquished country with an unbearable economic burden after the war. This kind of lesson is to be drawn, in the main, with regard to the extent of damage which a war does to an industrialized country, as compared with the extent of reparations which could be extracted from that country.

In wars which antedated World War I in the industrial epoch, cases can be cited when reparation payments or contributions greatly benefited the receiving country, without unduly burdening the country from which payments were extracted. A case in point is the settlement resulting from the Franco-Prussian War of 1871, which required the payment of five billion marks by France to Prussia. The payment of that sum resulted in the intensified industrialization of a unified Germany. Germany more than caught up with the degree of industrialization of France in the period following the Franco-Prussian War. France had been comparatively more industrialized before the start of the Franco-Prussian War, but the rate of its industrialization after that war was slower than that of a unified Germany. What has to be kept in mind, however, is that the Franco-Prussian War lasted only a few weeks and that the devastation of France during those few weeks was minimal. This is the reason why France was able to pay the sum of money, vast for that period, without unduly weakening its internal economic and financial position.

The misfiring, on the other hand, of the execution of the reparation provisions of the Versailles Treaty extended beyond the most immediate ill-effects of those provisions. In its wider impact, the attempt to carry out the reparation provisions of the Versailles Treaty contributed to a structural dislocation of the world economy. That structural dislocation was a result of the overly prolonged, overly devastating war, and of the elimination of one of the major belligerents, Czarist Russia, from the range of the world capitalist economy. That world-wide structural dislocation was an major contributing factor in bringing about an economic depression, unprecedented in depth and duration.

World War I, it should be recalled, was fought for the control of markets on a global scale. The war ended not only in the elimination of the vast market area of Czarist Russia from the Capitalist marketing range, but also in a comparative weakening of the economic and financial position of the major industrialized nations of Europe: France, Britain, and Germany. Though France and Britain were among the victorious powers, the duration and cost of the war reduced their economic and financial strength to a considerable degree. The reparation payments by Germany, financed partially through United States loans, delayed, if they did not arrest, the economic recovery of Britain and France. This is said with particular reference to the lag in the modernization of the plants of those countries. Furthermore, the financial and economic position which the industrialized countries of Europe had

182

maintained in relation to the non-industrialized countries of the world was greatly weakened. The world markets, for whose control World War I had been fought, had greatly shrunk as an indirect result of that war. In its economic aspect, World War I thus had the very opposite effect of what it was intended to attain. In the shrunken post-war capitalist world market, there was less to be shared than before the war.

The telling effect of the world economic debacle in the post World War I period may be seen in the loss of jobs for from twenty-five to thirty percent of the working force in the major Western industrialized countries at the end of the twenties. Production was cut to about fifty percent of the available capacity. Monetary manipulations, such as Britain going off the gold standard and the United States devaluating its dollar, had no appreciable effect in changing the situation. Nor did direct government intervention by way of sponsoring public works, reduce the rate of unemployment and unused productive capacity to any considerable extent.

It was at that time that a new approach to economic analysis was arrived at by John Maynard Keynes, who had warned against the adverse economic effects of the reparation clauses of the Versailles Treaty. The basis for Keynes' General *Theory of Employment, Interest and Money* was the realization that the lag in both investment and consumption could not be overcome unless the government took a direct hand in the operation of the economy. Keynes rightly considered that the end of World War I and its aftermath had brought the end of the *laissez-faire* period in the domestic national economies of the Western world, as well as in international economic relations.

What Keynes did not fully bring out is that the *laissez-faire* proposition had never fully worked. When Adam Smith came to rely on what he considered the "invisible hand", which implied a built-in ability of self-rectification of any economic ills, he was, for the most part, taking a negative stand against the survivals of pre-industrial economic restrictions which were present in his time. He expressed, in particular, opposition to the undue restrictions on the labor market by journeymen associations and on the market of goods by the privileged monopolistic foreign trade companies. In this opposition he was on a strict historical ground.

When Smith went beyond this historical frame of reference and implied that the absence of any government regulations and restrictions would by themselves guarantee continuous economic advancement, he landed in misty metaphysical territory. Smith never undertook to prove the implied postulation of continuous economic advancement and self-rectification of economic maladjustment on the basis of empirical tests. In a sense, Smith projected Leibniz' metaphysical notion of a best possible world into the economic sphere. He presupposed the best possible economic world, geared to technological progress, which is to be realized in the context of the forces of the market. He ignored the warning of Voltaire who, in Smith's lifetime, had ridiculed Leibniz' notion of the best possible world in his book entitled *Candide*. The characters presented by Voltaire in *Candide* are intended to demonstrate that no empirical evidence can ever be made available to show that mankind has been placed in the best possible world. Since there was never any other world, there is no basis for comparison available, Voltaire argued.

The postulation of the best possible world is, therefore, from an empirical point of view, as unsupportable as a postulation of the worst possible world. Conversely, one can say, Smith's notion of the best possible economic world, geared to an unregulated market, is likewise unsupportable on empirical grounds. So, for that matter, would be a postulation of the worst possible economic world, based on an untrammeled application of the *laissez-faire* proposition.

As an ultimate proposition, *laissez faire* constituted a myth in Smith's time, as it does in our time. One may grant that in Smith's time there was a need for a more unrestricted play of the market forces, which had been restrained by pre-industrial and pre-commercial practices. But such an interpretation of the *laissez-faire* proposition makes it an historically relative phenomenon, not an absolute category. Incipient industrialization required relative freedom from governmental and private monopolistic restrictions. This does not apply to the same degree in our time. It is to this relative decrease in the historical relevance of the *laissez-faire* proposition to which Keynes made reference. This is the historical perspective within which Keynes' disqualification of the *laissez-faire* proposition is to be placed.

Keynes did not specify any particular kind of government intervention in elaborating upon his anti-*laissez-faire* stand. He limited himself to arguing in general terms in favor of stimulation of investment and consumption. There is, in particular, no distinction, in Keynes' interventionist approach, between peacetime non-military expenditures and military expenditures. Interventionism, in regard to peacetime pursuits, in terms of stimulation of investment and consumption, fell far short of the mark of attaining any considerable degree of reduction of unused production capacity and an increase in consumer buying power during the great depression of the thirties. Only when non-peacetime economic pursuits, in terms of vast expenditures on arms production was undertaken, did the under-utilization of productive capacity and underemployment cease to be a problem in the Western industrialized countries.

The first country to turn from peacetime interventionist pursuits to military interventionist pursuits was Germany. The government of the

Weimar Republic had tried for years to stem the tide of under-utilization of productive capacity and unemployment by sponsoring public works and indulging in a deflationary monetary and price policy at the same time, but had had little success. It had not occurred to the policy making officials of the Weimar Republic, in particular during the period immediately preceding the ascendency of the Nazi regime, that an increase in productive activity and employment from depression levels cannot be attained by deflationary measures. Deflationary measures have at best a stabilizing effect on production and employment.

By sponsoring public works and pursuing a deflationary monetary and price policy at the same time, the government of the Weimar Republic operated at cross purposes, as far as the matter of overcoming the depression is concerned. But, regardless of the contradictory economic policy pursued by the government of the Weimar Republic, the magnitude of the public works program was entirely inadequate, as compared with the need to stimulate economic activity, in order to make the economy reach non-depression levels. The public works program undertaken by the government of the Weimar Republic during the depression years was no more than a token program.

When the Hitler government took over, it embarked, within a few months after the takeover, on a vast rearmament program. Within but six months, unemployment and the under-utilization of productive capacity practically disappeared from Germany. A vast rearmament program, it must be realized, is actually a program of subsidization of private industry. A rearmament program provides investment funds for the installation of plants to be utilized in the production of war goods. A rearmament program advances money for the purchase of raw materials and the hiring of laborers. A rearmament program guarantees the sale of the produced war goods to the government and thus removes any such war goods from the marketing nexus. A rearmament program further guarantees the war goods production contractor an acceptable profit rate, which is made even more acceptable by liberal depreciation charges and liberal cost allowances. The carrying out of a rearmament program – and this is a crucial point – makes the subsidization of private enterprise a matter-of-fact proposition.

Any commensurate subsidizing of private enterprise geared to the production of war goods is generally accepted, while the subsidizing of private enterprise via peacetime goods is always subject to heated controversies. The transformation of the government of Germany from a democratic to a dictatorial form made any political resistance to the undertaking of a vast rearmament program in the early period of the Hitler regime utterly impossible. This transformation was aimed not only at silencing political resistance towards rearmament inside Germany, it was aimed also to circumvent political opposition abroad by way of official Germany secrecy on matters of its rearmament.

No official pronouncements on the large-scale rearmament program was made by the Hitler government in its early stage, so that wide circles inside and outside Germany did not know about it. Informed persons inside and outside the country had, however, sufficient indication of what was actually taking place. Winston Churchill, at that time a private British citizen, and the present writer published articles on the stated matter in 1934, Churchill in England and this writer in the United States writing in *The New Republic* demonstrated, on the basis of an analysis of disguised German statistics, that a large scale armament program was under way in Germany.

In the United States and England, a vast rearmament did not get under way until the very outbreak of World War II. In the United States, full-scale armament production actually did not take place until 1942, the second year after the United States entered into actual combat in World War II. With large scale armament production in effect in the United States and England and millions of people drafted for military service, an acute labor shortage arose. Women had to leave their homes and take work in war factories to meet the increased demand for labor. Half of the total output in the United States was devoted to war goods, and about the same proportion prevailed in England. France succumbed early in the war; hence war production in that country had no chance to get into high gear. As far as the United States and England are concerned, it should be kept in mind that the depression of the thirties had been cured in the wake of the undertaking of the vast rearmament program.

In the economic sense, the rearmament program had basically the same effect on the economies of the United States and England which it had on the German economy in the early period of the Hitler regime. There was only a difference in the degree to which production facilities and labor were utilized for war production purposes in the United States and England during the actual combat stage of the war, on the one hand, and in Germany during the early period of the Hitler regime, in preparation for the war to come, on the other. The actual degree to which production facilities and labor in Hitler Germany were utilized for war production purposes during the pre-war tenure of office of the Hitler regime, however, is not fully known. What can be said, nonetheless, is that the German pre-World War II experience during the pre-war tenure of office of the Hitler regime shows that large scale war production in peacetime can eliminate large-scale unemployment and unused productive capacity.

In actual war time, a comparatively higher degree of war production and the calling up of millions of men puts a strain on the production facilities and the labor force of an industrialized country. In that sense one can say that in wartime there is an over-utilization present of the production facilities and the labor force of any fully mobilized industrialized country. The United States and England did not have to take recourse to a dictatorial kind of government, as was the case in Nazi Germany, in order to execute a full-scale war production program, because the war was actually in progress at the time when their vast war production program got under way. At that time opposition either in England or the United States to the execution of an all-out war production program could have been expected to be negligible, as it actually was.

Matters of rearmament and its economic effects are somehow different in a country like the Soviet Union, where large-scale private enterprise does not exist. In a planned economy with public ownership of the means of production, as is the case in the Soviet Union, all resources, and in particular production facilities and labor, are allocated on the basis of a government-authorized plan. In a country of that type, under-utilization of productive facilities and labor can take place only if the plan for the utilization of those facilities is not properly carried out. Such an improper way of the execution of the plans for the utilization of productive resources and labor in a country like the Soviet Union can, for instance, take place because of a lack of synchronization. Raw materials and labor may not arrive in time at the production facilities where they are supposed to be used. The production facility, the plant, may not be erected in time, and the raw material and labor will then remain unused, as a result. Those are but a few instances which indicate what kind of under-utilization of production facilities and labor can occur in a country like the Soviet Union. In a thoroughly planned and directed economy, a depression of the kind known in the West is institutionally prevented from taking place.

The aspect of the allocation of production facilities and labor in a planned economy, with public ownership of the means of production, in turn, shapes the market mechanism in such a country. The market mechanism in the capitalist countries of the West, in its turn, is in the main determined by a decision-making of privately owned production facilities. The adequacy of the decision-making by the multitude of private producers, in turn, is put to a test by a multitude of income receivers who are expected to purchase the products. The working of the so-called law of supply and demand, with the owners of private enterprises acting as suppliers and the private income receivers acting as demanders, is a highly fluctuating, and in many cases unpredictable, proposition.

The undependability of the market mechanism in the capitalist countries can be considered as a major contributing factor to the instability of the capitalist economies and their vulnerability to economic downturns. In a country like the Soviet Union, government planners predetermine supply as well as demand. In such a system, there is considerable economic stability and any steep economic downturn is made unfeasible, unless caused by natural disasters, such as drought and social disasters, such a war. It would not be correct, however, to say that the law of supply and demand does not operate at all in a country like the Soviet Union. It does operate, but its operation is, by and large, controlled. In the Western countries, where private ownership of the means of production and private decision-making prevails, the working of the law of supply and demand is largely uncontrolled.

In a country like the Soviet Union the shift from peacetime to wartime production has to be planned in the same way as the operation of peacetime production. The turning from the production of peacetime goods to the production of wartime goods is, therefore, in a country like the Soviet Union, a means of a planned reallocation of resources from one type of production to another. It is not, as in the case in the West, a matter of turning unused resources into used resources. Reference is made here to the change from the depression levels of production in the pre-World War II period to the non-depression level of production in the West during World War II.

It should be granted that, in the end, the turning of facilities and labor from employment in the production of peacetime goods to the production of war goods constitutes a deprivation of the sector of peacetime goods production for the benefit of wartime goods production. This happens, regardless of whether the production system is publicly or privately owned. The difference is seen in the way in which the economic benefits accrue. In privately owned productive undertakings, the economic benefits accrue to the private undertaking, while in the publicly-owned undertakings, the economic gains accrue to the publicly-owned undertakings. This is so, regardless of whether the production of peacetime goods or wartime goods is involved.

It so happens that in the West, the production of peacetime goods did not promise adequate economic benefits from a point of view of the private owners of those undertakings and that, therefore, there was under-utilization of productive capacity and unemployment. In turning from the production of peacetime goods to the production of wartime goods, the governments of the West came to underwrite the economic benefits, in terms of profits, for the privately-owned undertakings. The turning from peacetime production to wartime production in a country like the Soviet Union, where production facilities are publicly owned, is not accomplished by way of transformation of economically unprofitable undertakings into economically profitable undertakings, as was the case in the West. Full production and employment is underwritten in the Soviet Union for both peace goods as well as war goods production and their related employment.

In the pre-war depression stage, two major Western countries, the United States and England, tried public works projects to a wholly insufficient degree. It is still a matter of dispute in the United States whether government spending on public works does much to get a country out of a depression. Some economic conservatives in the United States point to the negligible effect which the public works program had on lessening the depression in the Franklin D. Roosevelt pre-World War II period. This argument of the economic conservatives is then extended to make it appear that the whole Keynesian proposition of government spending as a way to bring about a high degree of employment has allegedly proven to be ineffectual. Against the economic conservatives' attack on public works and the role they play in the Keynesian scheme, one has to point out that what was wrong with the public works program in the Franklin D. Roosevelt pre-World War II period is that there were not enough of those public works at that time.

Moreover, one of the main reasons why there were not enough public works in the post-World War I part of the Franklin D. Roosevelt era lies in the political difficulty to make enough money available for public works. Not enough money was made available for public works during the pre-war Franklin D. Roosevelt period, because economic conservatives of the same kind as the ones who attack the idea of public works in the United States today were busy in Franklin D. Roosevelt's time seeking to prevent and obstruct the financing of public works. Those very economic conservatives, and their followers among the United States populace, were making it politically unfeasible for the Roosevelt administration to get larger appropriations for public works than the few billions which had been made available for such purposes. Had the United States Government suggested that money be given to subsidize the operation of privately owned production facilities, one can be sure the economic conservatives of the pre-World War II Roosevelt period would not have been such sticklers for the economic orthodoxy of balanced budgets and hard currency as they professed to be at that time.

The monetary, financial and price policy of the governments of the United States and Great Britain were contradictory in the depression period preceding World War II. Outwardly, the governments of the United States and Great Britain pursued a policy of monetary and financial stabilization. The devaluation of the dollar in the United States and the going off the gold standard in Britain were, in their turn, bound to have inflationary effects. It should be kept in mind that any depression has by itself a deflationary effect. Any added deflationary effect, deliberately pursued by the government of a country where a depression is in effect, can, at best, stablilize the depression. The establishment of the National Recovery Administration in the United States, which constitued a nationwide price fixing measure, constituted but an additional aspect of the economic stabilization of the depression, though it was aimed at bringing about recovery.

All in all, the depression in the United States and England was not over until World War II was well under way. At the height of World War II production of war goods amounted to about half of the total output of each of the two countries. The populace of both, the United States and Britain, remained aware of the fact that it was only production of war goods on a gigantic scale which had made an end of under-utilization of productive facilities and large-scale unemployment. In Britain, the fear of the populace that a termination of hostilities of World War II might result in another depression was a major contributing factor in bringing the Labor Party into power in the last year of World War II. The prospect of the nationalization of major industries offered to many British electors the hope that the nationalized factories could be kept open, so as to guarantee full employment in those industries. In the United States, the re-election of Franklin D. Roosevelt for the fourth term, a year before the termination of hostilities of World War II, was in no small measure due to the expectation of the populace of the United States that, in case the hostilities should be terminated, the Roosevelt administration more than any other, would be more concerned with preventing under-utilization of productive facilities and large-scale unemployment.

What actually saved the situation, as far as the non-recurrence of large scale under-utilization of productive facilities and manpower in the post-World War II period in the United States and Britain is concerned, was the re-institution of the Cold War with the Soviet Union, which replaced the hot war with the Axis powers. Production of war goods and employment in war industries did not reach the proportion of war goods production and employment which it had reached during World War II. Instead of fifty percent of total production and employment allocated to the production of war goods, as was the case during the period of World War II, the production of war goods after World War II, in the period of the reinstituted Cold War reached about ten to twelve percent of total production and employment. The production of war goods thus was not far-reaching enough to prevent economic downturns in the post-World War II period in the United States and Great Britain. Economic downturns occurred several times during the post-war period in both of those countries. However, it can be stated with certainty that the downturn would have been much sharper without the production of war goods and the employment it created. The employment in the production of war goods in the United States, with the inclusion of drafted army personnel, can be put at ten to twelve million people.

Were this kind of employment non-existent, the economic downturns which took place in the United States after the end of World War II would have resulted in a much larger unemployment. Instead of the roughly six-seven million people who were out of jobs during the economic downturns in the post-World War II period in the United States, at least sixteen-nineteen million people may be expected to have been out of jobs during the economic downturns of the post-World War II period in the United States. By bringing a negative economic multiplier to bear, unemployment could have reached even higher levels and gone up to twenty-twenty-five to thirty million people. In that case, the proportion of people out of work in relation to people at work would have been about as high as it was during the depression of the thirties.

Production of war goods and employment in war goods production continues to serve as a cushion in the economic ups and downs of the economy of the United States and Great Britain. The long-term duration of this kind of production and employment has, so to speak, institutionalized it. To many people, whether directly engaged in war goods production, either as employees or employers, or not directly involved in war production and employment, the cessation of the production of war goods appears to have become unthinkable. To gain acceptance for even the possibility that war goods production and employment might have to be curtailed, should disarmament take place, it is necessary to bring more clarity into the economic aspects of war goods production and the opportunities which could be opened for its replacement.

First, one has to dispose of two arguments *in extremis*. One line of argument maintains that there is no way of doing away with war production and employment as a means of buttressing the economy, no matter whether or not such war production and employment is needed politically. The other line of argument maintains that war goods production and employment really is not essential for the operation of a capitalist economy and can be abandoned at any time, if the political circumstances permit it, without any deep-seated ill effects for the economy.

Both lines of argument are fallacious. The first line of argument is fallacious because ways are open to replace the range of production and employment which is now maintained through war production orders. The second line of argument is fallacious, because its implication, that the economy will readjust itself automatically, should war goods production and employment be abandoned, is based on unrealistic expectations. What must be stressed in the above stated context is that the economy could readjust itself, should war production and employment be abandoned, but not in a *laissez-faire* manner.

At this point, some basic reconsideration of economic theory must be brought into the picture. The reconsideration offered here is more drastic than the factors which have been illumined by Keynes. It appears to this writer that there was hardly any time in the history of the Western industrialized countries when there was a sustained full utilization of production facilities, coupled with full employment, except in times when large-scale transfers of public wealth to private ownership were effected. Within the framework of that kind of interpretation, the transfer of public funds to private enterprise, in preparation for war, or in the actual conduct of war, constitutes but one specific case. This writer has heard the noted American historian, the late Charles Beard, say shortly before World War II, that the United States knew prosperity only in preparation for war or in the conduct of wars, and in the immediate aftermath of wars.

In the comprehension of this writer, Charler Beard's statement is too narrow. Other forms of subsidized private production and employment have existed in the economic history of the United States. The turning of publicly-owned land into privately-owned land in the United States during the entire nineteenth century sustained United States agriculture financially, as well as other sectors of the United States economy, for extended periods of time. The turning of publicly-owned land over to the privately-owned railroads provided the basis for the sustained economic activity of the railroad industry for extended periods of time.

The turning of public funds over to private interests, in preparation for war, or in the actual conduct of war, appears to have been effective in bringing about the utilization of technological advances on a mass production basis. To take but a few spectacular instances, the pouring of public funds into production of tanks during World War I is closely related to the realization of mass production of automobiles in the post-World War I period. In the technological sense, there is very little difference between the production of a tank and the production of a truck or a passenger automobile. The boost for the mass production of automobiles came from the experience gained in the mass production of tanks. What added to the realization of the mass production of automobiles was the shifting of the financial burden by way of installment sales to the public at large. The public at large, in this instance, replaced the public as represented by the government.

While installment sales freed the mass production of automobiles from the necessity for continuous support from public funds, such was not the case in relation to the airplanes. The mass production of airplanes was brought about most directly through government orders for war planes in the period following World War I, and the more so since World War II and its aftermath. The government-ordered war planes were, of course, paid out of government funds and continue to be paid for out of government funds at the present time. Production of civilian airplanes constitutes but a small part of total airplane production. Airplane factories would be threatened with bankruptcy, were the government-financed production of war planes to stop or be greatly reduced.

What had been, and still is taking place with regard to airplanes, takes place, too, at present in regard to the development of the mass production of electronic equipment which is geared to defense purposes. The whole electronic industry in the United States on the present scale would not be here were it not for government orders and financing. Were those government orders and financing to cease, the electronic industry would shrink by a very considerable proportion.

What the three stated examples of the automobile, airplane and electronics industries signify, is that technological innovations, in order to get into mass production, require in their initial phases, financing by the government. In a sense, the railroads, too, which were a technological innovation at the time they were built, were made possible through public grants. In the United States those grants were not, however, for the most part, grants of money, but of land. The demonstration, undertaken here, that the initiation of mass production of important technological innovations requires government subsidies in a direct or indirect form, lends an ominous feature as far as the future economic development of the United States and other technologically advanced Western countries is concerned.

If direct or indirect subsidies by government are needed to initiate and maintain the mass production of technological innovations, the Western governments cannot be expected to be out of the picture of stimulating the technological advances of mass production, even if the production of war goods were to cease entirely. The reintroduction of a bill by the Nixon Administration, to grant tax reductions to firms which undertake the modernization of plants, testifies to the realization of the existence of this problem by United States officials. Whether mere tax credit alone will suffice to stimulate technological advancement on a mass production basis remains to be seen. It may be necessary to make government funds available to spurt technological advancement in privately-owned production undertakings.

In this context, one may well ask why government funds could not be used to establish government owned industries in which technological innovations will be put on a mass production basis. This could be done, of course, but it would involve the opting of the populace of the United States for socialism instead of for capitalism. As long as such opting does not take place, private enterprise, so long as it offers the prospect of efficient and profitable operation, will continue to have a claim on direct or indirect subsidies in the United States. Were this claim on government subsidies by private enterprise engaged in initiating and maintaining mass production geared to technological innovations to be institutionalized in the production of peacetime goods, it would lead to a fundamental reappraisal of the correlation of public and private revenue.

It had been the contention of the inaugurator of *laissez-faire* Political Economy in the industrial setup, Adam Smith, that public revenue, i.e., taxes, are collected in order to pay government officials, who are, in turn, to be pledged to steer clear of interference in the affair of business. That proposition was, by and large, adhered to in peacetime in most capitalist countries up to the most recent past, at least in theory. Were public funds to be used to stimulate the operation of private industrial undertakings in peacetime, the line dividing public from private revenue would have to be redrawn, not only as far as the practice is concerned, but also as to theory. The line of division between public and private revenue would, in the case of the subsidized enterprise, have to be drawn between the amount of taxes paid by the enterprise and the amount of tax money received directly or indirectly by that enterprise in terms of subsidies. As far as the social content is concerned, all subsidized enterprises must become mixed enterprises, because their operation will be made possible by mixing public with private funds. That some government control of the operation of subsidized industries will have to be instituted, stands to reason.

Government assistance in furthering technological innovations in industry, coupled with such assistance as would be required to further the distribution of technologically advanced products, could well prove to be an effective anti-depression measure. This form of government assistance to a technologically advancing industry could well become a potent built-in factor in reducing the steepness of economic downturns. If that were to be the case, the subsidization of a technologically advancing peacetime industry could be made to play the same role with regard to lessening the degrees of economic downturns, as is the case at present in regard to the government subsidization of the production of war goods.

The other side of the coin is presented in the case of the technologically and economically declining industries. The railroads, when they were built, it should be realized in the above stated connection, heralded a technological and economic advance in the modernization of the transportation system in the industrialized countries. In the course of the development of other mechanized transportation media, such as automobiles and airplanes, the railroads have become an ailing industry. In the United States, the railroads are financially unable to lay aside funds not only for modernization of equipment, but even for proper maintenance. What keeps the railroads in the United States from total bankruptcy is the transportation of defense freight and military personnel for which the railroads are reimbursed by the government.

Yet, even with that indirect subsidy, the United States railroads are becoming increasingly dependent on government funds in terms of long-term government loans for their continuous operation. The time will come when the United States taxpayers will increasingly ask the question, to what extent the taxes they pay are to be used for the continued operation of an apparently unprofitable line of privately-owned industry. Such questions on the part of the United States taxpayer could well result in shaping of public opinion in favor of government ownership and operation of the railroads. That such questioning had already begun is indicated by the statement of an influential member of the United States Congress. That Representative has recently expressed the opinion that if the United States continues the financial support of privately operated railroads on an ever-increasing scale, the question of transforming the privately-owned railroads into public ownership will have to be posed. The turning a few years ago of the Long Island Railroad in New York State from private to public ownership sets a precedent. The bankruptcy in 1970 of one of the largest railroads networks in the United States, the Pennsylvania Railroad, can well serve as a warning signal of what lies in store for other privately owned railroads.

Were United States public opinion to be shaped in the direction of favoring a government takeover of the railroads, it would mean that the United States taxpayer would have opted for socialism instead of capitalism. It would signify an opting for socialism, in specific cases when a line of industry could not be operated privately on a profit-making basis. Were public opinion to shape that way, one would be able to witness a division of the United States economy between technologically advancing profit-making undertakings, which were to be continued to be operated privately and controlled by the government, and technologically lagging profitless undertakings, which were to be owned and operated by the United States federal, state and municipal government agencies.

In Britain, war goods production and employment constitute proportionally about the same percentage of British total industrial output and employment as in the United States. The cessation of war goods production and employment, should a comprehensive disarmament agreement be reached, would create in Britain economic problems similar to those which could be expected in the United States in that case. The antidotes against the recurrence of deep-seated depressions could be the same as the ones suggested here for the United States. Direct and indirect financial support would be needed for the initiation and operation of technologically advancing industries on a profitable basis. The technologically advancing industries will in such case continue to be operated as privately-owned industries, but would, as far as the social aspect and economic substance are concerned, become mixed entities. Technologically lagging, profitless industries would, in turn, be slated for transformation to public ownership.

There are some distinctions between the prospects for the realization of such a program in Great Britain and the possibility of the realization of such a program in the United States. The range of taxation which would be necessary in Great Britain in order to provide direct or indirect financial support by the government for the initiation and operation of technologically advancing industries will constitute a relatively greater strain upon the average British taxpayer, since the average income in Britain is about half that in the United States. The subsidy program in Britain might, therefore, have to be carried out on a more curtailed basis. The proposal of practically profitless industries to be operated by the government, in turn, can be expected to make greater headway in England than in the United States. In the United States, greater difficulty will be encountered than in England to get public support for transformation into public ownership of profitless and technologically lagging industries.

In the United States, the question of public ownership of industries has, in the present generation, been somewhat sidetracked, due, in large part, to the practice of government financing of war and defense production. In nineteenth century America and in the first decade of the twentieth century, there appears to have been more popular support in the United States for government ownership of productive economic undertakings, than is the case at present. The idea of public ownership of productive economic undertakings has never reached, however, the extent of public support in the United States, which it had and still has in England and some other Western industrialized countries. The reason for this disparity lies mainly in the fact that enormous natural resources which were turned over to private exploitation, such as land, forests, oil, and minerals, coupled with the enormous absorption capacity of the internal United States market, made the operation of private economic undertakings in the United States more profitable for an extended period of time than in Western Europe. This made the factor of transformation of privately-owned productive properties into publicly-owned productive properties in the United States a more remote proposition than is the case in Great Britain.

There are, however, publicly-owned economic undertakings in the United States. The United States Post Office has since the founding of the United States republic been a publicly-owned economic undertaking. It continues to be publicly-owned in spite of its recently changed managerial setup. The Tennessee Valley Authority is a publicly-owned and operated economic undertaking. The reason why it was established in the period of the administration of Franklin D. Roosevelt was the absence of a privately-owned generating station in the Tennessee Valley. Privately-owned utilities considered it profitless to build and operate a generating station in the Tennessee Valley. The establishment of a publicly-owned generating station in Tennessee is to some extent in line with the suggestion made here, to put publicly-owned undertakings in place of profitless private undertakings. Similar is the case of public ownership of the New York City subways. These were turned from private to public ownership because private ownership and operation became profitless.

The Atomic Energy Commission, furthermore, is a publicly-owned and operated undertaking in the United States. It owns all atomic energy patents, the utilization of which it offers, in some cases, to lease to private operators. The reason why the Atomic Energy Commission was established as a publicly-owned undertaking was partly due to the fact that private operators did not consider, and still do not consider, the atomic energy field sufficiently profitable in order to risk any substantial investment. The other reason for the establishment of the Atomic Energy Commission as a publicly-owned economic undertaking was the necessity to keep the effectuation and utilization of atomic energy secret, in the interest of national security.

In connection with the suggested government subsidization of technologically advancing industries, the question must be asked how one determines what industries are technologically and economically promising. How does one determine the priority which one technologically and economically promising industry is to be accorded over another? Furthermore, how is one to determine how much money should be apportioned for one or another industry, and at what specific time? To determine all that, it would be necessary to establish a National Development Board as an agency to determine the technological and economic prospects of new industries and the amount of fiscal aid they are to receive at given periods of time. The same national development agency would have to be vested with authority to look into the sphere of technologically and economically lagging industries. With regard to such industries, the National Development Board would have to be authorized to make decisions, as to how much money is to be provided for the continuous operations of technologically lagging and economically deficient industries and for how long. Moreover, the National Development Board would have to be given the authority to decide at what point a technologically lagging and economically deficient industry is to be turned from private to public ownership.

The term "technologically lagging", in the sense in which it is here used, refers to the overall technological lag of a given industry, not a technological lag with regard to some specific technological device which could be introduced in a given industry. To state an example, let us take railroad transportation. Railroads have become a technologically lagging industry due to advancing technology in other spheres of transportation. Other mechanized means of transportation, such as automobiles and airplanes have been established. These alternate mechanized means of transportation operate in competition with the railroads and continuously reduce their total passenger and freight loads. By comparison, the passenger and freight load of the automobiles and airplanes is continuously increasing.

It should be granted that many new technological devices have been, and will continue to be introduced, in railroad transportation. The introduction of those devices could not be expected, however, to return to the railroads the passenger and freight load, which they continue to lose to other, more modern means of transportation. It can even be ascertained that the introduction of new technological devices in the operation of the railroads will, as time goes on, become more and more difficult if not impossible, from a financial point of view, were the railroads to continue to be privately owned. The transfer of the railroads from private to public ownership would, in turn, make it feasible to introduce some technological innovations which, for lack of available funds, could not be introduced under private ownership.

A development of the stated kind took place when the British railroads were turned from private to public ownership after World War II. Under private ownership, the operation of the railroads became so unprofitable in England that no money could be made available for modernization purposes. The privately-owned British railroads did not even earn enough to pay for current operating expenses. Only when the railroads became publicly owned did it become financially feasible to introduce Diesel locomotives. The British railroads are on the way of regaining financial potency since, due to public ownership, it became possible to reroute traffic with a view of maximum utilization of the whole national railroad network. The most inefficient and unprofitable railroad connections are being discontinued in the rerouting scheme. This is one particular advantage which public ownership on a national scale offers, as compared with private ownership. The recently undertaken rescheduling of privately owned United States railroads under the direction of a United States government agency is no match to what can be undertaken under public ownership.

Under public ownership on a national scale, the most inefficient and unprofitable undertakings can be shut down on short notice, as part of a national plan of operation. Under private ownership, the elimination of the least efficient and least profitable undertakings is a long, drawn out matter, which proceeds in a haphazard way. The presence of inefficient and unprofitable undertakings in a privately-owned industry reduces the average efficiency and the average profit rate of that industry on a national scale. Such was the case when the British railroads were privately owned. The deliberate elimination of the least efficient and least profitable undertakings in an industry under public ownership increases, in turn, the average efficiency and the average profit rate of a given industry. Such was the case when the British railroads were turned from private to public ownership.

Such was also the case, one should not forget, when other British industries were turned from private to public ownership. In addition to the railroads, the coal industry and the utilities were turned into publicly owned undertakings in Britain, because those industries, too, were found to be technologically lagging and practically profitless. In the case of the coal pits, as well as of the utilities, it was cut-throat competition which prevented technological and financial improvement. In the case of utilities, cut-throat competition resulted in price wars.

As a result of nationalization, the most inefficient and profitless undertakings in the nationalized coal and utilities industries were eliminated, as was the case with the nationalized railroads. With the determination of the rate of utilization of productive capacity and prices put under effective control by the public agencies, which assumed responsibility for the operation of the publicly-owned coal and utilities industries, efficiency and profits increased in both those industries.

There are other industries in Great Britain, such as the telephone and telegraph as well as ship building, which were established as publicly-owned undertakings. Private capital was not forthcoming to a sufficient extent to have those industries established as privately-owned undertakings though they were in the forefront of technological development at the time they were established. Such was in particular the case when the telephone and telegraph were introduced in Great Britain as publicly-owned communication media. The practice of establishing as publicly-owned those industries which are in the forefront of technological development continues in present-day England. The radio and televison communication system are among the industries which are in the forefront of technological development and which in out time have been established as publicly-owned industries in England.

Unlike Britain, the United States has not yet developed a politically oriented public consciousness in regard to matters of private and public ownership of economic undertakings. A most spectacular case of United States public innocence, so to speak, in regard to public and private ownership of economic undertakings took place comparatively recently. The case in point is the lack of public response to the legislation which authorized the transfer of the publicly developed and owned global satellites communication system to private ownership. A little band of four United States Senators, led by the then Senator Wayne Morse from Oregon, led a lonely battle to retain the right of public ownership of this system. There was hardly any public reaction to the filibuster which the little band of public-spirited Senators conducted in a vain attempt to forestall the transfer of the government owned global communication satellite system to private ownership and operation. The public at large appears to have been unaware that there was any issue at all involved in this matter.

Politics in the United States continues to be largely middle-class politics. Both the affluent and the not so affluent subscribe to the middle-class line in politics. Hardly any political division exists between the owners and operators of business, large or small, and between the people working for somebody for comparatively high or low wages. The comparative rapidity of the economic advancement of the United States, and the range of that advancement from which most sections of the United States population benefited, must be considered as the main reason for the lack of political differentiation in the United States.

It is quite possible that a further prolongation of the deep-seated depression of the thirties could have brought a political realignment to the United States. In it, politically oriented groups of business and business-minded people would have found themselves confronted by politically oriented groups of workers. The advent of World War II and the comparative prosperity, which the production of war goods during the war and its aftermath, the Cold War, brought about, muted existing social antagonism. The accentuation of social antagonisms, had the stated countering factors not been present, could have led to the establishment of a Labor Party in the United States, with mass union support, as opposed to a Non-Labor Party, with mass support from owners and operators of large and small scale business undertakings.

Whether such a political realignment could be obtained in the foreseeable future is difficult to tell. It is even more difficult to foretell whether the kind of transition from an economy geared to war goods production and employment to an economy wholly geared to the production of peacetime goods, in terms suggested in this essay, could be attained without a fundamental political realignment taking effect.

What one can predict, however, is that if a transfer of the economy geared to war goods production, to an economy fully geared to peacetime production is carried out, with sole reliance on an illusory self-adjustment of the economy, grave economic consequences are likely to result. The likelihood of the occurrence of a deep-seated depression cannot be ruled out in such a case – a depression more deep-seated than the one which occurred in the thirties. Under the impact of that kind of an economic disaster, a political realignment in terms of the formation of a Labor Party and a Non-Labor Businessmen's Party could conceivably take place. It is to be feared, however, that before such a democratic political realignment can ever get underway in the United States, a non-democratic form of political control of the United States economy will set in. That will then be the United States form of fascism.

It could be argued that such non-democratic political developments could also possibly take place in the United States if the economy continued to be geared to the production of war goods for an indefinite period of time. A nucleus of political non-democratic forces exists at present in the United States and can be expected to exist also in the future. That non-democratic political nucleus will most likely get a much better chance to grow and gain controlling political influence at the time when war goods production in the economy will come to an end in the wake of a disarmament agreement. In that case, mass unemployment and mass privation would present a much more fertile soil for the growth of a mass undemocratic political sentiment than is the case at the time when production of war goods constitutes a cushion against a deep-seated and prolonged depression. The way to prevent a steep economic downturn, with its attendant political consequences, is to provide for the smooth carry-over from the economy geared to war goods production to the economy geared fully to production of peacetime goods. The way to effect that kind of relatively painless transformation, from an economic point of view, is to embark on the kind of economic policy which has been outlined in this exposition.

Whether a politically oriented public consciousness in regard to matters of public and private ownership and operation of economic undertakings can be developed, in the absence of the kind of democratic political realignment which is suggested by this writer, one cannot be sure. For those Americans who do realize the urgency of the problem, it will be worth trying. The people of the United States could be aroused, if it were made clear to them what the continuous prevalence of political innocence in regard to matters of public and private ownership of economic undertakings would entail by way of an economic as well as a political breakdown which could ensue in the wake of massive disarmament.

The democratic character of the American economy in its political aspect could be significantly strengthened, if an economic policy geared to the interests of the private owners of economic undertakings were to be countered by an economic policy geared to the interests of the non-owners, the people who work for salaries and wages. Such polarization of the social sub-structure of the economic policy could be assisted by having the suggested National Economic Development Board Supplemented by a National Income Board. It would be up to such United States National Income Board to correlate propertied and non-propertied income. It would, furthermore, be up to the National Income Board to determine policies to be pursued in collective bargaining. Moreover, it would be up to this board to determine the line of division between an earned wage and a paid-out wage. The National Income Board would also set policy in regard to unemployment insurance, accident and health insurance, old age pensions, and public relief. It would further be up to the National Income Board to decide manpower policy, which includes setting educational standards for jobs and the channeling of available manpower into available positions. Within the stated institutional framework, the execution of a manpower program would make it possible for the National Income Board to set up an employment policy as well as a retirement policy.

It might be of interest to note that both types of agencies suggested here for the United States the National Economic Development Board and the National Income Board had been set up some years ago by the conservative government of England. The two boards had been continued in operation by the Labor Government. The two types of boards set up in England have, however, no more than advisory functions. Unlike those British prototypes, the boards suggested here for institution in the United States would make policy and have the administrative power to put the policies into effect. The two types of boards which have been set up in Britain have paid but lip service to the idea of government direction of national economic development and a national income division policy. The boards suggested for institution in the United States are, by contrast, to provide for an effective direction of the American economy.

What is needed, in case a widespread disarmament agreement takes effect, is not economic demobilization, followed by an attitude of "everybody for himself and the devil takes the hindmost." A return to a "do nothing" policy by the government would lead only to economic stagnation which might end in disaster. What is required is an orderly demobilization of the economy geared to the production of war goods, to be followed by an orderly remobilization of the economy geared to the production of peacetime goods.

A number of trained and untrained economists in the United States think that spending for the production of war goods and its impact on economy are merely incidental. Those people are prepared to argue that the elimination of the war goods production can be disregarded, as far as the functioning of the economy is concerned, if and when production of war goods can be abandoned, in the wake of a widerange disarmament agreement. Those economists should be reminded, however, of the magnitude of the spending for war goods production in the United States. The former United States President, General of the Army Dwight D. Eisenhower, in his farewell address as United States President, reminded the American people that the money spent on war goods production since the beginning of the fifties amounts yearly to more than the total profits of all the United States business enterprises. To cite another figure, the money spent yearly on war goods production in the fifties amounted to more than the total amount of money which was yearly spent on the expansion of United States industry. Or, to put the latter factor in a different form, the money spent yearly for production of war goods in the United States amounted to more than the yearly amount of net capital formation in the United States. Net capital formation, one should remember, constitutes the sinew of economic growth.

The elimination of such vast spending cannot but have a most devastating effect on the economic well being of the people of the United States, if it is not parried by concerted government-directed action. The institution of the counter measures suggested here can be expected to neutralize the economic shock, which economic demobilization is likely to bring about. What will be needed in the United States and other Western nations, in the wake of a comprehensive disarmament, is not just economic demobilization. In place of economic mobilization geared to the production of war goods, economic remobilization, geared to the production of peacetime goods, will have to be effected. The institutional change involved in this connection will signify a turn from the "invisible hand" of *laissez-faire* economics to the visible hand of a directed managerial economy.

A number of trained and untrained economists, it should be admitted, do not put their sole reliance on the allegedly self-regulative powers of the economy. Those economists bring up the matter of public works as a means of countering the economic downturn which they expect in the wake of a comprehensive disarmament agreement. The execution of such a program no doubt has some merit. Public works, such as the building of roads, houses, schools, and hospitals, are likely to take some of the slack off an economic depression. The impact of the production aspect of public works can be compared with the impact of the production aspect of armaments. Both public works and the manufacture of armaments produce goods which do not have to enter the market. In that sense, public works production is preferable to production of goods which have to be disposed on the market. Public works production is bound to remain, however, peripheral as far as total national production is concerned.

Public works production, it should be realized, is, by its very nature, production effected by way of utilization of derivative social capital. This derivative social capital owes its very existence to the productive social capital employed in non-public works production. Productive social capital is, in its turn, embodied in plants producing goods to be acquired by individual income receivers. The extent of derivative social capital depends upon the extent of non-derivative productive social capital. If non-derivative productive social capital is not formed, or is formed to an inadequate degree, derivative social capital also cannot be formed or cannot be formed to any adequate degree.

The subsidization, direct or indirect, of technologically advancing industries, which is suggested in this exposition would guarantee a proper degree of formation of non-derivative productive capital. This, in turn, could serve as a basis for a proper degree of utilization of derivative social capital in public works operation. The maintenance of a proper correlation between non-derivative and derivative social capital could permit public works to be instituted, not only as emergency measures, but on a permanent basis. Such development would be in line with Kenneth Galbraith's advocacy of an increase of the role of social capital, which constitutes the main thesis of his widely read book, *The Affluent Society*.

As far as the Soviet Union is concerned, the impact of economic demobilization will, of necessity, lead to social and economic changes in that country, too. Shifting of production from the military to the non-military sphere would be the immediate impact of large-scale economic demobilization. Acceleration of technological progress, in the production process, such as intensification of the drive to install automated machinery, could as well be anticipated. Increased mechanization of agriculture could also be expected to take place at the same time. Furthermore, a shift from the overemphasis on the production of producers' goods to the production of consumers' goods could well be expected to follow. A redistribution of income, with emphasis on increases of the lower income levels, would be in line with the changes suggested above. Increase in pensions would, in turn, be in line. Extension of existing social services, such as free medical, maternal, and child care could, and probably would, also take place. Introduction of hitherto non-existing free social services, such as free intra-urban transportation and free water and electricity in use in homes could be expected too.

As far as structural institutional changes are concerned, the motivating force which would be present in the United States cannot be expected to be present in the Soviet Union. In an economy fully planned there are no obstacles in the way of a deliberate shift of material resources and manpower from one sector to another. Thus, the threat of an economic depression which one can expect in the United States as a result of the discontinuation of large scale production of war goods cannot be expected in the Soviet Union. The elimination of the threat of an economic depression thus cannot be regarded as a factor which is to guide economic mobilization for peace in the Soviet system of the national economy.

Chapter 7

INTERNATIONAL ECONOMIC COOPERATION

This chapter will consider the correlation of the economic policies of the United States and of the Soviet Union in the wake of the demilitarization of their economies with those of their respective allies. To be meaningful, such a reprojection of the correlation of the economic policies of the United States and the Soviet Union must be placed in a historical perspective. In bringing in the historical perspective, one must make reference to the world economy as it has existed in the past and to the world economy as it exists at present.

When the Commercial Revolution came into its own in the sixteenth century, the world capitalist economic order was established. It became an order in which economic domination was matched by economic subjugation. The commercially advanced countries established themselves as the dominating countries. The countries that were not commercially advanced had to put up with economic subjugation by the commercially advanced countries. Thus was formed the world economic system, in which the countries that were not commercially advanced were assigned the role of colonies. The economies of the colonies were expected to serve the economic interests of the mother country. Thus enrichment, i.e. capital accumulation in the mother countries, was accomplished at the cost of capital decumulation in the colonies, i.e., impoverishment of the colonies.

The policy aimed at enriching the mother country at the cost of impoverising the colonies, by way of legal restrictions, was a latter-day policy, as far as the Commercial Revolution is concerned. During the early period of the Commercial Revolution, traders from the commercially-advanced countries engaged merely in raids. In such raids, which can be termed as hit-and-run undertakings, the traders tried to get hold of as many wares as possible, preferably precious metals, and at best gave trinklets in return. Those piratic expeditions of the fifteenth and sixteenth centuries were not conducted with a view towards establishing permanent settlements in the raided countries. The piratic expeditions constituted what one can call the pre-colonial stage of the Commercial Revoluion.

The colonial stage, in which permanent settlements in the commercially non-advanced countries were established, was a later phase of development. In that later stage of development, the perpetuation of the economic backwardness of the commercially non-advanced countries became a matter of a continuous, uninterrupted policy. The policy to be pursued towards the colonies was made in the mother country. That policy placed the colonies into a web of economic restrictions, which were to perpetuate the relative economic backwardness of the colonies.

The earlier pre-colonial economic policy of the commercially advanced nations in regard to the commercially non-advanced nations is known in economic history as the Bullionist policy. *Bullion* is the name for chunks of gold. It was the aim of the early foreign traders to bring bullion from the commercially backward countries into the commercially advancing mother country. Bullion in that period was regarded as an embodiment not only of private wealth, but of national wealth as well. In the later period of the Commercial Revolution in the seventeenth and eighteenth centuries, the acquisition of bullion was still considered a supreme factor in the trading of a commercially advanced country with a commercially non-advanced country. Yet, at that later period, factors other than acquisition of bullion were considered worthy of consideration. The use to be made of bullion entered into the range of economic discussion.

Such writers as Thomas Mun and Josiah Child suggested the investment of bullion in furthering foreign trade in goods other than bullion. The promotion of multilateral trade with a number of commercially non-advanced countries became the declared policy of the commercially advanced countries in the later period of Commercialism. Such was the so-called Mercantilist system, in the later phase of which the acquisition and retention of colonial territories became an integral part.

The promotion of economic domination of one set of countries, matched by the promotion of economic subjugation of another set of countries, did not end with the Commercial Revolution. When the Industrial Revolution succeeded the Commercial Revolution, the promotion of economic domination by one set of countries, matched by the promotion of economic subjugation of another set of countries, concentrated on keeping that very Industrial Revolution out of the subjugated countries. The economically subjugated countries were to be forced to buy industrial products from the dominating industrialized countries. In turn, the economically subjugated were made to serve as suppliers of food and raw materials to the dominant industrialized countries.

What runs through the patterns of promotion of economic domination and its matching counterpart of economic subjugation, during the periods of both the Commercial Revolution and the Industrial Revolution, is the presence and active participation of the national state. The national states of the dominating countries played a highly active role in setting and executing the particular economic policy, in regard to the countries which were to be made and kept economically subjugated.

In the period of the Commercial Revolution, the governments of the economically dominating countries licensed the foreign trade companies, which carried out set state policy. In carrying out the state policy in subjugated countries and keeping them economically subjugated, the privileged foreign trade companies operated as quasi-agents of the state. The economic benefits which accrued to the privileged foreign trade companies from the foreign economic operations were, in turn, shared by the licensing governments of the economically dominating states.

When, in the period of the Industrial Revolution, the monopolistic power of the foreign trade companies was reduced, state power took another form in establishing and perpetuating economic domination and its counterpart, economic subjugation. The economically dominating countries instituted discriminatory import and export tariffs, which placed high duties on the imports of non-agricultural products from the economically subjugated countries.

In turn, the economically dominating countries set comparatively low import tariffs for the importation of agricultural products from the economically subjugated countries into the economically dominating countries. This discriminatory tariff policy forced the subjugated countries to remain agricultural. Furthermore, the discriminatory tariff policy made it possible for the economically dominating countries to become more and more industrialized. The discriminatory tariff policy resulted, moreover, in making the economically subjugated countries accept a comparatively low price for their agricultural products.

The policy of tariff discrimination by the economically dominating countries made it impossible for the economically subjugated countries to diversify their production. Lack of economic diversification and dependence solely on the sale of agricultural products weakened the bargaining position of the agricultural countries in their dealings with the industrialized countries. This weakening of the comparative bargaining position of the agricultural countries made itself felt in the necessity to accept a comparatively unfavorable price for their own products and to grant a comparatively favorable price for the products of industry, which had to be imported from the industrialized countries.

In their dealings with the economically subjugated countries, during the period of the Commercial Revolution, the foreign trade companies used more direct pressures to the disadvantage of the economically subjugated countries. Less direct, and more indirect, pressures were applied in deals with economically subjugated countries by the comparatively less monopolistic foreign traders of the economically dominating countries in the period of the Industrial Revolution. What took place in both cases, however, was most definitely a decumulation of the wealth of the economically subjugated countries in favor of the economically dominating countries. Only the form of the decumulation of the wealth of the economically subjugated countries by the economically dominating countries is changed from the period of the Commercial Revolution to the period of the Industrial Revolution.

It can be stated, as a valid proposition, that the decumulation of wealth in the economically subjugated countries during the period of the Commercial Revolution was a preconditioning factor for the Industrial Revolution to take effect in the economically dominating countries. It is likewise a valid proposition that the decumulation of wealth in the economically subjugated countries, in favor of the economically dominant countries, during the period of the Industrial Revolution, intensified the industrialization of the economically dominating countries.

The proposition which calls for the accumulation of wealth in a dominating country at the expense of a subjugated country has not been expressed outright in a representative school of economic thought. During the period of the Commercial Revolution, the then prevalent Mercantilist school of economic thinking introduced the propositions of balance of trade and of balance of international payments. In both of these propositions, the word *balance* constitutes a misnomer. The actual experience to which the word *balance* was meant to refer represented itself as an imbalance.

The proposition named *balance of trade* referred to an imbalance based on the principle that the economically dominant country should enrich itself at the expense of the economically subjugated country. This principle was brought to life in the early period of the Commercial Revolution, by hit-and-run tactics. The adventurous foreign traders of the commercially more advanced countries were expected to, and did, stage raids on the commercially less advanced countries in order to take possession of valuables, particularly precious metals. Little, if anything, was offered in return. It is that kind of foreign trade to which the proposition of balance of trade referred during the early period of the Commercial Revolution.

At a later stage, when the Commercial Revolution fully matured, the so-called foreign trade turned more and more from bilateral to multilateral trading. In the multilateral trade, one set of nations were the commercially maturing nations, while the other set of nations were the commercially retarded nations. It is with reference to this kind of multilateral trade that the proposition of balance of international payments was introduced. Again, the word balance represented a misnomer. What actually took place was the reapplication, in a slightly varied form, of the principle of enrichment of the commercially advanced countries at the expense of the commercially retarded countries. The variation in the application of this principle, in the period of the fully matured Commercial Revolution, consisted in the institution and perpetuation of an imbalance in the relative economic position of the respectively advanced and non-advanced countries, in multilateral instead of bilateral trade.

This particular imbalance was expected to be, and was actually, instituted and perpetuated, by using the wealth imported from one commercially retarded country to a commercially advanced for re-export. This re-export, in turn, was expected to, and did, take place in order to augment the trade by the commercially advanced country with another commercially retarded country. If, in the total multulateral trade between the commercially matured country and several commercially retarded countries, the commercially advanced country could show a balance in its favor, that balance fell within the range of the proposition of balance of international payments.

When the Commercial Revolution was superseded by the Industrial Revolution, the proposition of balance of trade and balance of international payments became subject to another variation. The variation did not affect the basic principle of enrichment of the economically advanced country at the expense of the economically retarded country. That principle was retained. The variation presented itself in the inclusion of industrial goods in the flow of foreign commerce.

Industrial goods were included in the flow of commerce between the advanced and non-advanced countries, however, with the stipulation that the economically retarded countries were to be prevented from becoming industrialized. The imbalance in this case was shifted to the institution and maintenance of a division of the world between economically dominating industrialized nations and economically subjugated non-industrialized nations. The reformulation of the propositions of balance of trade and balance of international payments to bring them in line with aspects of industrialization and non-industrialization, respectively, was undertaken by Adam Smith and David Ricardo.

In Smith's comprehension, the balance of trade came to be viewed as favorable to the technologically advancing country when that country exported more goods to the technologically retarded country than it imported from it. This application of the proposition of balance of trade brought out, though in an indirect manner, that the balance was expected to be favorable to the technologically advanced country and unfavorable to the technologically retarded country.

The balance of international payments, in the form reformulated by David Ricardo, was made to include, in addition to the factors of export and import of goods, the factors of export and import of capital. The economically advanced countries were identified in the balance of payments proposition, as it was reformulated by Ricardo, as the capital-exporting countries. The economically retarded countries came to be identified, in turn, as capital-importing countries. This division reflected the actuality of capital movements in the era of nascent industrialization. In its wider range of interpretation, the reformulated balance of payments proposition implied the stipulation that capital exports from the economically advanced countries must not lead to the industrialization of the economically retarded countries.

The capital exported from the economically advanced countries to the economically retarded countries, the implied stipulation provided, was in the main to be used to provide increased credit for the economically retarded countries, in order to assist them in exporting their non-industrial products to the industrialized countries. In this sense, the new version of the proposition of balance of international payments was aimed at perpetuating the economic backwardness of the non-industrialized nations and, in turn, at furthering the economic advancement of the industrialized nations. The principles according to which the economically advanced nations were to enrich themselves, at the expense of the economically retarded nations, were kept intact in this new version of the balance of international payments proposition, as the above provided exemplification readily shows.

To take account of the changed form of international economic relations brought about by the introduction of industrial products in the flow of foreign commerce, a new proposition was added. In response to this new development, David Ricardo provided the proposition of comparative costs. At its face value, the comparative costs proposition appears to state that each country exports the goods which it produces most cheaply. Thus the proposition, on its face value, treats all countries as equal in terms of economic development. That, however, is not the implied meaning of this proposition. The implication carried by the proposition of comparative costs is one which makes a definite distinction between economically developed and economically undeveloped countries. The implication, furthermore, connotes the stipulation of the perpetuation of a division between the economically developed and the economically undeveloped countries.

David Ricardo, the economic theorist of the Industrial Revolution in the capitalist countries who had introduced the proposition of comparative costs, provided apparently innocuous examples which were to demonstrate the applicability of the proposition. Portugal, Ricardo begins his exemplification, has been known since times immemorial as a wine-producing and wine-exporting country. Portugal's climate, its soil, and the particular skill of its population, were conducive to wine-production and wine-export, Ricardo continues by way of an apparent explanation.

On its face value, the example means that the specialization of Portugal in the production and export of wine is due to favorable economic pre-conditioning factors prevailing in that country. Those favorable economic pre-conditioning factors are, in turn, to be interpreted, on their face value, as leading to favorable economic results.

In a matching example of the applicability of the comparative costs proposition, Ricardo refers to the case of England, as an industrialized nation. England, Ricardo states, has paid a high price for becoming industrialized. The English entrepreneurs, who became manufactures, entered an untried sphere of economic activity. It was a pioneering economic task to which the English manufacturer subjected himself. At first, the pioneering manufacturer did not know whether the introduction of a new, revolutionary technology would pay off economically. Nor did the pioneering manufacturer know whether the production of a new kind of product, through the application of the new revolutionary technology, would pay off. The pioneering manufacturer could not have known in advance whether a worker who had been taken off his farm and put to work in a factory could adjust himself to the tempo of production in the new type of production organization. Nor, for that matter, could the pioneering manufacturer know in advance where, and under what conditions, the new kind of products, produced by the application of the new revolutionary industrial technology, could be sold. Yet the pioneering British manufacturers took the plunge; they braved the risks.

It took two to three generations, Ricardo further relates, before the English manufacturers knew what particular goods to produce and with what particular machinery. It likewise took two to three generations for the English manufacturers to find out whether the new products produced by way of the new revolutionary technology could be sold, and under what conditions. Similarly, Ricardo continues to relate, it took two to three generations for the English factory worker to acquire the ability to work in an efficient manner in a manufacturing production unit. Thus, one is to conclude, England had established itself as a manufacturing nation at a cost.

Accordingly, Ricardo's proposition of comparative costs stipulates that England, having borne the costs of industrialization, has deservedly ascended to the role of the sole industrialized nation in the world. As such, England has ascended to the role of the supplier of industrial products for the rest of the world. It is this claim of England to industrial world economic superiority, matched by the clamor for economic non-industrial inferiority to be foisted upon the rest of the world, which constitutes the real meaning of the comparative costs proposition and its application, the way it had been advanced by Ricardo. Thus, the comparative costs proposition, in its wider implication, constitutes a perfect

213

example of how the principle of the division of the world into economically advanced countries and economically retarded countries, came to be geared to the age of the Industrial Revolution.

On its face value, the application of the comparative costs proposition appears to demonstrate the principle of economic equity. But in its application the comparative costs proposition turns out to demonstrate blatant economic inequity. Inequity is seen particularly in the stipulation that the application of the comparative costs proposition calls for a division of the world into a relatively small industrialized part and a relatively large non-industrialized part.

This division of the world into a few economically dominating countries and many economically subjugated countries, which originated in the age of the Commercial Revolution, was given a new lease of life in the age of the Industrial Revolution. This then was the bearing of the proposition of comparative costs, which underlay the social and economic polarity of the world up to World War I.

An anti-colonial movement came to the fore in the wake of a world war. World War I, which was a war between the economically dominating countries, ended in the weakening of the hold of those countries upon the economically subjugated parts of the world. It can be said that all the belligerents in World War I lost that war. They lost it because none of them was able to attain its implicit aim. The aim was directed towards the extension of the range of economic domination by one set of belligerents among the economically dominating countries at the expense of the reduction of the range of economic domination by another set of belligerents. This implicit aim was not attained by any of the two sets of belligerents of the economically dominating countries, because economic subjugation came to be resisted on a world-wide scale.

In the economically subjugated countries, leaders arose and began to challenge the validity of the stipulation of the comparative costs proposition. The stipulation of that proposition, which condemned the economically subjugated countries to perpetual economic backwardness, was met by a growing defiance on the part of the representative leadership of the non-industrialized part of the world. With that defiance went resistance to the way in which the proposition of balance of payments had been applied. The stipulation that the capital exported from the economically dominating industrialized countries to the economically subjugated non-industrialized countries was not to be used for the industrialization of the economically retarded countries became unacceptable to the spokesmen of the non-industrialized part of the world.

The defiance of the stipulation of the comparative costs proposition, as well as the stipulation of the balance of payments proposition, by the leadership of the economically subjugated non-industrialized part of the world, led to active resistance. The economically subjugated, non-industrialized nations took countermeasures to prevent the continuation of economic discrimination against them. The economically subjugated countries served, in particular, notice on the dominating, industrialized countries, that any use of capital exported from the industrially advanced countries to the non-industrialized countries will become subject to specific regulations to be promulgated by the governments of the economically subjugated, capital-importing countries.

Those regulations came to be promulgated with a view towards using the imported capital for the furtherance of industrialization of the non-industrialized nations. The regulations, addressed to those who exported capital from the industrialized countries, included either a limitation or a prohibition of the transfer of economic gains accrued to the capital thus imported. This limitation or prohibition of the transfer of economic gains accrued to foreign capital came to cover the interest and profits derived from capital exported from an industrialized and imported into a non-industrialized country. With the limitation and prohibition of the transfer of economic gains accrued to capital imported into a non-industrialized country from an industrialized country went the stipulation that such economic gains were to be channeled by the governments of the non-industrialized countries into industrial investment spheres in those countries.

This stipulation, which the authorized representatives of the non-industrialized nations attached to the operation of the balance of payments proposition after World War I, constituted a reversal of the stipulation which the representative interests of the industrialized nations had attached to the operation of the balance of payments proposition before World War I. This institutional reversal signified, in turn, a qualitative reversal in international economic relations. This qualitative reversal signified in particular a change in the character of the flow of capital from the capital-rich to the capital-poor countries.

Before World War I, the operation of the balance of international payments by the capital-rich countries was aimed at forestalling, or at least slowing down, capital formation in the capital-poor countries. After World War I, the operation of the balance of international payments by the capital-poor countries became aimed at preventing the forestalling and slowing down of capital formation in the capital-poor countries. This change in the character of operation of the balance of international payments signified, moreover, that capital investments by capital-rich countries in capital-poor countries were prevented from bringing about additional accumulation of capital in the capital-rich country at the expense of capital decumulation in the capital-poor country.

The attempt to redress the character of economic relations between the capital-rich and capital-poor countries by replacing economic domination and dependence with economic interdependence did not, however, have smooth sailing. The flow of capital from the capital-rich countries to capital-poor countries started to drop, in the wake of the stipulated change in the operation of the balance of international payments. The drop could be ascribed mainly to the reluctance of owners of capital in capital-rich countries to forego the extraordinary gains which they could and did make prior to World War I from investments in capital-poor countries. This reluctance was heightened because the owners of capital in capital-rich countries realized that their capital, invested in the capital-poor countries, was likely to be used for capital formation in those countries.

The reluctance turned to outright abstention from foreign investment when the owners of private capital in the capital-rich countries learned that the formation of publicly owned social capital was to be given priority over the formation of private capital in capital-poor countries. The priority given to the formation of social capital, i.e., public funds, was exemplified in the capital-poor countries by the transformation of real-invested-capital owned by foreigners in those countries into publicly owned social capital. This transformation was effected by turning productive undertakings which were owned by foreign investors into publicly owned productive undertakings.

As time passed, the emphasis placed in the capital-poor countries on capital formation within the range of publicly owned social capital continued to increase. The increase in emphasis on publicly owned social capital came to be matched by increasing control over the channeling and the earnings of private capital in the capital-poor countries. As a result, the flow of private capital from the capital-rich to the capital-poor countries for investment purposes fell to a trickle in the period following World War II. With the flow of private capital from the capital rich to the capital-poor countries almost eliminated, publicly owned social capital of the capital-rich countries was called upon to fill the gap. The flow of publicly owned social capital, i.e., of public funds, from the capital-rich countries was to make it possible to add to the publicly owned social capital formed in the capital-poor countries. In this case, the role of capital influx from the capital-rich countries to the capital-poor countries was to become totally reversed as compared with pre-World War I period. Capital accumulation in the capital-poor countries came to be attained at the cost of capital decumulation in the capital-rich countries.

The new character of capital accumulation in the economically underdeveloped countries has to be considered a key factor in the reshaping of the world economy. It is a factor in which neither the balance of

216

trade nor the balance of international payments play any decisive role. Both those propositions were related in the past to the factor of foreign commerce. The balance of trade proposition was related to foreign commerce in terms of the movement of commodities. The balance of international payments was, in turn, related to foreign commerce in terms of the movement of capital. Neither of the two propositions was directly keyed to economic development in terms of the industrialization of underdeveloped countries. The balance of international payments did make some allowance for the economic development of underdeveloped countries, but economic development was considered only as an incidental factor, which was kept on a restricted basis in the period before World War I.

In the post-World War I period, and in particular in the post-World War II period, economic development in terms of industrialization became a primary factor. The balance of international payments was reduced to the role of the intermediary factor, of channeling publicly owned social capital from the economically developed countries into the economically underdeveloped countries. In their relations with the economically developed countries, the economically underdeveloped countries thus dropped out, for the most part, of the competitive marketing economy geared to profit-making by private capital. Economic gains, in a context in which social capital, i.e., public funds of a developed country, are added to publicly owned social capital in an underdeveloped country, came to count primarily as gains in productive capacity. The gains in productive capacity are expected to express themselves in an increase of the total production, technically called gross national product. The increase in the gross national product, in turn, is expected to result in an increase in national income, which in its turn, is expected to express itself in the improvement of the standard of living.

Profits in all these instances are to be considered as social profits, i.e., public economic gains, not private profits in terms of private economic gains. The reason for referring to the difference between costs of production and prices realized from effected products as social profits, i.e., public economic gains, are twofold. First, the stated profits accrue in productive undertakings which utilize social capital, i.e., public funds. They thus accrue in a productive sphere, which is designated as the range of publicly owned social production. Second, the profits accrued in the productive undertakings geared to social capital, i.e., invested public funds, are, as a rule, used to increase the social capital, i.e., invested public funds, of the given underdeveloped country. The increase in social capital, i.e., invested public funds, makes, in turn, for an augmentation of social production, i.e., production in publicly owned undertakings.

The detachment of the basic form of capital formation in the economically underdeveloped countries from direct contact with the sphere of private profit and private capital formation has a most distinct effect on the relationship of the economically underdeveloped countries with all the economically developed countries. The designation "all economically developed countries" includes countries in which only part of the productive capital is publicly owned social capital, as well as countries in which all productive capital is social capital. Within the first range of countries, one finds the United States; the second range of countries is represented by the Soviet Union. It thus comes to pass that, in their relationship with the underdeveloped countries, in which publicly owned social capital forms the basis for economic development, the United States and the Soviet Union find themselves in identical roles. Thus, a firm basis for cooperation between the United States and the Soviet Union could be established, as far as their respective active participation in the economic development of the underdeveloped countries is concerned.

The change in the forms of capital transfer from the developed to the underdeveloped countries could not, in turn, fail to have an effect on the relationship of the developed countries to each other. The changed position of the developed countries in relation to the underdeveloped countries made it imperative to have the relationship among the developed countries changed. This need for a changed relationship between the developed countries had been taken account of by the former Chancellor of the Exchequer of Great Britain Selwyn Lloyd, when he specified the reasons why Britain found it necessary to apply for membership in the European Common Market. The explanatory part of Selwyn Lloyd's state paper stated correctly, that in the nineteenth century Britain's earnings from its capital exports augmented its earnings from commodity exports. A balance of international payments favoring Britain thus was added to a balance of trade in Britain's favor. As a result, Britain had a high rate of capital formation. In the twentieth century, in particular after World War I and, more so, after World War II, Britain's earnings from capital exports reached an unprecedented low level. Gains made by way of the favorable balances of trade were insufficient for Britain to outweigh the losses suffered through the shrinking of the economic gains derived from the balance of international payments.

From the realistic assessment of the changed position of Britain in the world market of capital, as compared with the world market of goods, the British state paper, submitted by Selwyn Lloyd, drew an unrealistic conclusion, however. The unrealistic conclusion drawn by Britain in the stated state paper is to be seen in the expectation to have the losses suffered from the dwindling earnings from capital export to the underdeveloped world recouped by increasing its trade with developed countries. Such expectations are to be regarded as unrealistic, because the increase in the sales of Britain's products in the European countries, which constitute the European Common Market, could not be expected to be so substantial that it could even make up for the loss of British earnings from capital exports. At best, the sales of British products in the European countries, which constitute the Common Market, – were those sales to be weighed against the prospective increase of sales of products in Britain of the European countries, which constitute the Common Market, – could increase the rate of capital formation in England only insubstantially.

The economies of the Continental European industrialized countries, which constitute the European Common Market, as well as the economy of industrialized Britain, have not been developed as complementary economies. The industries of each of those countries have been established on a competitive international basis, not on a cooperative international basis. If one were to take one of the most industrialized countries of Western Europe of the Common Market countries, Western Germany, and compare its industrial plant with that of England, one will find very few West German industries which are not duplicated in England and, the reverse, is conversely also the case. Were one to ask, what, in terms of industrial products, does England not have to offer, what West Germany has, or conversely, what, in terms of industrial products, does West Germany not have to offer, what England has, it would be difficult to find any such product.

Were Germany to have had a greater opportunity to sell its industrial products to England, in case England were to become a European Common Market country, England would, in turn, be given a greater opportunity to sell its industrial products to Germany. The gains for either West Germany or England from the sales of industrial products to each other, were England to be admitted to the Common Market, would about cancel each other out. West Germany could, however, be expected to gain an edge over England since wages in West Germany are lower than in England. In addition labor productivity is, on the whole, higher in Western Germany than in England, since German plant equipment is newer than British plant equipment. Western Germany had had to re-equip almost its entire industrial plant, in the wake of the almost total destruction of its industrial plant during World War II.

In their relation to the less industrialized countries of the European Common Market area, such as Italy, West Germany and England would have to engage in a fierce competition, were England to become a member of a Common Market country. England is likely to lose out in the stated competition, because, again, the comparatively lower labor costs and the comparatively higher labor productivity of West German industry were to make West Germany get the edge over England in its exports to Italy.

The lowering and the eventual elimination of tariffs, which constitutes the raison d'être of the establishment of the European Common Market, cannot be considered an adequate basis for a cooperative international integration of the West European economies. Just the opposite of a cooperation can be expected to happen, the fiercest kind of competition between the industries of the various European countries, which constitute the Common Market countries, can be expected to take place. As a result, certain industries in some of the member countries could be expected to be slowed down in their development and some of the same kind of industries might, in their turn, become more rapidly developed in other member countries. In the long run, some industries in some of the member countries of the Common Europan Market might be entirely eliminated, while in other European Common Market countries the same kind of industries would be likely to become overdeveloped.

It is only through monopolistic cartel agreements that an international relocation of industries within the Common Market countries could be prevented. Such prevention of the relocation of existing industries within the Common Market area could, in turn, be attained only at the expense of the narrowing of the range of demand and the freezing of the income level of the broad masses of the population, not a bright prospect for their industrial growth and economic expansion. The only substantial increase in trade for the European countries, which at present constitute the Common Market countries as well as England, which only recently was granted permission to enter the Common Market, can be seen in a substantial enlargement of the trading area extending beyond the borders of all those countries.

Only the extention of the tariff free area to the extent of the possible inclusion of the whole world could lead to a sustained industrial growth of England as well as the European countries which at present constitute the European Common Market. Such worldwide extension of the tariff free area would then embrace all industrialized countries. That area will then include Western, Southern and Northern Europe, which are now members of the Common Market countries, as well as the Free Trade Association countries in addition to the socialist countries of Europe and Asia as well as the United States, Canada and the Latin American countries. All those countries would thus become part of a worldwide free tariff zone. All African countries as well as Australia and New Zealand would as well become part of that worldwide free tariff zone area.

In that worldwide tariff free zone there would still be room for regional organizations of nations, such as the Continental Western European Common Market countries (the Six) with the subsequent addition of England and the Free Trade Association (the Seven) as well as the Comecon, the regional international organization of the Soviet Union and most of the European socialist countries. Regional economic organizations of the four non-European continents could also be expected to continue to exist. On the American continent a closer international trade relation between the United States, Canada and the Latin American countries could, in particular, be expected to develop within a regional tariff free trade organization of that range.

The above stated pattern in international economic relations is, however, far from being realized. Up to very recently, almost all Western countries have conducted economic warfare against the Soviet Union as well as other socialist countries of Europe and Asia. With the aim to prevent the increase in the military potential of the Soviet Union and other socialist countries of Eastern Europe, as well as Asia, those countries were subjected close to an economic boycott by the Western countries. More recently some European Western powers, notably England and France and Western Germany, have made moves to increase their trade with East European countries, notably the Soviet Union. Thus a move got under way, on the part of the major European Western powers to break with the policy of economic warfare and economic boycott in their relations with the Eastern European socialist countries and, in particular, the Soviet Union.

In the United States, authoritative spokesmen for the United States Chamber of Commerce have urged a re-examination of the list of United States goods which are withheld from export to the Soviet Union and other East European countries. Influential business circles in the United States have thus gone on record in favor of a relaxation of economic tensions in the relations of the United States with the Soviet Union and other East European countries. The United States administration has only reluctantly followed suit. Some products have been removed from the list of those goods which had been previously placed on the list of strategically important items. Some items have been declared free from export restrictions to the Soviet Union and other Eastern European countries. This move, however, is not more than a gesture in the direction of revitalization of trade between the United States and other East European countries, in particular, the Soviet Union.

Against such gestures the attempt of United States officials to make the Western European countries slow down their trade relations with the Soviet Union is to be brought up. Pressure was put upon officials of

Western European countries by representatives of the United States State Department, not to have long term credits extended to the Soviet Union in its trade relations with the Western European countries. To what extent the pressures put by United States officials on the officials of Western countries has been successful has not been reported. It is doubtful, however, that the pressure exercised by United States officials was very effective in the stated respect.

What was effective, however, was the pressure recently brought to bear on Henry Ford, to abstain from an agreement with the Soviet Union to build a factory there for the production of trucks. As against the non-realization of that project, the realization of plans by Italian and French automobile manufacturers to have automobile factories built in the Soviet Union is to be cited. It appears that the policy of non-cooperation in the economic sphere with the Soviet Union, spearheaded by the United States, has come to be pierced as far as the Western European states are concerned.

Chapter 8

NEGATION OF THE COLD WAR

Hardly any of the proposals made in the previous chapters could be agreed upon and put into effect if the Cold War atmosphere continues to prevail. It is, therefore, fitting to examine what the Cold War is all about and what its course was in a period which spans more than a half of a century. With a view to putting the Cold War into a historical perspective, an account of the origination and the conduct of the Cold War, as undertaken here, should be very much in order.

In all the attempts to eliminate the Soviet state from the concert of powers, the so-called Cold War, as a war fought short of the use of military weapons, was but a preliminary to its transformation into a hot war. In that sense, the Cold War must be considered as but an intermittent factor between a potential and an actual hot war against the Soviet Union. At the early period in the existence of the Soviet state the intermittent period of Cold War practices as against hot war activity was shorter than at a later period. The Western powers, however, had not for a moment specifically given up the ultimate aim of destroying the Soviet power. During the fifty years of the existence of the Soviet state, the Cold War tactics have changed, as have the formulations of Cold War policies, but never was the Cold War, as a preliminary to its completion in terms of the ultimate aim of the destruction of the Soviet state, given up in any specific form.

The first phase in the period of intermittent cold warfare followed by hot war activity was highlighted at the Versailles Peace Conference which followed the termination of hostilities after World War I. The agenda of the Versailles Conference included a provision aimed at the dismemberment of Russia. The dismemberment was to be attained under the guise of granting self-determination to the various ethnic groups which lived within the borders of the former Russian empire. This policy was approved by all the Western Allied leaders who masterminded the Versailles Conference, and was duly implemented. Within a very short time after its establishment, the Soviet government found itself besieged on all sides by Russian troops opposed to the Soviets. Their invasion of Russian territory was to a great extent masterminded in the Allied chancelleries. Those anti-Soviet troops, which fought to overthrow the Soviet government, were in the meantime establishing secessionist regimes in all but the most central parts of the Russian territory.

It was only over that central part of Russian territory that the Soviet government had retained continuous control. In a sense, the anti-Soviet interventionist armies took off where the defeated German army had left it. The Brest-Litovsk *diktat* had forced the fledgling Soviet government to accede to the loss of sovereignty over the Ukraine, part of Byelorussia, and the Baltic Russian provinces.

With the defeat and capitulation of the German army on the Western front, the German occupation troops stationed in the part of Russia over which the Soviet government had been forced to renounce its sovereignty were withdrawn. The anti-Soviet Russian interventionists' armies tried immediately after the German military defeat on the Western front to fill the gap left by the withdrawal of the German occupation armies on Russian territory, by establishing anti-Soviet occupation regimes with pro-Western backing on the part of Russian territory which had previously been held by the Germans. Moreover, the secession of Russian provinces brought about by the anti-Soviet Russian occupation troops was vastly extended beyond the area which the Germans had occupied in Russia. The vast Siberian territory was added to the regions which were forcibly detached from the sovereignty of the Soviet government. The extreme North, as well as the Northwest of European Russia, was also added to the territory over which anti-Soviet occupation armies held sway.

All those anti-Soviet armies were amply supplied with munitions and provisions by the Western Allied government. In some regions, as in the extreme North and the Far East, allied occupation armies, the United States expeditionary corps among them, themselves descended upon Russian territory. When the tide of the Civil War which was forced upon the Soviet government appeared to be swinging in favor of the Soviet government, the Polish government was egged on by the Allies, and most noticeably by France, to threaten the existence of the Soviet regime by making war on Russia.

When, after more than two years of civil war and foreign intervention, peace was finally restored over most of the territory which had come under Russian sovereignty during the Czarist regime, a cold war strategy was devised which was to signify but a lull in the hot war. The so-called *cordon sanitaire,* which had been fathered by Clemenceau, was devised in terms of a long-term assault upon the existence of the Soviet government. For the time being, the *cordon sanitaire* policy was to be kept short of direct military intervention. The so-called *cordon sanitaire* policy had marked as its advance position the establishment of so-called buffer states which were to encircle the Soviet state. The states of Eastern Europe were designed to form the outer ring of encirclement, with defeated Germany to be kept as an outpost of that ring of encirclement.

Within a short while after the establishment of almost all of the Eastern European states on the borders of Russia, those states came to be ruled by Fascist and semi-Fascist regimes, which assumed an extremely hostile position towards the Soviet government. Those Fascist and semi-Fascist East European states were lavishly provided with funds and military supplies by the Western governments. The degree of hostility of those East European states in their official and semi-official policy towards the Soviet government was but one step short of the outbreak of open military hostilities. The Soviet government in its own foreign policy in the entire period between the two World Wars had to take into consideration the possibility, and even the probability, that any of the Eastern European states, either singly or in concert with each other, might begin a hot war without any forewarning. Acts of provocation against the Soviet regime by almost all the Eastern European states were numerous, and those provocations provided the Soviet government with a sufficient indication that the warlike policies of those states were but a prelude to the outbreak of an open war between the Eastern European states and the Soviet government. Nor, may we forget, in this connection, the continuous economic and political support which all the Eastern European states received from the Western governments.

Unexpectedly, Germany breached the solid anti-Soviet front in which it was accorded a place of an outpost of the anti-Soviet *cordon sanitaire* of the Eastern European states. In Rapallo, defeated Germany signed an agreement with the Soviet Union which opened the way for economic relations between Germany and the Soviet regime. Economic relations between the Soviet government and Western Allied powers, such as England, had not been ruled out by the allied governments, but defeated Germany was not expected to maintain those relations. By signing the Rapallo agreement, Germany somehow entered into competition with the Western allied governments, as far as taking advantage of the prospective trading gains which the maintenance of economic relations with the Soviet government promised to entail.

There were moments when the Western allied governments allowed humanitarian considerations to guide their relations with the Soviet Union. A striking example of a humanitarian allied action was the free distribution of food on the territory of the Soviet Union under the guiding hand of Herbert Hoover of the United States. Against that humanitarian gesture has to be pinned the implacable enmity of President Wilson towards the continuous existence of the Soviet regime, fully matched by the anti-Soviet zeal displayed by Clemenceau and Lloyd George. Lloyd George's foreign secretary, Curzon, established himself as a kind of official propaganda chief of the Western allied governments. Curzon's stream of notes, which were dispachted to the Soviet capital, were not diplomatic notes in any strict sense, they were to score propaganda points; no other meaning could be attached to them.

President Wilson's implacable enmity towards the very existence of the Soviet regime was most blatantly expressed in the employment of United States troops in the military intervention in the far north of European Russia and in the far eastern part of Asiatic Russia. In both cases, the aim of the direct military intervention by the United States was to support the operation of the Russian armies opposing the Soviet forces on Russian soil. In that respect, United States military intervention failed because the peripheral role assigned to United States interventionist forces could not be maintained as such after the core of the anti-Soviet forces, the Russian anti-Soviet armies, started to disintegrate in the wake of the military defeats which were administered to them by the fledgling Red army.

In retrospect, it might be of interest to say a few words as to why the amply supplied and military well-trained anti-Soviet armies succumbed to the blows of the poorly supplied and poorly trained Soviet armies. The answer to that puzzling phenomenon lies in the comparative level of the morale or fighting spirit which animated each of the two armies. The men in the Soviet armies were fighting for the preservation of the revolutionary gains, which were, in brief, the right to retain common ownership of land and other natural resources, and the retention of common ownership of manufacturing undertakings. The anti-Soviet armies were fighting, in turn, for what may be called the re-privatization of the common ownership of land and other natural resources, as well as for the re-privatization of manufacturing undertakings.

Re-privatization, were the civil war to be won by the anti-Soviet forces, would not have directly benefited any of the mass of soldiers and officers who were fighting on the anti-Soviet side. On the other hand, the soldiers and officers fighting on the pro-Soviet side regarded the retention of public ownership as directly benefiting each of them. In addition, the vast majority of the soldiers and officers who were fighting on the Soviet side probably were afraid of punishment to be meted out indiscriminately against the whole population which remained loyal to the Soviet regime. The memory of the pacification expeditions of the period following the 1905 revolution were yet alive in many of the soldiers and officers who rallied to the defense of the Soviet regime. In addition, the threat of punishment, including the mass execution of supporters of the Soviet regime, were openly hoisted on the banners of the Russian anti-Soviet troops. In the parts of formerly held Soviet territory and intermittently occupied by anti-Soviet troops, those threats became a reality. Thus, in the eyes of the defenders of the Soviet regime, the anti-Soviet soldiery and its officers came to appear as but a vanguard of executioners' squads.

226

After the high morale of the forces fighting on the Soviet side and the comparative low morale of the forces fighting against the Soviets utlimately decided the issue of the civil war in favor of the Soviets, the war aims were not given up by the anti-Soviet side. The Western governments realized that a lull in the struggle for the overthrow of the Soviet regime had to be accepted for some time, but the ultimate goal, the elimination of Soviet power, was in no way reversed.

The lull in the struggle for the elimination of Soviet power took a zig-zag course. Undeterred in the aim to have Soviet power destroyed, the allied governments took several steps which outwardly resembled a policy of rapprochement with the Soviet regime. Britain, first among the big Western powers, extended *de facto* recognition to the Soviet regime and engaged in trade relations with the Soviet government. This minimal recognition of the reality of the existence of the Soviet state was within a few years reversed by the denial of *de facto* recognition of the Soviet state, as exemplified by the expulsion of the Soviet representative, and by the curtailment of trade relations with the Soviet government. The same policy of partial recognition of the existence of the Soviet state and limited trade relations was also pursued at first by France, which later also reneged on the *de facto* recognition and curtailed trade relations.

The breaching of the allied anti-Soviet front, in granting *de facto* recognition to the Soviet government, as well as the opening of trade relations with the Soviet regime by Germany, had a most telling effect on the policy of the Western governments towards the Soviet regime. The Western governments, which did not have it within their power to prevent Germany from dealing directly with the Soviet government, decided to beat Germany at that game. The Western European governments came to realize that they could not postpone indefinitely normalization of diplomatic relations with the Soviet state. As a result, one witnesses the establishment of full diplomatic relations with the Soviet state by the two major Western European powers, Great Britain and France. The United States, on its part, insisted on extending no more than a *de facto* recognition to the Soviet state and engaged in strictly limited trade deals with the Soviet government. Only with the rise to power of Hitler Germany, which presented a potential military threat not only to the Soviet state but to the Western powers as well, did the United States, under the administration of Franklin D. Roosevelt, extend full diplomatic recognition to the Soviet regime.

To match the pro-Soviet move which Germany made in Rapallo, the Western European powers prepared a counter-offensive of their own, which was designed to wean Germany away from the overtures it had made to the Soviet government and to lure it back into a firm anti-

Soviet position. The Western European powers consummated that move in the Locarno Pact, which was aimed at tying Germany's foreign policy to that of the Western European powers with the specific understanding that only the Western borders of Germany were to be kept inviolate, while the Eastern borders of Germany were to be implicitly regarded subject to revision in favor of Germany. Thus the Western powers, in the Locarno Pact, tacitly reaffirmed Germany's quest for expansion towards the East. The Locarno agreement must be seen as an attempt to tie Germany to the anti-Soviet bloc of the Western powers. That attempt can well be regarded as but the beginning of a Western European policy which in less than a decade culminated in the Munich agreement between Prime Minister Neville Chamberlain of Britain and the head of the Nazified German government, Adolf Hitler.

In Munich, Chamberlain but reaffirmed what had been offered to German foreign minister Stresemann in Locarno, namely, that Germany is to feel free to move against the Soviet Union with the tacit support of the Western powers. That Hitler bit off more at the start of his move against the Soviet Union than Chamberlain had bargained for, did not exactly do credit to Chamberlain's declared policy of "peace in our time." As far as Poland was concerned, Britain, in particular, was not prepared to transfer that country out of its and France's implicit sphere of influence into Hitler's outright sphere of influence. This was the political basis for Britain's pledge to come to the defense of Poland in case of an attack by Nazi Germany. Yet, Chamberlain was prepared to have Czechoslovakia dismembered and turned into Nazi Germany's outright sphere of influence rather than see an attack on Czechoslovakia by Nazi Germany made a *casus belli,* as the Soviet government had suggested. The United States went along with the Chamberlain policy. Yet, the Franklin Roosevelt administration did sense that the reliance for the prevention of a war in Western Europe on the diplomatic and extra-diplomatic moves of the Hitler government was a risky proposition. The United States administration under Franklin D. Roosevelt, therefore, undertook to extend full diplomatic recognition to the Soviet regime.

An ocean of words has been printed to prove that full diplomatic recognition of the Soviet state and the apparently conciliatory policy which ensued during the Franklin Roosevelt administration was the kind of policy which was and allegedly continues to be inimical to the essential national interest of the United States. What all the writers who attempt to disparage the foreign policy of Franklin D. Roosevelt and his aides in regard to their dealing with the Soviet state forget is that the very existence of the United States, along with the existence of its Western allies, was threatened by the war aims of the Hitler regime. What all those defamers and would-be defamers of the patriotism of Franklin

D. Roosevelt do not care to mention is that, given an early defeat of the Soviet state by the Hitler regime during World War II, the continuous existence of the United States and its Western allies could have been assured only on the condition that they were to accede to becoming dependencies of the Hitler empire. Short of that, no deal would have been possible with the Hitler regime, had it been victorious over Russia. The alternative to a deal with the Hitler empire after its victory over Russia would have been the conquest of the Western states, and in particular of England and, in due time, the United States by the Hitlerian armies and navies. If that kind of insight is applied to the foreign policy of Franklin D. Roosevelt and his aides, he will have to be recognized as the greatest and most realistic political and military leader which the United States has had since George Washington.

The conciliatory policy which Franklin D. Roosevelt and his closest aides pursued towards the Soviet Union by no means had a smooth sailing during his tenure in office. The policy proclaimed by the then United States Senator, Harry S. Truman, that Russia was to be left to bleed to death from the mortal blows which the Hitlerian armies were preparing for it, had quite a few supporters in official and non-official circles in the United States. It should be remembered that the strategic United States war plan, which was prepared under the direction of the Chief of the United States General Staff, George Marshall, took it for granted that the Soviet state would go out of existence within a few weeks, at best, a few months, after the initial attack on it by the Hitlerian armies. The first strategic plan laid down by the United States General Staff at the beginning of World War II was a plan to fight the war against Germany without, and not with, the Soviet Union.

The British General Staff, under the direction of Winston Churchill, seconded the initial strategic war plan of the United States General Staff by devising such strategic war moves which, in the very midst of the war against Hitlerian Germany, were aimed at weakening the Soviet Union. The delaying of the Second Front in Western Europe up to the time when the bulk of the Hitlerian armies were destroyed by the Soviet armies, and the insistence on landing troops in Italy and the Balkans, where Hitler could not have been decisively defeated, are but stark illustrations of the sinister plan which was aimed at weakening the Russian ally of the Western powers. The plan had as its goal the preservation of as much and for as long as possible the power of the Hitlerian armies, so that they might take the heaviest possible toll of the Soviet fighting forces.

It is to the credit of Franklin Roosevelt and his aides that they were among the most ardent supporters of the complete surrender policy towards the Hitlerian regime. Franklin D. Roosevelt succumbed, it should be granted, to the delaying tactics used by Winston Churchill and the British General Staff, as far as the postponement of the opening of the Second Front and the granting of primacy to the secondary fronts in Italy and the Balkans is concerned. However, Franklin D. Roosevelt and his aides never wavered, as far as the pursuit of the policy of unconditional surrender towards the Hitler regime was concerned. Had Churchill and the British General Staff had their way completely, it can well be assumed that, in the face of the possibility of an added weakening of the Soviet fighting strength, there would have been the temptation to use the partially preserved Hitlerian military power in a combined assault of Western and German military forces, presumably under a post-Hitler regime in Germany, to pursue the aim of a military conquest of the Soviet state. The miracle of Russian military resistance and the brilliant military offensive which the Soviet Russian armies developed against the Hitlerian forces put an end to all those anti-Soviet military and political speculations. The possibility of another Versailles-type conference at the end of World War II, in which Russia was again to be denied a political and military representation, as it had been the case at the Versailles Conference after World War I, had come to naught.

The direct millitary aid, in terms of munitions and provisions, which was given to the Soviet state by the United States could not turn the tide of the war. The tide of the war was turned by the military strategy of the Soviet General Staff and its massive execution. The military aid of the United States can be considered as a contributing factor in hastening the complete defeat of the Hitlerian armies. Had this direct aid from the United States not been forthcoming, victory over the Hitlerian armies would presumably have been delayed. That the complete absence of the United States military aid could have resulted in the defeat of the Soviet armies by the Hitlerian forces cannot be argued convincingly.

What is, however, demonstrably convincing, is the argument that the undermining of the strength of the Hitlerian armies by the repeated massive assaults of the Soviet armed forces had reached such considerable proportion at the time when the Second Front was opened in France, that it became possible for the United States forces and the forces of its Western allies to cut through German lines the way a knife cuts through butter. The United States forces, and those of its Western allies, cut through German lines with such ease as to make persistent fighting almost unnecessary, except in such isolated pockets as the Battle of the Bulge. The millions and millions of dead and wounded Soviet citizens, armed and unarmed, had saved hundreds of thousands, if not millions, of American and West European lives which would have had to be spent to defeat the Hitlerian forces, had they not been decimated and weakened by the persistent assaults of the Soviet forces.

The Teheran and Yalta agreements which were negotiated by Franklin D. Roosevelt, Winston Churchill, and Joseph Stalin, it should be kept in mind, were agreements made under wartime conditions, as a means of attaining victory. Assurance was to be given to the United States and British governments by the spokesman for the Soviet government that the Soviet Union was able and willing to remain in the war to the very end. In addition, agreement was sought by the allied powers, and in particular by the United States, that after the defeat of Germany, the Soviet Union would enter the war against Japan on the allied side. The Soviet Union, as represented by Joseph Stalin and his aides, wanted, in turn, to be assured that the United States and Britain were to remain in the war until the proclaimed war aim, the unconditional surrender of Germany, was attained.

Mindful of the long years of the policy of the *cordon sanitaire,* which had the support of the Western allied powers in the period between the two World Wars, Stalin was not satisfied with a mere declaration of good faith on the part of Franklin D. Roosevelt and Winston Churchill, who represented the Western powers. In Yalta, he made sure that a political climate was to be prepared in post-war Europe, and in particular in Eastern Europe, which would make it impossible for the Western powers to use the Eastern European states as territories on which Cold War policies were to be bred and hot war policies were to be prepared against the Soviet Union. Stalin insisted in Teheran, and more so in Yalta, on the transformation of the Eastern European states from centers of anti-Soviet activities to citadels of pro-Soviet policy.

The envisioning of such a transformation was the only tangible part of a *quid pro quo* which the Western powers could offer the Soviet Union in return for its continuation of the all-out war effort on the side of the Western allies. The Soviet government kept its part of the agreement by contributing the major share to the complete defeat of the Hitlerian armies and by entering the war against Japan at the period specified in the intra-allied agreement. The allied powers fulfilled their part of the intra-allied agreement by withdrawing from those parts of Germany which had been occupied ahead of schedule by the allied armies and by letting the Soviet armies enter those parts of Germany. The Soviet government reciprocated by letting the occupation forces of the Western allied armies enter Berlin, which, in turn, had been occupied ahead of schedule by the Soviet armies.

At the Potsdam Conference, Truman, acting as Roosevelt's successor, and Atlee, acting as Churchill's successor, did not go further in any of their dealings with Stalin and his aides than the Teheran and Yalta agreements had provided for. Truman and Atlee lent themselves exclusively in Potsdam to the implementation of those agreements. Truman and Atlee might have been tempted to reverse some parts of the agreements which had been made by their respective predecessors in Teheran and Yalta. Such a temptation was probably great on the part of those two representatives of the Western powers, in particular in view of their realization that victory over the Germans had been attained and victory over the Japanese was in sight. At the Potsdam Conference, however, no such direct attempt to reverse the Teheran and Yalta agreements was made. The resumption of Cold War strategy was deferred in this instance.

The United States did not keep faith with the Soviet Union when it prevented Soviet Russian military forces from taking decisive action against the Japanese after the Soviet government entered into open hostilities against Japan. The dropping of the atom bombs on Hiroshima and Osaka was hardly justifiable from a military point of view, as far as the aim of defeating the Japanese military forces was concerned. Japan was on the verge of military defeat anyway. Massive assaults of the Soviet military forces against the Japanese would have hastened the complete military defeat of Japan. Instead, the dropping of the atomic bombs on Japan upon instruction of the then President of the United States, Harry Truman, and his aides, was aimed at effecting a political blow against the Soviet Union.

The Soviet government was to be kept out of the settlement, and in particular out of sharing the military occupation rights in Japan. The dropping of the atomic bomb accomplished that political aim. In this sense, the dropping of the atomic bomb on Japan, which brought about the end of hostilities on a world-wide scale and thus ended World War II, signifies at the same time the resumption of the Cold War. The Truman administration took off where the pre-Franklin D. Roosevelt administration had left it. The Soviet Union was again to be treated as an adversary, as a political enemy. The period of wartime cooperation of the United States and the Western allies with the Soviet Union had ceased and the Cold War policies were resumed. President Truman and his aides did not waste any time reinstating the Cold War in the high policy councils of the United States.

Winston Churchill was called upon by President Truman to sound the bugle and to re-intone the Cold War shouts in the United States. In his Fulton, Missouri speech, the former Prime Minister of England refashioned the *cordon sanitaire* proposition of Clemenceau by supplanting it with the iron curtain slogan. Churchill was not original in his use of the words "iron curtain." The words had been used before, but not with the same aplomb as the *cordon sanitaire* proposition. In a sense, it was necessary to replace the *cordon sanitaire* slogan, since the countries which had been designated as the embodiments of the *cordon*

232

sanitaire proposition had slipped out of the anti-Soviet orbit. The East European states, in conformity with the Teheran and Yalta agreements, had become states pledged to friendship with the Soviet Union. The iron curtain slogan which, on Churchill's call, was to replace the *cordon sanitaire* proposition, paid due attention to the change in the international situation which had taken place in Eastern Europe as a result of the defeat of Hitlerian Germany. The Eastern states had become outposts of Soviet power in Europe instead of being outposts of anti-Soviet power in Europe. By calling for a replacement of the slogan of *cordon sanitaire* by the slogan "iron curtain," Churchill inferentially acknowledged that, as far as the Eastern European countries were concerned, the policy of *cordon sanitaire* had failed.

Churchill's call for the lowering of an iron curtain not in front of the borders of the Soviet state, but in front of the eastern borders of the Western European states, constituted, in a metaphorical form, a reaffirmation of the change in the geographical position of the Western powers vis-à-vis the Soviet Union, which had taken place as a result of the defeat of Germany in World War II. The change in the relative geographical, as well as military and political, position of the Soviet Union, to which Churchill's use of the iron curtain slogan has made reference, did not deter Churchill, as the spokesman for the Western powers, from calling for the re-fanning of the Cold War which had been kept to some extent in abeyance during the period of hostilities in World War II.

With the United States as the undisputed leader of the Western powers during World War II and its aftermath, it was up to the United States to take a lead in the implementation of Churchill's call to re-fan the Cold War. In pursuance of that task, the foreign policy advisor during the first term of office of the Truman administration, Kennan, took it upon himself to restate the Cold War strategy. In an article published anonymously in the influential magazine *Foreign Affairs,* Kennan provided a mode of operation for the implementation of Churchill's iron curtain device. Kennan called his mode of operation "containment policy." It was the same kind of policy which was pursued during the *cordon sanitaire* period of the pre-World War II era. The policy aimed at the isolation of the Soviet Union from the Western world. The policy of isolation as it had been pursued in the *cordon sanitaire* period was, in turn, meant only as a temporary device, to be used until a direct assault on the Soviet Union was made possible. The variation presented in the containment policy and the method of isolation which it was to pursue makes the continuous operation of this method contingent upon the expectation of an ultimate breakdown of Soviet authority within the borders of the Soviet state and/or the Eastern European states which lie within the Soviet sphere of influence.

The containment device proclaimed by Kennan in his article was made the official policy of the United States Government. Its implementation may be seen in the rollback provision, also called "liberation policy", which was aimed at the specific reversal of the internatonal agreements made in Teheran and Yalta. Those agreements had conceded that after the defeat of Germany the East European states were to lie within the Soviet sphere of influence. To place these states once more within the sphere of influence of the Western powers had thus become the declared aim of the United States foreign policy, which was backed in its essentials by the other Western powers. The rollback, or so-called "liberation" policy, in regard to the Eastern European states, became embodied in United States presidential election programs of both the Democratic and Republican parties.

The Cold War policies of the Western powers, and of the United States in particular, as their undisputed leader, have been conducted in the same zig-zag fashion since World War II as they were in the pre-World War II period. The Truman administration implemented agreements made during the war by extending United States relief aid to the Soviet Union through the United Nations Relief and Rehabilitation agency. The Truman administration did not go as far as to break diplomatic relations with the Soviet Union when the Cold War brought about a hot war in Korea. It can well be argued with a high degree of certainty, however, that the Korean War either would not have broken out at all or would have been quickly terminated, if an atmosphere of enmity and suspicion had not been fostered in the relations of the Western powers with the Eastern and Far Eastern socialist states, and in particular in the dealings of the United States with the Soviet Union. That the Soviet Union and the other socialist states started to promote enmity and suspicion on their part in their dealings with the United States can be taken as but an answer to policies of the United States and the other Western powers.

The losses of men and material incurred by the Soviet Union in the conduct of World War II were far larger than those incurred by the Western countries, and in particular the United States. There was therefore less of a material basis for enmity and suspicion of the Western powers in their relations with the Soviet Union than vice versa. The hard line policy of the Soviet Government towards the Western powers, and in particular towards the United States in the last years of the Stalin regime, can well be explained with regard to the weakened material condition in which the Soviet Union found itself in the period immediately following the cessation of hostilities. Some of the irresponsible acts of the Stalin regime, as far as internal policies of the Soviet Union were concerned in the years immediately preceding Stalin's demise, can well be understood in the light of the nightmare which Stalin and his close aides had to go through in taking into consideration the possibility that the Western powers, led by the United States, might resume a hot war against the Soviet Union. In view of the refashioning of the Cold War under United States leadership, with its proclaimed aim of attaining a breakdown of Soviet power, Stalin and his entourage could not rule out the possibility of such a war. The weakening of the comparative economic and military position of the Soviet Union as compared with that of the Western powers, and in particular of the United States, at the end of World War II, made even speculation on the possibility of such a war enough of a nightmare to block any clear political vision, even in a statesman with as much *sang-froid* as Stalin had been known to have.

Under the conditions of extreme international tension, the proposal of the United States Government to turn atomic fission over to the control of an international body, as had been suggested in the Baruch Plan, could not have been expected to be greeted with warm welcome by the political leadership of the Soviet Union. Regardless of the technicalities of this move on the part of the Truman Administration, and regardless of what the document prepared under the direction of Bernard Baruch contained or did not contain, it appears improbable in retrospect that the Soviet Government could have seen anything more in the proposed agreement than an effort to prevent it for all time from coming into possession of an atomic fission device on its own accord. The Truman Administration could still continue to claim in retrospect that its endorsement of the Baruch Plan was a means of rapprochement with the Soviet Union. Outwardly, the Baruch Plan to internationalize atomic fission devices was no doubt a peace move. Yet, in the Cold War atmosphere, even its United States proponents could not have expected it to be accepted by the leaders of the Soviet Union.

The Truman Administration's tenure ended in an atmosphere of a highly intensified Cold War which had given rise to the hot war in Korea. Internally, the outbreak of the hot war in Korea resulted in the strengthening of the anti-democratic forces within the United States. The smear campaign which was conducted by the Junior Senator from Wisconsin, Joseph McCarthy, was conducted with a view towards intimidating all those who did not take the most extreme position in the Cold War between the United States and the Soviet Union. That campaign of intimidation was, in turn, extended from the civilian branches of the Government, which shaped and executed foreign policy, to the military establishment of the United States. In the guise of fighting alleged Communist influences, McCarthy pursued a devious policy aiming at matching the powers of the constitutional government of the United States with his own high-pressure political campaign conducted from the rostrum of the United States Senate Committee on Internal Security. Truman, who complained about the irresponsibility of the McCarthy outbreaks, was probably not fully aware that he himself, as President of the United States, as well as his close aides, could well have been regarded as the godfathers of McCarthy's extramural policies, which flourished in the shadow of a world-wide Cold War and the hot war in Korea as its matching counterpart. With the end of the Korean War and the replacement of the Truman Administration by the Eisenhower Administration, McCarthy's power waned, and the junior senator from Wisconsin died shortly thereafter.

During the Eisenhower administration, a lull set in in the Cold War. Eisenhower kept his election promise and went to Korea to initiate the signing of a truce. Although the Truman Administration formally presented the Korean War to the American people as but a "police action", that so-called "police action" cost the United States only slightly less in killed and wounded men than the casualties which the United States suffered in World War I. A sigh of relief went over the whole United States when the Korean War was formally ended. Eisenhower followed up the ending of the Korean War by going with his Secretary of State, John Foster Dulles, to Geneva to meet Bulganin, then the Premier of the Soviet Union, and Nikita Khrushchev, the then First Secretary of the Communist Party of the Soviet Union. Though as far as agreements were concerned, the Geneva meeting of the political leaders of the United States and the Soviet Union resulted only in the drawing up and subsequent signing of a cultural exchange agreement, the international political atmosphere, particularly as it affected the United States and the Soviet Union, became perceptively discharged. As a follow-up of the Geneva meeting, Nikita Khrushchev, who had in the meantime replaced Bulganin as Premier of the Soviet Union, visited the United States at the invitation of the Eisenhower Administration. Premier Nikita Khrushchev's tour through the United States, in spite of the sniping attacks on him by implacable emigre groups and extreme United States rightists, was an event which abated to a high degree Cold War frenzy in the United States.

Eisenhower's private conversations with Khrushchev resulted in what used to be called the "Camp David spirit." That was the spirit, which, if consistently pursued, could have brought about an end to the Cold War. Things, however, turned out differently. The political forces in the United States which were bent on the continuation of the Cold War started an intensified drive in favor of the Cold War, which resulted in the double-crossing of the Eisenhower peace policy. The shooting down of a United States spy plane on the eve of the convocation of a conference between the heads of the governments of the Western powers and the head of the government of the Soviet Union in Paris constituted but the culmination of a drive by the pro-Cold War forces in the United States not to permit the Cold War activities to cease. Under these circumstances, the Paris conference could not take place, and the end of the Cold War became a rather remote proposition. One does not properly assess cause and effect relationships when one attempts to put the blame for the torpedoing of the Paris conference on the then Premier Khrushchev. The conference had been torpedoed before the Western and Soviet leaders had even assembled in Paris. Among the influences which led to the torpedoing of the Paris conference, we must mention the pro-Cold war activities and the proclamation of the executive of the Congress and Industrial Organization and American Federation of Labor, the central United States labor organization, on the eve of the convening of the Paris conference, as well as the sharp speech favoring the Cold War delivered on the eve of the Paris conference by the then Under Secretary of State, Dillon. The Paris conference was torpedoed not the least by the shooting down of the United States spy plane as it flew over Russia.

The last year of the Eisenhower Administration, the year which followed the torpedoing of the Paris conference, was marred by an intensification of the Cold War. The establishment of a leftist regime in Cuba was seized upon by the Eisenhower Administration to put additional coals into the fires of the Cold War. When the Kennedy Administration took over, the Cold War was raging with the fury it had reached in the Truman period. Kennedy himself was quite active in fanning the fires of the Cold War with an unprecedented zeal. Kennedy, one is to keep in mind, was quite willing to turn the Cold War into a hot war over the issues of Berlin and Cuba. John Kennedy, it can be said, went Dulles, the shaper of foreign policy during the Eisenhower Administration, one better. John Foster Dulles is known for having instituted and pursued a so-called *on the brink* policy, which meant that measures short of actual war were expected to attain United States foreign policy aims. John F. Kennedy was not satisfied, however, with pursuing *on the brink* tactics; he actually went *over the brink* by having authorized actual timed battle orders for a general United States military assault on the Soviet Union over the issue of Cuba. Only the decision of the then Premier Khrushchev to avoid a military conflict prevented a nuclear war at that time.

One can well say that by threatening atomic war over Cuba the Kennedy Administration had caused more anxiety to millions of Americans than any other administration in the whole history of the United States.

Never in any previous threat of war or actual war in which the United States became involved was the prospect of wholesale annihilation of the entire American population ever raised, as had been the case during the crisis over Cuba in the fall of 1963. John F. Kennedy had made some contribution, it should be granted, to the abatement of the Cold War, but those were rather incidental factors in the Cold War frenzy, in which he personally and his administration indulged. He made a conciliatory speech at the commencement exercises at the American University in Washington on June 10, 1963. He was instrumental in bringing about an agreement on a limited nuclear test ban, it should be added. The conciliatory commencement speech was, however, countered by a belligerent speech delivered subsequently at a rally in West Berlin. There was no time to test whether the test ban agreement was considered by Kennedy a genuine change in policy direction or just an incidental gesture in the frenzied pursuit of the Cold War. In the meantime, the American population continued to be in a state of high agitation and great anxiety lest a further overheating of the Cold War were inadvertently to lead to a hot war and a nuclear war at that. It is reported that John F. Kennedy fancied himself to become another Napoleon; if he did, he would possibly have been given a chance to become a Napoleon manqué, had he lived longer.

President Lyndon B. Johnson took over the reins of government in the aftermath of the signing of the limited nuclear test ban agreement, which could have provided a basis for some abatement of the Cold War. The Johnson Administration had played Cold War policies in regard to the Soviet Union on a low key, though some of the hotheads among the policy makers in the Kennedy Administration were kept in office by President Johnson. Those hotheads spent their time heating up the Cold War atmosphere by blowing up Cold and hot war issues with regard to Asia and in particular, Southeast Asia.

The intensification of the armed conflict in South Vietnam was one of the results of the activity of some hotheaded advisors to President Johnson. The Secretary General of the United Nations, U Thant, had made it clear that the increased military activity in South Vietnam, with the aid at an earlier period of United States material and military advisors, was in no way a means to solve the political and social problems which beset that country. The United Nations is the organization to which a peaceable solution of the situation in South Vietnam could be referred, the Secretary General of the United Nations suggested. In addition, there was a Geneva Agreement of 1954 in existence which had been reached at the time when Vietnam was partitioned. That agreement could have been invoked for the settlement of the outstanding issues in Vietnam. The larger aim should have been the neutralization of the whole of Vietnam, as well as the whole Southeastern region of Asia. The Vietnam conflict nonetheless escalated through United States air bombing raids on the territory of North Vietnam. The continuation and intensification of the military conflict in South Vietnam constituted a continuous danger of boiling over and embroiling the whole Southeastern region of Asia as well as areas beyond it, in a military conflict. It became one of the danger spots over which World War III could have erupted.

The often invoked so-called Domino strategic theory which, as referred to South Vietnam, is based on the argument that the loss of South Vietnam will lead to the fall of other United States strategic strongholds in the Far East, is not tenable. The Domino strategic theory is not applicable to the conflict in South Vietnam for the very reason that South Vietnam lies definitely outside the basic strategic perimeter of the United States in the Far East. That South Vietnam is of no fundamental importance to the United States strategic military position in the Far East has been admitted by one of the chief United States policy makers of the Kennedy and Johnson Administrations, McGeorge Bundy, during a talk at the Radcliffe Club at the beginning of March 1965.

In a sense the entry and presence of the United States military forces in South Vietnam is more of a Cold War than a hot war issue. It revolves around the issue under what conditions a coalition of leftist parties known under the name of the National Liberation Front is to be given the opportunity to take part in the formation of a post war government in South Vietnam. Around that issue, the Paris Peace Conference convened during the last stage of the Johnson Administration became deadlocked. The matter has thus been once more removed from the political negotiating sphere to the military sphere.

At this time, Vietnamese are made to meet Vietnamese on the battle field with gradually diminishing United States military participation. Under the so-called policy of Vietnamization, the Vietnamese conflict comes to assume the character of a Vietnamese civil war, as which it should have been recognized by the United States from its beginning. Had that recognition come during the Kennedy and Johnson Administrations, the United States could have and possibly would have stayed out of a direct involvement in military operations in Vietnam. This writer had sent a letter to the above stated effect to President Johnson at the very beginning of the Johnson Administration. No acknowledgment or reply was received.

At this stage it might be in order to present in retrospect a brief comparative evaluation of the respective stands of the Democratic and Republican parties in regard to the Cold War. In the period which preceded World War II, the Cold War was initiated under the Democratic administration of Woodrow Wilson, and was continued under the Republican administrations of Harding, Coolidge and Herbert Hoover. Under the Democratic administration of Franklin D. Roosevelt, a kind of truce was declared in the Cold War during the fighting period of World War II. In the post-World War II period, the Cold War was reignited under the Democratic administration of Truman, while a kind of lull in the Cold War prevailed under the Republican administration of Eisenhower.

Franklin D. Roosevelt had sensed the real danger which a victorious Nazi Germany would have presented to the continued existence of the United States as an independent nation and chose the Soviet Union as an ally of the United States in the common fight against the Nazi onslaught. On the other hand, Truman also a Democrat, reverted to the policy of another Democrat, Wilson, because in Truman's time as in Wilson's time, defeated Germany lay low and did not present any danger to the United States. Truman and Wilson ignited the Cold War in United States relations with the Soviet Union since they came to regard Germany, respectively defeated in World War II and World War I, as a power vacuum. John F. Kennedy, a Democrat, kept the Cold War for the most part of his short tenure of office at a boiling point, except for the brief span of his tragically terminated life which followed the signing of the Atomic Test Ban Agreement.

President Lyndon B. Johnson, a Democrat, had refrained from reigniting the embers of the Cold War as far as the Soviet Union is concerned. The escalation of the war in South Vietnam could not fail, however, to be reflected in an increase of the tension between the United States and the Soviet Union. Were it not for the Vietnam conflict, President Johnson could have reverted to the policy of Franklin D. Roosevelt, for whom he had great admiration. If that would have come to pass, the Cold War tension could have abated. Had Franklin D. Roosevelt lived to see the end of World War II, it appears likely that the Cold War between the United States and the Soviet Union would not have been reignited. Thus, a period of international cooperation between the United States and the Soviet Union would have ensued. It is not too late, even at present, for the successor of Lyndon B. Johnson to the Presidency of the United States, Richard M. Nixon, to revert to such a policy. President Nixon's declaration that the period of confrontation of the United States with the Soviet Union is to be replaced during his administration with a period of negotiation can be taken as an encouraging sign in the above stated direction, were it to be followed through.

That such a reversal of policy would get support from influential persons in the United States is indicated by the publications and pronouncements of Senator J. William Fulbright, the Chairman of the Foreign Relations Committee of the United States Senate. Senator Fulbright expressed interest in "building bridges of accommodation" between the United States and the Soviet Union. Senator Fulbright is not alone among United States senators and congressmen as well as other influential persons in the United States outside of the Congress, who want to see the Cold War terminated.

In the wake of the prosecution of the Vietnam War, more than a goodly half of the United States electorate have turned against hot and Cold War policies and could be counted upon to support the termination of that policy. The wide popular response to the appeal of the anti-war stand expressed by such candidates for the nomination for the office of the President of the United States in 1968 as Eugene McCarthy and Robert F. Kennedy had borne testimony to the effect that Cold and hot War policies were becoming more and more unpopular with the average American. The resolution adopted June, 1971 by a majority of United States senators led by Majority Leader Mike Mansfield which demands complete withdrawal of United States military forces from Vietnam at a fixed date can well be regarded as the highlight of the anti-war sentiments among the top echelons of the elected representatives of the American people. The Administrative branch of the United States Government will, in due time, have to follow suit.

West Germany has arisen from the ashes of World War II and is becoming an increasingly potent military, economic and political power. France is keying its role as a military and political power center by turning into an atomic power. Britain, in its turn, is trying to prevent West Germany or France from becoming the preponderant military power in Western Europe. The United States is forced to maneuver between the three major powers in Western Europe, in an attempt to retain its position of military, political and economic leadership among the Western nations.

The Berlin crisis which had arisen in 1962 and which had again flared up at the beginning of 1969, over the question of the international status of the city of Berlin, constitutes in actuality a phase in the struggle between the Western powers and the Soviet Union over the question of the role of Germany in the sphere of international relations. Germany had become a focal factor in the Cold War. As such, it could well have become the country over whose future World War III could have broken out. It is to be hoped that the four occupying powers will come to some agreement in the near future which will ease the tension between the East and the West as centered on Berlin.

A peaceable solution of the German problem has become imperative. A guarantee of the inviolability of the Oder-Neisse border between Germany and Poland on the part of all Western powers had long been overdue. First France among the Western powers has specifically guaranteed the inviolability of the Oder-Neisse border. Second, most recently Western Germany has recognized the inviolability of the Oder-Neisse border which constitutes a significant step towards the pacification of the European continent.

With the guaranteeing of the Oder-Neisse border by Western Germany should go the recognition of the existence of the Eastern German state, the German Democratic Republic. The Eastern German state, it should be admitted by all the Western powers, has as much right to exist as the Western German state, the Federal Republic of Germany. It is a United Nations principle to recognize the existence of any state regardless of its political complexion. That principle is to be made applicable to the Eastern German state as to any other existing state.

From all that has been said in this Chapter, the conclusion has to be drawn that the stipulation of the Cold War as but a phase preliminary to a hot war has to be discarded. With that realization, the continuation of the Cold War will tend to become meaningless. It is quite possible that a negation of the Cold War will come about in the course of disarmament agreements and its attendant measures. The very thaw in the Cold War which came about as a pendant to the signing and ratification of the ban on atomic test explosions testifies to the interrelationship between a rapprochement on military matters and a rapprochement on other than military matters. Were a live and let live attitude come to govern the relations between the United States and the Soviet Union, the Cold War will fade away,

INDEX OF NAMES*

* Index prepared by Elaine A. DeGrood.

AFTERWORD

The signing of the agreements in Moscow on May 27, 1972 on the curbing of an increase in defensive and offensive atomic weapons took place after this book had gone to press. Those agreements have been signed by President Richard Nixon for the United States and General Secretary Leonid Brezhnev for the Soviet Union. The above stated agreements are to be considered as constituting a step in the direction pointed to in the present volume.

PHILOSOPHICAL CURRENTS

1. D'ANGELO, Edward. – The Teaching of Critical Thinking, Amsterdam 1971, X, 78 pp.

2. PYUN, Hae Soo. – Nature, Intelligibility, and Metaphysics. Studies in the Philosophy of F. J. E. Woodbridge. Amsterdam 1972, X, 108 pp.

3. CROSSER, Paul K. – War is Obsolete. The Dialectics of Military Technology and its Consequences. Amsterdam 1972, VI, 244 pp.

The series will be continued, standing orders for forthcoming volumes accepted.
Leaflet with full description free on request.

B. R. Grüner Publishing Co.
P.O.B. 70020
Amsterdam (Holland)